GOLF

THE ESSENTIAL COMPANION

GOLF
THE ESSENTIAL COMPANION

Dawson Taylor

Illustrated by Taylor Jones

Robson Books

First published in Great Britain in 1988 by Robson Books Ltd, Bolsover House, 5–6 Clipstone Street, London W1P 7EB.

British Library Cataloguing in Publication Data

Taylor, Dawson
  [How to talk golf]. Golf: the essential companion.
  1. Golf
  I. [How to talk golf] II. Title
  796.352

ISBN 0–86051–502–8

Printed in Great Britain by Billing & Sons Ltd., Worcester

CONTENTS

INTRODUCTION

Where did anyone ever get the idea of striking a little ball a number of times with ridiculous looking implements so as to drive it great distances and then putting it into a little round hole only 4¼ inches in diameter? Where did it all start? How long ago?

'Way back in the 1600s in Holland, the Dutch played a game called "Het Kolven." There are contemporary paintings and literature which tell us that the game was played in wide open spaces such as on frozen lakes or rivers, or roads and that a ball was struck from a tee and flew long distances in the air from one stake or marker to another similar stake or marker. We also know that the ball had to be played from the exact spot where it happened to come to rest on the ground or ice.

The clubs used then were startlingly like the wooden shafted golf clubs of the late 1800s. They were slender wooden instruments with leather grips and graceful heads of metal or wood that were attached to a supple shaft by "whipping" or wrapping with closely laid cord or line. The ball then in use was small and light but there is no doubt that it flew long distances when struck properly. We assume that in the 1600s the Dutch were playing a game closely related to the game of golf as we know it today.

The earliest reference to golf in Scotland occurs as early as 1457 in a decree by King James II that "anyone who wasted his time at fut-ball and the golf should be punished."

In 1776 the links of St. Andrews, Scotland were being used for golf and one William Gib was given permission to use the links for the raising of rabbits but the links were "not to be spoiled where the golfing is used." The rabbits multiplied, as rabbits are apt to do. In a few years the golfers of St. Andrews were permitted a "free drop" from any rabbit burrow that entrapped their golf balls. That is, they could pick the ball up and move it away from the trouble, and strike it from a fairer lie.

In 1754 the rules of golf were formally introduced by golfers who called themselves the Royal and Ancient Golf Club, Royal because one of their members was the King of England himself. Their rules, with surprisingly few modifications, continue to govern the game of golf today no matter where it is played all over the world. There is one simple rule in golf—you take your club (you have quite a selection of clubs with faces of various "lofts") and attempt to strike a round rubber or super-polymer golf ball (1.68 inches in diameter and weighing 1.68 ounces) from here to there in the least number of strokes. The "there" is represented by a hole in the ground 4¼ inches in diameter.

Over the centuries the language of golf has evolved in much the same way as the game itself came to be refined into beautifully-kept garden-type golf courses ranging from 6,000 to 7,000 yards with 18 individual holes which the golfer is expected to play "from tee to green", the tee being the starting spot and the green the closely cropped area where the hole is.

The language is colorful and descriptive. A "whiff" or complete miss of the ball is certainly a word that comes from the sound of the act itself. A "dub" is probably another one for the golfer who is a dub, a weak player who hits the ball with a sound like "dub."

Over the several hundred years of golf history many unusual terms and expressions have found their way into the language of golf. Some of them, such as the word "dormie" (which describes the situation where one player is so far ahead of another he cannot lose) is so old that no one really knows its origin.

The game of golf was brought to this continent in the early 1870s. The Royal Montreal Golf Club was formed then by Scots who had come over to the New World and brought with them their baffies and gutties and their knowledge of how to lay out a demanding golf course on rolling hills and dales.

In 1884 Russell Montague, a New Englander who had studied law in London, came to the White Sulphur Springs area in West Virginia.

He had played golf in Scotland and loved the game. He laid out a rudimentary 6-hole course at Oakhurst, West Virginia and with a few friends began the first true golf club in the United States where regular tournaments were played and silver medals awarded to the lowest scorer.

From the 1890s on interest in the new game grew rapidly. At first it was a social game meant primarily for the rich. Golf balls were expensive and the common man could not afford to play the game. In 1898 Coburn Haskell had the brilliant idea of making a golf ball by winding rubber-bands around a core. The result was the Haskell ball which replaced the hard "billiard-ball" gutta percha which had been in general use for a number of years.

With the invention of the rubber-wound Haskell ball the cost of golf balls was reduced drastically and many more players could afford the game.

In the early 1900s Harry Vardon, a great English golf champion, visited the States and played a number of exhibition golf matches. His slashing style, his accuracy, his long-driving ability caught the fancy of the Americans. Golf took off in America.

In the 1920s the most charismatic golfer of all time appeared in the person of Robert T. Jones, Jr. A soft-spoken Southerner, he was a boy wonder of golf and by the time he retired from golf competition at the age of 28 he had set records that would never again be equaled. Furthermore he had captured the hearts of America with his charming personality. When he returned from Scotland after winning both the British Open and Amateur Championships he was greeted by a tremendous ticker-tape welcome in New York with several million people shouting their acclaim for his accomplishments.

"Bobby" Jones, Walter Hagen and Gene Sarazen dominated the golf scene in the 1920s and then came the era of Ben Hogan, Byron Nelson and Sam Snead. The 1960s saw the rise of Arnold Palmer, Gary Player, Billy Casper and Gene Littler. Lurking in the wings was a stout, stocky young man from Ohio. In 1959 and 1961 he had won the U.S. Amateur Championships. He said he was not interested in playing professional golf but when he changed his mind and turned professional in 1961 Jack Nicklaus came to dominate golf as it had never been done before. Not long afterward another marvelous golfer, Tom Watson, came on the scene to challenge the King and as the 1980s march on we have seen an invasion of great foreign players in the persons of Severiano Ballesteros of Spain, Bernhard Langer of Germany and Isao Aoki of Japan, among others.

Early on all men golfers wore knickers. The roughs were deep then and oftentimes were brambly. Long trousers with cuffs could get in the way of a golfer deep in the "jungle." Knickers did not.

Golfers then wore shoes with smooth rubber soles or else wore shoes with rubber cleats, not unlike those on the shoes football players wear today. The teeing area was frequently a bare twelve-by-twelve-inch square of hard-packed grassless ground. There, the golfer teed his ball upon a conical mound of sand. At every tee there was a tee-box full of sand with a bucket of water suspended above it. It was the caddie's duty to wash the player's ball using the sand to scrub it and then to make the tee for his player. He did this by pouring some of the water onto the sand, and then, with a gob of wet sand in his hand he would form a miniature volcano-like structure on the hard ground and tee his player's ball on the top of it. He had to know his player's preference, too, as to tee height to insure a good tip after the round was over.

In the 1920s a wooden tee, the Reddy Tee, was invented. The teeing ground became softer with short cut grass on ground that would accept a wooden tee. Tee-boxes then gradually disappeared, never to be seen again.

In the early 1900s a serviceable set of nine wooden-shafted clubs could be bought for the equivalent of $75.00 today. The average golfer carried a driver, a brassie (named for the brass plate on its bottom), and a spoon with greater face loft than the brassie. Iron clubs were wooden-shafted of hickory—a midiron, mid-mashie, mashie, mashie-niblick, niblick and a putter, the counterparts of today's 2-iron, 4-iron, 5-iron, 7-iron, and 9-iron. A set of clubs like this was not heavy so most golfers carried their own clubs in what were called "Sunday" or "Pencil bags" with a diameter of eight to ten inches.

Not until the days of Jones in the late 1920s and early 1930s was there any thought of matching clubs in weight and flexibility. Bobby Jones is credited with having one of the first sets in which the clubs were closely matched to each other.

Golf club manufacturers produced matched sets of clubs with irons from 1 to 11. Walter Hagen once used a set with twenty-four clubs, numbered 1, 1½, 2, 2½, 3, 3½ and so on. The Spalding company had made a deal with Bobby Jones to manufacture clubs with his imprint. They were so fearful that the golfers of that day would not accept the shiny appearance of the steel-shafted club that they colored them yellow to simulate the look of the hickory shafts. But the chromium plated shaft was accepted and is the standard of today.

Then the United States Golf Association, the ruling body of American golf, stepped in and decided that the golfer would be allowed to carry no more than fourteen clubs in regulation play. The USGA also began to study the effect of different materials and compressions in golf balls. Golfers were driving "hot" golf balls prodigious distances. Courses which had bunkers designed to trap the player's ordinary drive were being by-passed as the ball flew over them more frequently than not. The USGA in cooperation with some of the golf club and golf ball manufacturers developed a mechanical golf driving machine dubbed "Iron Byron" because it seemed to duplicate the wonderful swing of great golfer Byron Nelson.

Thousands of hours of testing of balls and equipment brought standardization in equipment and rules governing the initial velocity of the golf ball. Today no golf ball is allowed in play with an initial velocity of more than 255 feet per second.

Most of the professional golfers of early days came from the ranks of the caddies. Few of them were college-educated. Nowadays most of the good golfers of the United States, both men and women, come from Junior Golf programs and from intensive college golf programs that grant scholarships to likely golf prospects. Golf is now recognized as a serious college competitive sport. College golf matches act as great training grounds for the golfers of today and tomorrow. But players who want to gain admission to the PGA tour still must obtain their playing cards by successfully completing a qualifying school course.

Prize money in the early days of golf was scandalously low. In the early U.S. Open Tournaments the winner was awarded a medal. In 1931 the USGA awarded Billy Burke, the winner, a prize of $1,000. Twenty-first place that year brought Olin Dutra $25.00. It was not until 1947, when Lew Worsham beat Sam Snead at St. Louis Country Club, that first prize money was increased to $2,000. That year thirty-first place paid $75.00. As late as 1946 the prize for the winner of the British Open Championship was £150, worth $600 at that time. Sam Snead won it that year and gave the entire sum to his caddie. In 1984 Severiano Ballesteros' purse for winning the British Open was £55,000, about $70,000 in American money.

Today golf purses have grown astronomically large. Recently, in an unofficial golf match TV audiences watched Jack Nicklaus win a quarter of a million dollars in a "Skins" game, a kind of winner-takes-all format.

Here are some unusual facts about the way purses have improved over the years in both mens' and ladies' professional golf.

In 1948 Mildred "Babe" Zaharias was the leading money winner with $3,400. In 1984 Betsy King won $266,771.

In 1941 Ben Hogan was the leading money winner with $18,358. In 1984 Tom Watson won $476,260.

In 1965 the U.S. Walker Cup team defeated the team of Great Britain-Ireland. On the U.S. team were six young players who soon turned pro—Gary Koch, Curtis Strange, Jerry Pate, George Burns, Craig Stadler and Jay Haas. As of the end of 1984 these six golfers had won prize money totalling nearly $7,000,000.

How high is the prize money going? Million dollar purses have been put up but so far no golfer has won one because they usually involve the winning of two or three designated tournaments in one year.

But while golf fans would like to see this happen, true afficionados would rather make successive pars or birdies or fire an ace.

LEXICON

Ace

n: a single shot from the tee ending up in the cup. Also known as a hole~in~one. If the ball comes to rest against the flagstick, the flagstick may be removed (gently) so as to allow the ball to fall to the bottom of the cup. Billy Joe Patton scored an ace in that man~ner on the 6th hole of the Augusta National course in the 1954 Masters.

address

v: to take one's stance and adjust the club preparatory to hitting the ball.

air shot

n: a whiff, a complete miss of the ball. One of the most embarrass~ing shots in golf at any time, but especially so on a first tee with an au~dience looking on.

Gary Player

TEE HEE HEE

alternate stroke

n: a variation of the game of golf in which two partners take turns in striking the ball. A very old golf game, it still is played in modern times in International Ryder Cup (Professional), Walker, and Curtis Cup (Amateur) matches as well as at many golf clubs that uphold the traditions of golf.

amateur golfer

n: one who plays the game for pleasure rather than for financial benefit or professional reasons.

Ben Hogan

away

n: after the initial shots off the tee, the expression used to designate the golfer farthest from the hole who always plays first. He is said to be "away." This is true even if one player's ball is on the green and the other's is in a bunker. It is also said to have been Ben Hogan's favorite expression. Jimmy Demaret, who played with Ben a great deal, was asked if Ben ever spoke to him during a round. Jimmy said, "Sure, on every hole when we reached the green he'd say, "You're away."

Back nine

n: the second nine of an 18-hole golf course. On many early golf courses the first nine holes were laid straight out from the clubhouse and then the golfer turned and came back "in." See "turn" and "in."

backspin

n: the reverse spin imparted to the ball as the grooved club strikes down on it at impact. The depth of face grooves is governed by the Rules of Golf. In the early days deeper grooves were allowed and the result was that a good golfer could do tricks with backspin and side spin (imparted by

(backspin cont'd)
a "cut" shot).

baffy

n: a wooden club of the early days of golf with greater loft than a spoon (3~wood). It would be considered in the 4~ or 5~wood range in today's game.

Bakspin mashie

n: a wooden~shafted club with 5~iron loft and deeply grooved face. The club was declared illegal in the 1920s, but as it could make the ball do wondrous things golfers gave it up reluctantly.

banana ball

n: a slice, that is, a ball that curves quickly to the right for a right~handed golfer or to the left for a left~handed golfer, as a result of an outside to inside swing that causes the ball to rotate counter~clockwise.

best ball

n: the selection of the lowest sin~ gle score of a foursome on a hole as the score of the entire four~ some for that hole. In foursome competition it is a favor~ ite game of American players who have high handicaps that bring their scores down close to those of the bet~ ter players. Example: Players A, B, and C have 5s while player D has a 4. The "best ball" is the 4.

better ball

n: the selection of the lower of two scores on a hole as the score of a twosome for that hole. "Better ball" is always used in twosome play, "best ball" in foursome play.

between the markers

prep. phrase: the teeing ground is always designated by two markers placed on a line perpendicular to the line of play. The golfer may tee up directly on the line between the markers or anywhere in the rectangle made by two club-lengths on a line straight back of each marker. If he plays his ball from in front of the marker, he may not count the stroke, must re-tee it properly, and is charged a penalty stroke for the error.

birdie

n: a score one less than par on a hole. Also called a "bird."
Note: You don't "make a birdie" today, you "make bird," or you are not "cool."

Chi Chi Rodriguez

bisque

n: a handicap stroke given by one player to another. The player getting the stroke may apply it to any hole he wishes, but must notify his opponent in advance of playing that hole that he is "taking his bisque." (Pronounced bisk).

bite

n: "bite" results on a well-struck iron shot when the

(bite cont'd)

blade of the club strikes the ball on the downswing and causes the ball to rotate with backspin, that is, from the bottom of the ball backward toward the top. When such a ball hits the green it bites. Usually the momentum of the ball will cause it to travel forward for a first hop and then the backspin bites and pulls it back.

Billy Casper

blade one

v: to hit the ball across its center line with the bottom edge of an iron club. The result is a ball that rockets off the club like a line drive in baseball.

blade putter

n: a straight~faced metal putter, sometimes with a small flange at the bottom, but always with a square top edge no more than a half~inch in width.

JoAnne Carner

blast

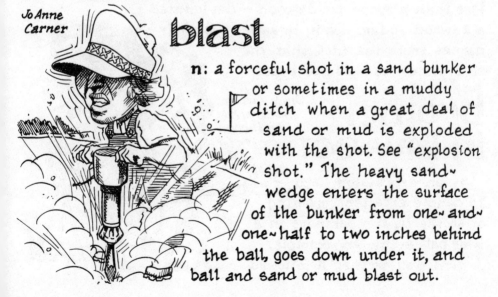

n: a forceful shot in a sand bunker or sometimes in a muddy ditch when a great deal of sand or mud is exploded with the shot. See "explosion shot." The heavy sand~ wedge enters the surface of the bunker from one~ and~ one~half to two inches behind the ball, goes down under it, and ball and sand or mud blast out.

bogey

n: a score of one over par on a hole. In the early 1900s a British golfer one over par, mindful of Colonel Bogey in the marching song, "Colonel Bogey March," popular at that time said, "Even Colonel Bogey could have done better than that!" The name stuck from that time on. Playing "bogey golf" means playing at a one over par pace per hole, 45~45=90 on a 36~36=72 par course.

borrow

v: to aim the ball when on a sloping green a distance to the right or left of the cup depending upon the slope, so as to compensate for the amount of slope, and putt on the proper line to the cup. The amount taken in feet or inches is the "borrow." "I had to borrow six inches to get in on the high side of the cup."

brassie

n: a fairway wood with more loft than a driver but less than a spoon or 3~wood — designated a 2~wood today. Early brassies got their names from the fact that the sole~plate was made of brass.

brother~ in law act

Bruce Lietzke and Jerry Pate, brothers~ in~law for real.

n: an expression used to denote excellent meshing of scores by two partners in a two~ball event. An example: A birdie by partner A followed

(brother~in~law act cont'd)

by a birdie by partner B and then another birdie by part~
ner A. Sometimes you will hear the losers moan, "They
brother~in~lawed us to death."

bull's~eye putter

n: a brass blade putter with an unusual curved~up heel.
It is nearly center~shafted, giving it excellent balance.
With the success of the original model some flanges have
now been added. Developed about forty years ago by
the Acushnet Company, it became one of
the most popular putters of all time.

bunker

n: any obstacle, as a sand trap or
grassy depression, constituting a hazard.
The golfer is not permitted to rest the
sole of his club on the ground or sand
of a hazard as he prepares to play. Bun~
kers vary greatly in size, shape, and depth.
Hell Bunker at St. Andrews is about 50 yards wide, 25 yards
long, and 15 feet deep. On the other hand, the tiny "Devil's
ass~hole" bunker at Pine Valley in the United States is
more like a pit 6 yards deep and sloping at the bottom
like a funnel.

buried lie

n: the unfortunate situation that
occurs when a ball hits soft turf or
sand and practically burrows down
out of sight. If it is truly out of sight
the golfer is permitted to uncover the
top of the ball so as to identify it as

(buried lie cont'd)

his own. A moderately buried lie in a sandtrap is called a "fried egg" in the United States because that's just what it looks like.

buttonhook

n: a putted ball that hits the cup on one side, goes around the back of it, rolling on the edge and shoots back out from the front edge of the cup toward the golfer. Bobby Jones once said, "When I saw my putt buttonhook, I knew I had lost the match."

Bobby Jones

Calamity Jane

n: the name Bobby Jones gave to his favorite wooden~shafted blade putter made for him by famous Scottish club~maker, Tom Stewart. Later in Jones' career a duplicate of the original was made for him when it was discovered that the center of Calamity Jane #1 had worn down from so many perfect putts on the face of the club. Jack Nicklaus recently had a number of duplicates of Calamity Jane made for some of his friends.

carried the hazard

v: the successful negotiation of a shot over a water hazard or a bunker. Also heard as "flew the bunker" which means the golfer successfully drove over it.

cash~in putter

n: a blade putter first manufactured by the Wright &

(cash~in putter cont'd)

Ditson Company in the 1930s, then by Spalding. Several professionals on the tour today, notably Johnny Miller and Andy Bean, use the extremely popular cash~in putters.

casual water

Tom Watson

n: rain water in a fairway or rough. If the ball lies in casual water, the golfer may lift it and drop it without penalty in a dry place (if he can find one) nearby, but not nearer the hole. The rule is that if the golfer can see visible water under his shoes, he may declare the area cas~ ual water. On the green, when casual water lies between the golfer's ball and the hole he may lift the ball and circle around, keeping the same distance to the hole, and attempt to find a dry path.

Chapman system

n: a method of partner play after the drive off the tee in which golfer #1 hits golfer #2's drive and vice versa. Then a choice is made as to which ball will be used for the final alternate stroke to the hole.

Lee Trevino

chili dip

n: a faulty "dipping" stroke on a short chip in which the club hits the ground first and then the ball. The result is usually a bad one with the ball moving only a few inches or feet.

chip~and~run

n: a shot played with a club that has a low loft such as a 4~iron or 5~iron that carries the ball over fringe or rough ground around a green and then allows the ball to run the rest of the way toward the cup. The ratio is usually one~third chip to two~thirds run.

chip shot

n: a delicate shot around the edge of a green usually made with a club of 4~iron, 5~iron, or 6~iron loft and intended to carry in the air and on the green and roll toward the hole.

cleek

n: a wooden~shafted club in the 4~iron or 5~iron range. Used for chip~and~run shots.

club

n: the implement used by the golfer to strike the ball. Has a head, a hosel, that connects a shaft to the head, and a grip of leather or a combination of rubber and cork. Today, a golfer is permitted to carry no more than 14 clubs in his bag. Walter Hagen played in the days before the 14 club rule went into effect. He used a set with 26 in all. He rewarded his caddie handsomely for carrying that monstrous load.

v: many golfers rely on their caddies to advise them about choice of clubs. In fact, many caddies are better golfers than the weekend players whose

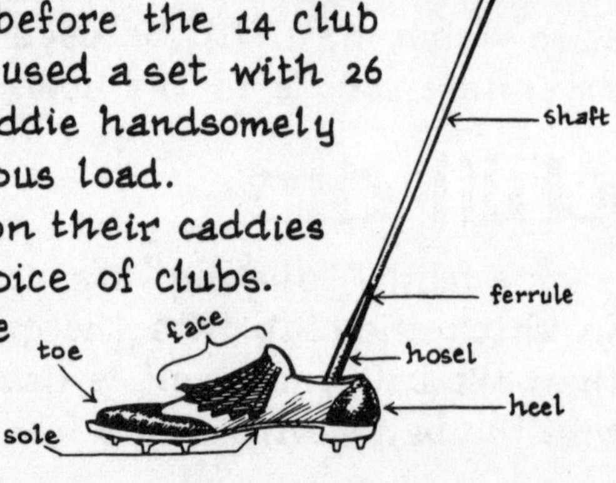

grip

shaft

ferrule

face

toe

hosel

heel

sole

(club cont'd)

bags they carry. When a caddie recommends a 5-iron or a 6-iron for a particular shot, he is "clubbing" the player. In the British Open of 1960 Arnold Palmer bogeyed the par-4 Road Hole, the 17th at St. Andrews, three times in a row after hitting 6-iron seconds. On the last day he had the same shot into the green. He asked caddie "Tip" Anderson to give him his 5-iron. Tip said, "You'll go over the green with it!" Arnie insisted on the 5-iron. He hit and ran the ball over the green onto the road. But he chipped up then within a foot of the hole and made his 4. Arnie said, "See there, Tip, you've been giving me the wrong club all week."

concede

vt: to assume that your opponent can make that very short putt to win the hole and therefore count the ball in the cup as if he had taken and made the shot. Example: A hits out of bounds on his drive on a par-3 hole. B puts his ball on the green a foot from the hole. A, who would be hitting his 3rd shot to the green on his second ball would have good reason to "concede" the hole. On the green, when an opponent's putt is close to the hole for a sure win, it is polite for the other player to concede it by knocking it away.

cuppy lie

n: a ball in a cup-like depression. Usually on bare ground in the rough between

(cuppy lie cont'd)

two hanks of rough grass. Frequently an "impossible lie." All the golfer can do is hack and hope.

cut

v: to slash the cover off the golf ball. Until the invention of the solid "cut~proof" ball, the outer cover of a golf ball was frequently cut by the sharp edge of an iron hitting it "in the middle." Golf balls with cuts in them became unplayable because they were out of round. Today only the professionals and good amateurs play the wound~rubber, Surlyn~covered golf ball which still may be cut by a poor stroke.

n: the "cut" is the score in a golf tournament at which the field is narrowed after two days of play (three in the British Open). Usually the low forty (sometimes as many as sixty) players including ties make the cut and play the last two days.

cut shot

n: a shot played with any iron from a 4 to a wedge. where the golfer takes his club outside his normal line on his backswing and returns it from outside to in so as to impart spin to the ball. The cut ball spins in a clockwise fashion, stops quickly on the green, and rolls to the right.

A cut shot is a trick shot or a "top drawer" shot by a pro.

Doug Sanders

Dance floor

n: the green or fairway. A ball that lands safely on the cut grass is said to be "on the dance floor."

dawn patrol

n: early morning golfers are the dawn patrol. From the famous old movie "Dawn Patrol" with Richard Arlen where the fighter planes went off at 5:00 a.m. in fog.

defender

n: an interesting betting game for three players in which each golfer "defends" against the other two on every third hole. Example: A, the defender, has 4 against B's 5 and C's 5 on the first hole. A wins 2 points, having defended the hole. If A had had a 6, he would have lost the hole and B and C would have won a point apiece. On the next hole B defends against A and C, on the third hole C defends against A and B, and so on.

dogleg

n: a golf hole shaped like a dog's leg. In fact, in Scotland the term is dog's leg. The dogleg hole can bend either way.

Fala

dormie

n: when one player is as many holes "up" or ahead of the other player as there are holes left to play. Example: A is 3 up on B with 3 holes to play. B would have to win all three holes to tie. A is said to be dormie. The player "up" is dormie. It is not the other way around.

double-eagle

n: a score 3-under par on a hole. The most famous

Gene Sarazen

(double~eagle cont'd)

double~eagle, "The shot heard around the world," was made by Gene Sarazen on the Par~5 485~yard 15th hole at Augusta National in the 1935 Masters. It enabled him to catch Craig Wood and tie for the lead. Gene then won the championship in a playoff.

driver

n: the longest club in the bag, 42 to 44 inches long, with a face from one~and~three~quarter inches to two~and~one~quarter inches deep and shallow loft (9° to 11°) in order to enable the golfer to "drive" the ball low and far. In recent years driv~ er heads have been constructed of metal which leads to the anomaly of the name "metal wood."

driving iron

n: a long shafted iron club with a heavy head and very little loft. In the early days of golf, in the 1800s, all the golf clubs were made with wooden heads. In the 1870s the Scots began to make clubheads out of forged steel and thus the "iron" was born. With it came the driving iron.

driving range

n: a location from which practice shots may be played.

drop

n: to place a new ball or reposition the one in play

(drop cont'd)

when a golfer loses a ball, hits it into a hazard, or into an unplayable lie. The golfer must add a penalty stroke to his score. Then he is allowed to "drop" the ball nearby where he will have a chance to advance it. He holds the ball out at arm's length and makes his drop. Watch how the good players in televised golf make a drop and try to choose a good "lie" for the next shot. Sometimes they get fooled when the ball rolls into another bad lie.

Horton Smith

dual-purpose wedge

n: one that can be used on the fairway as well as in the sand.

dub

v: to mishit a shot and cause it to dribble along the ground.

n: the golfer who mishits a lot of shots.

duck hook

n: a shot in which the ball "ducks" to the left as soon as it is hit. Much more dreaded than a slice or banana ball. Ben Hogan once said, "I get nauseated every time I hook."

duffer

n: a poor golfer, also known as a dub.

duffer's delight

n: the easiest club in the bag to use is a 5~iron because it has a moderately short shaft and is of medium loft. Because it sometimes is the only club a duffer can use well, it has come to be known as "duffer's delight."

dunch shot

n: a short shot into crunchy sand that makes a sound like "dunch" as the club strikes. The shot has little or no follow through.

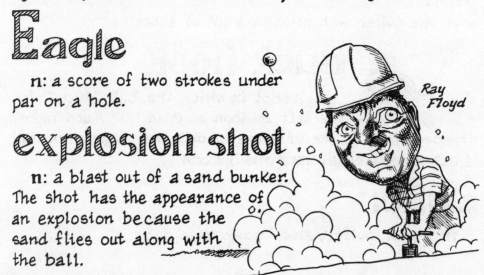

dying putt

n: a putt that just barely reaches the cup and then falls in or stops very close to the hole. On very fast greens it is sometimes necessary to use this style of putt so that the ball will not run by the cup and result in a three~putt coming back.

Eagle

n: a score of two strokes under par on a hole.

explosion shot

n: a blast out of a sand bunker. The shot has the appearance of an explosion because the sand flies out along with the ball.

Ray Floyd

Face grooves

n: grooves cut into the face of a club par~
allel to the sole to make it possible to put
spin on the ball. In the early days of golf
the faces of the iron clubs were
smooth. Then, clubs were
grooved, deeper and deep~
er until the 1930s when
the Royal and Ancient de~
creed that face grooves can
be no deeper than .035 inches.

Arnold Palmer

fade

n: a gentle, controlled slice, only a few yards from
left to right. To be distinguished from a banana ball
which is a great big slice out of control.

fairway

n: the closely cropped grass that lies between the tee
and the green. The fairway is bordered by the "rough,"
grass which is cut longer, ranging from an inch~and~a~
half to six inches or more.

fat

adj: hitting the turf behind the ball instead of the ball.
A ball hit "fat" will have no spin and usually the golfer suf~
fers a loss of expected distance on his shot.

feather

vt: to put a delicate fade on a shot into the green. The

(feather cont'd)

shot floats to the left of the hole and then "sits down" as light as a feather, working its way toward the hole with left to right spin.

featherie ball

n: in the early days of golf, the 1800s, golf balls were made out of leather stuffed tightly with goose feathers and then sewn, not unlike the way a baseball is sewn in modern times. The ball maker would boil a pound of feathers until they were softened and then, using a special tool, would stuff the leather cover as tightly as possible through a small hole in its side. The featheries were expensive, so golf then was a rich man's game. The invention of the gutta-percha (see "gutty") helped to bring down the cost so that the average man could enjoy the game.

flub

vt: to strike the ball poorly and move it only a few feet. "He flubbed the ball trying to get it out of the deep rough."

fluffy lie

n: a ball sitting high in the grass with considerable room for the club to get "under" the ball. A dangerous lie in the rough because it is practically impossible to impart spin to a ball from a fluffy lie.

foozle

vt: to make a bungling stroke, a complete mess of a shot. For example: In trying to loft a shot over a bunker to top the ball or "hit the ball in the head" and dribble it into the bunker.

fore...

n: the warning cry to the golfers on the course ahead to let them know that they are in danger of being hit by a golf ball. The usual response is for the golfer ahead to cover his head and duck.

fore~caddie

n: a caddie who is sent on ahead to stand near the driving area to observe where the tee shots land. fore~caddies are used in tournaments where the rough is deep. In this way the players' balls can be found readily thereby avoiding delays due to long hunts for the sometimes hard to find golf balls.

forward press

n: the body movement with the hands and arms or with the body (sometimes an inward kick of the right knee), which initiates the backswing. The movement starts the body slightly forward toward the ball and then there is a reverse movement which lets the clubhead be backward away from the ball in a smooth motion.

four~ball

n: a match in which four golfers used all four scores to determine the winning and losing of holes. There are many variations of four~ball matches including the high and low scores of a pair being matched against those of the other pair; or "aggregate"—the low score plus the total of the two scores of a pair.

fried egg

n: a ball in sand, slightly buried, and with a ridge of sand all around it.

fringe

n: the short grass just off the closely cut surface of the green.

frog hair

n: same as fringe. An expression popularized by Jimmy Demaret on early TV golf commentating.

Funston's rule

n: "Always expect your opponent to hole out on his next stroke and you will never be surprised." Attributed to Irv Funston, a Michigan Seniors Champion.

Gallery

n: the cluster of spectators around the green in a tournament.

Ginty

n: a modern day version of the cleverly designed wooden club (see "baffy") with a V-shaped sole plate to help the clubhead get through heavy rough.

Give, give?

vt: what your opponent asks when his ball and your ball lie equally close to the hole on the green. It means, "I'll concede your putt if you will concede mine." Used most frequently by weak putters who are afraid of short putts.

gooseneck putter

n: a putter whose head is offset to the right as a result of an "L-bend" in the shaft near the hosel.

go to school

v: learning about the speed or direction of a putt by carefully observing another player's putt on the same line to the cup.

grain

n: the direction in which the grass grows on a green. Some greens are very "grainy," which means that instead of the blades standing straight up they lie in one direction or another like hair on a person's head. Grain

36

(grain cont'd)
can help to move a putt several inches one
way or the other as it travels toward the
cup. Watch the pros inspect the inside
of the cup before they putt. They're
trying to determine which way the
grain of the grass lies. They also look
for the shine on the green. If they
can see it, it tells them the grain
grows with the shine and the putt
will roll faster with it than
against it.

Judy Rankin

Grand Slam

n: winning all four major championships
in one year—the United States and British
Opens, the United States Professional Golfers
Association championship, and the Masters
Tournament.

Jan Stephenson

graphite

n: a recently developed golf club shaft material
of spun carbon, lighter than its counterpart in
steel, but subject to greater torque. Used
mainly by women golfers.

green

n: the closely cut grassy area that surrounds the flagstick and hole.

greenie

n: a bet as to who will be the first player to get his

(greenie cont'd)

ball on the green. On par~3s the "greenie" usually is won by the golfer whose ball is closest to the flagstick after all the players have made their tee~shots.

green jacket

n: the coat awarded to the winner of the Masters Tournament.

Jack Nicklaus, winner of five Masters.

gutty

n: also "guttie." In the 1870s an idol of the Indian God Vishnu was shipped to England protected by a gummy substance called gutta~percha. An enterprising Scot rec~ognized its possibilities as a material for golf balls. Those fashioned out of it were called gutties. They were hard, like billiard balls, and had a low trajectory and they were used for a number of years until the invention in the late 1890s of the Haskell rubber~wound ball.

Halve

v: to tie the score on a hole in a match. Both A and B, playing a head~to~head match, have 4s on a hole. "A has halved the hole with B." The word is pronounced as if it has no "l," "have."

ham~and~egging

n: same as the Brother~in~law act. Two partners alternately winning holes for their side.

handicap

n: an allowance of strokes intended to even competition between two golfers of unequal ability. Example: A's usual game is at even par~72. B's game is at 82. B's handicap would be calculated at 80% of the difference between par~72 and 82 or 8 shots. When A plays B he has to "give" B 8 strokes, that is, lower B's score by one stroke a hole on eight different holes. The holes where strokes are "given" are determined by the degree of difficulty of a golf course with the hardest hole usually designated as the "#1 stroke hole."

hand mashie

n: an illegal, cheating toss of the ball by hand. Years ago sand traps were often deep enough to obscure a player from the view of his opponent. Cheating golfers were known to pick up the ball in a trap, pretend to make a golf swing, and then release the ball at the same moment throwing it toward the hole. Now that bunkers are shallower, the shot is not seen much anymore. More often it is now a "foot mashie" that moves a ball out of a bad lie in the rough when the opponent is not watching.

Haskell

n: Coburn Haskell was the inventor of the wound-rubber golf ball in 1898. The invention revolutionized golf. It brought the cost of balls down so that everyone could afford to play the game.

hazard

n: a golf course obstacle whether a bunker of sand or grass or a water-course (lake, pond, ditch). A golfer may not "ground" his club in a hazard. That is, he may not set it down on the sand, grass, or water behind the ball before he makes his stroke. If he does so, he suffers a penalty of one stroke.

hickories

Bobby Jones

n: the strong wood of the hick-ory tree, used for many years for the shafts of golf clubs. The golfers of the early days found the shafts strong enough to withstand a hard blow at a golf ball and yet flexible enough to give the shot some whip or kick at impact. In the late 1920s the steel shaft replaced the hickory shaft. However, it is still seen in "classic" re-productions of old putters such as the famous "Calamity Jane" of Bobby Jones.

high side

n: any cup not on level ground has a high side as well as a low side. Since gravity helps the ball to fall into the cup, it is desireable for a putt to approach the cup on the high side, so it will have a better chance of falling in — also known as the "Pro side" of the

(high side cont'd)
cup because professionals are always using
it to their advantage. The low side of the
cup is also known as the "wrong
side," the "duffer's side," or the
"amateur side."

hit it in the head

n: an expression meaning to top the ball, hit it above the middle.

hole~in~one club

n: a group of golfers at a golf club agree that each of them will contribute a dollar or two to the member of the group who scores the next hole~in~one.

hole~in~one contest

n: a contest among golfers, all driving from the same tee to the same cup, to see who can make a hole~in~one. Usually the winner is the golfer whose ball is closest to the cup. However, there have been instances of golf~ers actually holing out in such contests. The odds against making a hole~in~one are approximately 44,000 to 1, depending, of course, upon the length of the hole.

honor

n: the right to drive first from the next tee goes to the golfer with the lowest score on the previous hole. On the first tee golfers usually toss a coin to determine honor. In club matches the golfer whose name is on the top of match schedule has the honor on the first tee.

hook

n: a ball hit with a right to left curve caused by counter~clockwise rotation of the ball. A smoth~ered hook is one that takes off to the left as soon as it leaves the club face. A normal hook occurs at the tail end of the flight of the golf ball. A hook adds distance to a drive, about 17 yards on a 200~yard drive hit straight with the same power.

horseshoes

n: a putting game between two players, each one putting two balls. Scored like the game of horseshoes with single points for the closest ball or balls and 3 points for an ace. The win~ner is the one who reaches a total of 21 first.

hosel

n: the hollow part of an iron club into which the shaft is fitted.

hot~dog pro

n: an "unknown" professional playing in a competition with other better known pros. The name originates from the dialogue, "Who's the pro coming up to the hole now? He's a nobody, let's go get a hot dog."

hunching

n: the illegal "stealing" one~half to one inch closer to the hole in replacing a ball marked on the green.

(hunching cont'd)

Under the rules the ball must be replaced exactly where it was when first marked. Cheaters try to take an illegal advantage and move the ball forward.

hustler

Lee Trevino

n: a con~man on the golf course who will hide his true ability in order to get favorable betting odds. Lee Trevino was an acknowledged hustler in his early days and one time pretended to be the locker~room boy at a golf club in order to "take" Raymond Floyd. Lee walked away with the money. Lee says that "A true hustler is one who can bet a hundred dollar Nassau without any money in his pocket.

Imaginary cup

n: coined by Horton Smith, one of the greatest putters of all time, the possessor of "The Velvet Touch." He said "all putts are level except sometimes the cup isn't where it's supposed to be." On a breaking putt, he would move the cup in his mind's eye to one side and putt straight for that imaginary cup allowing the break to carry the ball into the hole.

immaculate shot

n: a perfect shot, straight, and heading for the hole.

impossible lie

n: a lie from which the ball cannot be advanced

(impossible lie cont'd)

successfully. Occasionally a golfer finds his ball in such a terrible place that the shot is "impossible." Examples: lodged under the lip of a bunker, under a tree with the tree trunk obstructing the backswing, or a pitch to a severely sloping green with no chance to stop the ball near the cup.

impregnable quadrilateral

n: the name that Grantland Rice, sports writer, gave to the four major championships won by Bobby Jones in 1927, the United States and British Opens, the United States and British Amateur championships.

in

n: the second nine of a golf course, the "in nine." Early golf courses went "out" and then turned around and came "in."

Craig Stadler

in jail

prep. phrase: when a golfer's ball is in an impenetrable jungle, or behind a tree or trees directly on the line to the green, he is said to be in jail.

in your pocket

prep. phrase: when your ball lies within a foot or two of the hole, it is said that "you have your birdie on par in your pocket."

in the leather

prep. phrase: originally "within the leather," the phrase denotes the boundary of "gimmie" putts in some friendly matches not played under the strict rules of golf that require all putts to be holed. The clubhead is put inside the hole on the side near the ball with the shaft on the ground pointed toward the ball. If the ball is within the length of the shaft, but does not reach the "leather" or bottom part of the grip, the putt is conceded. Hustlers have been known to shorten their putter grips so as to gain an extra inch of advantage when putts "in the leather" are given.

irons

n: golf clubs with either forged or cast iron heads. They range from the #1 iron to the #9 iron with lofts from nine or ten degrees for the #1 iron to as much as thirty-five degrees for the specialty clubs such as the pitching wedge or sand wedge. In the early days of golf the clubs had distinctive names which were lost when the steel shaft came into vogue in the late 1920s. The early names were mid-iron, mid-mashie, mashie, mashie-niblick, niblick, and putter.

Jigger

n: the old name used for a cleek, an iron club with 4-iron or 5-iron loft. Often used for chipping to the green.

Knee-knocker

n: a putt in the 2-to 4-foot range

(Knee-knocker cont'd)

which causes the golfer mental and physical problems. His knees "knock" in fear that he may miss the putt. It is also called a "white knuckler" because of tension in the fingers.

Lag

v: to putt cautiously so that the ball does not run by the cup if you miss the hole. This generally indicates that the golfer is attempting to get down in two putts for sure and does not worry if he misses his first putt.

lay off

v: a golfer "lays off" his golf club when he breaks his wrists improperly at the top of his back swing.

leader board

n: a large billboard type of display showing the current standing in relation to par of the leaders of a medal tournament. Originated at the Augusta National Golf Course for the Masters Tournament. Red and green numbers are used to show scores under or over par. A Red 3 means that the golfer is 3 under par, a Green 3 means that the golfer is 3 under par.

leave it

v: the order to "leave the flagstick in the hole" so the player can use it in making his shot. The golf ball cannot be on the putting surface when this order is given.

lift and clean

v: under wet conditions the ball often will embed itself or plug in the fairway and mud will adhere to it. When this happens, a "lift and clean" rule is put into effect by the Golf Committee. The player may pick up his ball, clean it, and return it close to its original spot.

links

n: sandy, undulating land built up along a coastline. Since early golf courses were built on links the name came to be designated the golf course itself, "golf links."

lip

n: the edge of the cup.

v: the act of rimming the cup, that is, the ball rolls around the edge, but does not fall into the cup.

loop

n: a peculiarity in the golf swing in which the golfer performs an exaggerated clockwise motion with his hands at the top of the swing to bring the club back to the ball on an inside track. Miller Barber, Hubert Green, and Gay Brewer are notable examples of good golfers with loops in their swings.

Gay Brewer

low side

n: when the cup is not on level ground, the one side lower than the other is called the low side. See "high side."

Make the cut

v: in tournament play the score among the low 40 or 60 players, depending upon the Committee's ruling as to the cut-off score — usually determined at the end of the second day of a 4-day medal tournament

mallet-head

n: a barrel-shaped head on a putter, flat on the striking surface and usually rounded at the rear.

marker

n: (1) an official scorer who not only records the player's score but also observes the play to see that the rules of golf are obeyed.

n: (2) a coin or similar object which is placed directly behind the ball so that its place can be "marked" when the ball is lifted. The stymie rule (see "stymie") is no longer played, so any ball on the putting green that may interfere with the line of another player's putt is lifted and marked at the request of that player.

Nancy Lopez

marshall

n: traffic directors for the gallery.

mashie niblick

n: the name in the early days of golf for an iron now in the 7-iron range.

Masters

n: the name assumed by the Augusta National Invitational Golf Tournament a few years after its first tournament in 1934. Because Robert T. Jones, Jr. wanted champions and other excellent players, the "masters of golf," to partici~ pate, the tournament came to be called the "Masters."

meat off my fork

n: when a player unexpect~ edly holes out a putt, a bunker shot or a chip to tie a hole he appeared to be losing, the player who has been tied will say, "You took the meat off my fork," meaning he expected to win the hole but either a good shot or fate ruled otherwise.

midget~killer

n: a drive that travels very low to the ground and never rises more than a foot or two in its flight.

mid~iron

n: in the early days of golf, the name for a 2~iron.

mid~mashie

n: old name for the 4~iron of today.

miss the cut

v: fail to qualify for the last two days of tournament play. See "cut."

mixed foursomes

n: play in which there are two foursomes, each consisting of a man and a woman.

move your mark

v: a request that a golfer move his marker out of the line of the requester's putt. The opponent will then lift the coin, measure one club head to the right or left of the line, but the same distance from the hole, and move the marker there. The reverse procedure is carried out when the ball is returned to its original marked spot.

muckle

adj: an old Scottish term for the broken down part of a cup. "He was always going in the muckle side of the cup.

Mulligan

n: a free second shot off the first tee if the first shot is bad. Fergus O'Shaughnessy Mulligan was a famous Irish golfer of the 1890s. He was Club Champion of Parknasilla links in County Kerry no less than fifteen times. But he had one peculiarity. If he had a poor drive from the first tee he would insist that he could call the round off and start over again with another ball. His opponents tolerated this peculiar custom and soon everyone claimed to be entitled to a "Mulligan" on the first tee. Even Ben Hogan has been known to take one once in a while. Sometimes players even allow

(Mulligan cont'd)

"choosies" which means that if the Mulligan shot is not as good as the first one, the golfer can elect to play his first instead. Incidentally, at Franklin Hills, a prominent Jewish club in Birmingham, Michigan a Mulligan is called a "Rosenberg."

Nassau

n: the name for a system for scoring or betting that originated in the Bahamas in the 1920s. Ryder Cup, Walker Cup and Curtis Cup matches are conducted at match play on a Nassau style of scoring. Three points are at stake. One point is awarded to the winner of each nine and one point for the overall match. Many golfers often make bets on a Nassau basis with one dollar riding on each point and in a few cases larger amounts.

never up, never in

n: an expression meaning unless you hit the ball at least as far as the hole, you will never hole it. Also stated as "never up, never down."

niblick

n: the old name for the 9-iron.

O.B.

n: stands for "out-of-bounds"——a ball that carries

(O.B. cont'd)

beyond the boundary of the golf course. Costs the player one penalty stroke and he must play again from the spot where the unfortunate shot originated. The expression is believed to have been coined in Ireland in the 1930s at Ballybunion where there is a graveyard to the right of the first hole and Finbar O'Brien's farm beyond it. Many a tee~shot was either "in the graveyard" or "O.B."

one~iron

n: the straightest faced iron of all, meant to drive the ball far and low. Often used off the tee for greater accuracy. Therefore, it is also known as a "driving iron."

"The Open"

n: the name given to the open golf tournament held in the British Isles.

U.S. Open

n: the annual golf tournament conducted by the United States Golf Association. "Open" to all, amateurs as well as professionals. Actually, an amateur must have a handicap of 3 or better in order to attempt to qualify for the tournament.

out

n: the first nine holes of an 18~hole course constitute the "out nine."

outside agency

n: anything outside the golf course and not part of it that unfairly affects the golf ball by moving it. A dog, for instance.

Paddle grip

n: the name of the grip of a flat~sided putter in which in order to propel the ball toward the hole the flat~sided plane is at the same angle a ping~pong paddle would have.

par

n: the score an expert player would be expected to make on a given hole, allowing for two strokes on the putting green. Yardages for par per hole:

	Men	Women
Par~3	up to 250	up to 210
4	251 to 470	211 to 400
5	471 and over	401 to 575
6		576 and over

peg

n: the name first given to wooden tees. Until the invention of the wooden tee in the 1920s golfers used wet sand to form a conical mound from which they struck the tee~shot.

pick it up

v: what your opponent says when he concedes your putt.

pin

n: the flagstick.

ping

n: a currently famous and very popu~
lar putter which features a "cavity
back" or hollow which spreads the effec~
tive power of the club over a wider face
surface.

pipe

n: another name for the hosel or neck of an iron.
"He hit it on the pipe," means he shanked it.

_hosel

Der Bingle

pistol~grip

n: a putter grip with a curved han~
dle at the top not unlike that of a
pistol.

pitch

v: to loft the ball in the air to the
green from a spot not very far from
the green, usually in order to avoid a
hazard or uneven ground between the
ball and the green. "There are
no bunkers in the air," is an
old expression which explains
why golfers like to pitch the ball rather than run it to
the hole.

pitch~and~run

n: to be distinguished from the chip~and~run. In
this shot the ball is pitched, or lofted from just off
the green, in the air one~half to two~thirds of the way
to the cup and then allowed to run to the hole. The
different lofts of 8~iron, 9~iron, or wedge permit great

(pitch~and~run cont'd)
variations in the results of the shot.

pitching wedge

n: a lofted club with a flange on the bottom specially designed for pitch shots from the fairway or rough.

playing the odd

n: the act of causing your opponent to play his shot after you have played yours. Bobby Jones was a master of this strategy and would intentionally play his tee~ shots short of his opponent's. Jones would hit his next shot close to the hole. The pressure was then on the opponent to match the shot.

play through

v: one group of golfers steps aside and allows the follow~ ing group to play the hole the first group was on—usually as a result of some delay such as an unsuccessful search for a lost ball. This is golf etiquette—the fact that slow players realize they may be holding up faster players— and allow them to play through as a matter of courtesy.

plugged lie

n: a ball embedded in its own divot~mark in the ground.

plumb bob

v: the act of sighting "through" a putter shaft suspended per~ pendicularly to the ground. By using one eye and closing the other some golfers can

(plumb bob cont'd)
determine the amount of slope from ball to hole.

practice tee

n: the separate practice area where golfers may use every club in the bag. A practice green and practice bunker often adjoin the practice tee.

press

v: to add another bet, basically a double or nothing bet, to the one that is in effect.

n: "I'll give you a press," means I will bet you the same amount as the original bet for the remaining holes. Example: A wins the 5th hole of a nine hole match and becomes 2 up with 4 holes to play. B presses him for the last 4 holes, thus making an equal but a separate bet for the remaining holes. If B can win the press bet he can offset a loss of the bet for the nine holes and come out even. Usually a press bet cannot be offered unless one player or the other is two holes ahead.

An "automatic press" is one that is agreed in advance and need not be further discussed between the players. It goes into effect any time there is a two hole differential.

pro

n: one who plays golf or teaches golf for money. A professional golfer.

pull

n: a shot that is moving toward the left as a result

(pull cont'd)

of an incorrect swing from outside to in.

push

v: the act of pushing the ball toward its target. The left wrist is not broken but remains firm through the shot which travels low and often has considerable backspin.

Jack Nicklaus

Reading the green

n: a phrase that indicates inspection of the contours and slopes of a green to arrive at a decision about the speed, distance, and direction necessary to putt a ball successfully into a hole.

ready golf

n: in order to speed up play, golfers sometimes play "ready golf" which means that they don't wait to see which player is farthest from the hole, but proceed to strike their ball when they are "ready" to do so.

Red Grange

n: a score of 77 on the tour is a Red Grange, the number that former football star Red Grange wore on his jersey.

red numbers

n: red numbers are used on a scoreboard to show the number of strokes a player is under par. Green numbers are used to denote scores over par. On an electronic

(red numbers cont'd)
display the symbols (-) and (+) are used to denote scores under or over par.

rough

n: areas, usually of long grass adjacent to the tee, fairway, putting green, or hazards. "Short rough," grass cut two to three inches in height, is close to the fairway and "deep rough," where the grass can reach four to six inches in height, is farther away from the fairway.

rounders

n: the act of moving the ball in a circular fashion to the right or left on the green, keeping the same distance from the hole, in order to avoid casual water which lies between the ball and the hole. It is done without penalty.

rut iron

n: a short-headed club, an iron that was developed to enable a golfer to get a ball out of a track or rut. In the early days of golf wagons were used in the maintenance of the course. Their wheels left narrow, deep tracks or ruts. Also called a "track iron."

St. Andrews

n: the "Auld Grey Toon" in Scotland where it all started in the 1500s when Mary, Queen of Scots, played golf there. It was said that she whiffed her first five shots and lost sixteen golf balls on the round. Saint Andrews is not pronounced

Mary, Queen of Scots

(St. Andrews cont'd)

the way it looks. Say "Sin Andrus" and the Scots won't know you are a visitor. Originally, St. Andrews had 12 holes. The first 11 traveled straight out to the end of a small peninsula. After playing these the golfers returned to the clubhouse by playing the first 10 greens in reverse order plus a solitary green by the clubhouse. So, originally a "round of golf" consisted of 22 holes at St. Andrews. In 1764, the Royal and Ancient resolved that the first 4 holes should be converted into two and since the same 4 holes became 2 on the way back the "round" was reduced from 22 to 18 holes. Since St. Andrews was the arbiter of all that was correct in golf, 18 holes came to be accepted as the standard of the world.

sand-bagger

n: a hustler who keeps his handicap artificially high so that he can win tournaments or bets. Also known as a "mug-hunter" because of the mugs or trophies he collects.

sand trap

n: a hazard in which sand is used — usually a pit whose depth can vary from a foot in a shallow sand trap to as much as 6 to 8 feet in such bunkers as Hell Bunker at St. Andrews. Also called a bunker.

Gene Sarazen

sand wedge

n: a specially constructed club with a broad, low angle face that gives a great deal of loft and with a flange on the bottom that allows the club to slide through the sand under the ball. Gene Sarazen is credited with

(sand wedge cont'd)

making the first wedge-type club. The invention of the sand wedge revolutionized sand bunker play.

sandy

n: an "up and down" out of a sand bunker, a blast and then one putt into the cup. When agreed upon in advance, each member of a foursome contributes a specified sum to the player who makes a sandy.

save

n: the act of scoring a par that seems to be in doubt because the player had missed the green and was in the rough at greenside or in a bunker. It is also called "getting up and down," getting on the green and down in one putt.

sclaff

vt: the act of hitting the ground behind the ball before striking the ball— usually with a poor result.

Scotch foursome

n: a game in which two partners take alternate strokes to advance the ball. Sometimes with "selected drives" in which the partners will choose the better drive of the pair.

scramble

n: the name for a modern day game in which all members of a foursome drive and then select the best drive of the foursome

(scramble cont'd)

for a second shot. All four players then take second shots from that place. That type of play continues until the ball is in the hole.

shag

v: the act of retrieving golf balls driven out onto a golf~driving range. Hence, "shag~bag," the bag that holds the practice balls.

shank

v: to strike a ball on the hosel so the ball comes off at a sharp right from the inside curve of the blade or inside curves of the club. It is one of the most disturbing experiences any golfer can ever have. It is also known as a "Chinese lateral," an "out~shoot," or a shot "on the pipe." Even the greatest of golfers have shanked a ball at one time or another. The great Harry Vardon once had the habit so bad that he seriously considered giving up golf for good.

CLANG!

shooting lights out

vt: the act of scoring sensationally well with lots of birdies and eagles, no bogeys. The expression comes from Western movies where the hero in command of the situation shoots out the lights in a saloon.

Don January

skins

n: a game played by three or four golfers where the low score on a hole wins

(skins cont'd)

the bet provided no other player has the same score. When two players tie for low score, the bet carries over, in effect, doubling the bet for the next hole. An outright win on a hole is called a skin. A win of a carryover that goes three holes is a win of three skins.

Lee Elder

sky

v: to hit under the ball and hit it high but not far. Not unlike a pop-up in baseball.

slice

n: a ball that curves to the right (for a right-handed golfer) because of the clockwise spin imparted to it by the clubhead. Most duffers slice the ball because they do not make a proper turn of the body away from the ball but use only their hands, arms, and upper body. Also called a "banana ball."

smother

v: to close the clubface at impact, that is, rotate the blade in clockwise fashion which lowers the effective loft of the face and causes the ball to take off in a low trajectory to the left.

snake

n: a long putt that finds the bottom of the cup after traveling at least thirty feet over several different breaks in the green. As it heads for the cup it looks like a "snake."

socket

n: the opening in the neck of an iron club into which the club shaft is fitted. In Scotland when a player shanks the ball he is said to have "hit it on the socket." In the final round of the British Open of 1932, which he won, Gene Sarazen "socketed one" on an early hole. His caddie put the iron away in the golf bag and said, "We won't be requiring the use of that club anymore, will we, Mr. Sarazen?"

Old Tom
Morris

spoon

n: a lofted face fairway wood of early day golf comparable to the 3-wood of today.

spot

v: to mark the position of a ball on the green by placing a coin behind it.

spot putting

n: the act of picking out a discoloration or imperfection on a green and using that as a target to shoot at on the line to the cup. The spot may be a few inches or a few feet in front of the ball.

stance

n: a player places his feet in position preparatory to making a stroke. He takes a stance.

steel shafts

n: the invention of the steel shaft in the late 1920s

(steel shafts cont'd)

outmoded the old wooden shafts. Steel shafts were more responsive to feel and could be manufactured to consistent tolerances. This made matched sets of clubs possible, matched in weight and flexibility.

steer

vt: to attempt to drive the ball with a stiff wrist action, not a freely released swing. A golfer will try to "steer" the ball when he fears trouble on one side of the hole or the other. Results generally are not good.

stiff

adj: describes a ball hit close to the hole on an approach shot. "He hit it stiff to the pin."

stony

adj: a ball so close to the flagstick that an easy putt will be made. The ball is said to be "stony" or "stone dead."

stymie

n: a ball lying directly in the path of another player's ball on the line to the cup. In the early days of golf, such an obstruction was "played," that is, the ball had to be by-passed or jumped. In the 1930s the rule was finally abandoned. A ball closer than six inches had to be lifted under the stymie rule. Many golf course cards were made exactly six inches long so that a stymie could be measured easily.

sudden death

n: when a medal tournament or the qualifying round

64

(sudden death cont'd)

for a tournament ends in a tie between two or more players, they begin a playoff of as many holes are necessary until one player wins a hole and thereby the tournament and the loser is eliminated by "sudden death."

Fuzzy Zoeller, defeated Ed Sneed and Tom Watson in the 1979 Masters.

swing weight

n: the artificially designated physical relationship of clubhead, shaft, overall weight, and club length. A swing weight of C~1, which is light, is suitable for a woman player while a man might use a D~1 to D~5 swing weight.

Take advantage of the flagstick

v: when a player's ball is not on the putting surface he has the right to ask that the flagstick be left in the hole. Sometimes this can work to the golfer's advantage especially on a slippery downhill approach. Hitting the flagstick may help to stop the ball near the cup, might even allow it to fall into the hole.

take it

v: when your opponent says "take it," it means that he is conceding your next putt—also "pick it up" and "that's good." It also means "take the flagstick" out of the hole.

tap~in

n: a very short putt usually of no more than a few

(tap~in cont'd)

inches which can be tapped lightly into the cup. Holing a "tap~in" is not a certainty, however. Hale Irwin went to tap in a 2~inch putt in the 1984 British Open and whiffed the ball. He lost the championship by a single stroke. Even the great Arnold Palmer has been known to miss a tap~in.

tee

n: the specially designed close~cropped area from which the first shot on a hole is taken. The marker for the tee is on a horizontal line perpendicular to the line to the hole. The golfer may tee his ball any~ where in the rectangle formed by the line between the markers and a line two club~lengths depth be~ hind the markers.

Also, the wooden peg on which the ball is placed before it is struck from the tee area.

temporary green

n: in winter and early spring or when greens are under repair, temporary greens are often mowed out of the fairway grass near the permanent green in order to protect the regular green from abuse. Temporary greens are usually rough and difficult to putt on successfully.

that dog will hunt

an expression that indicates an es~ pecially long straight drive down the fairway.

TOP DOG

that's good

statement: what your opponent says when he

(that's good cont'd)

concedes your putt. When this happens, reach down and pick up the ball quickly for if you attempt to putt it you surely will miss.

three-fifty club

n: a club comprised of some of the world's longest hitters. To qualify for the group, a golfer must have driven the ball more than 350 yards in a long drive competition.

tiger tees

n: the tees that are far~ thest away from the hole are said to be deep in "tiger country." The Scot~ tish name for "Blue tees" or Championship tees. Country club members in the U.S. usually play from white tees and women from yellow tees even closer to the green.

Everybody's a critic!

tight lie

n: a lie in which the ball sits right on a bare or bald spot where there is no grass at all.

top

vt: to hit the ball above the middle and hit a poor shot that travels a short distance.

turn

v: after a golfer finishes the 9th hole and proceeds to the 10th, he is said to "make the turn." This expres~

(turn cont'd)
sion stems from the early days of golf when the first nine holes went "out" and the second nine went "in" toward the clubhouse.

Also, an expression of body movement away from the ball in the backswing. The greater the turn, the more power generated.

two-ball

n: a golf event in which two partners play together against another pair of golfers. Scoring in a two-ball event is varied—low ball of the pair, combined total of the pair, low ball and low total of the pair.

two-club wind

n: a twenty miles per hour wind that affects the distance a ball will travel. A 5-iron with a two-club wind will have the effect of a 3-iron. A 5-iron against a two-club wind will have the effect of a 7-iron.

Waggle

v: moving the clubhead back and forth over the ball in preparation for a swing. Cary Middle-coff, Masters and U.S. Open Champion, was known to waggle as many as twenty-four times before he struck the ball.

whiff

v: to miss the ball completely, to "fan"

Cary Middlecoff

(whiff cont'd)

the ball. The expression is believed to have originated in 1876 when Lord Gormley Whiffle completely missed a 4~inch putt to lose the Silver Medal at St. Andrews Old Course by one stroke. The spectators kept remarking to one another, "Did you see that Whiffle?" Later the phrase was shortened to its present form.

whipping

n: strong black twine used as a tight wrapping to attach a wooden shafted club to its hosel.

Hale Irwin

wind~cheater

n: a ball which is hit on a lower than normal tra~ jectory in order to lessen the effect of a head wind.

winter rules

n: a local rule providing for the lifting and cleaning of a ball lying in the fairway and placing it within six inches of where it originally lay, but not nearer the hole.

woods

n: the name given to wooden~headed golf clubs. The driver is the #1 wood and customarily golfers of to~ day carry three or four wood clubs in their bag, the #3 (with greater loft) and the #5 (with even more loft). Older golfers sometimes carry a #7 wood. The ori~ ginal names for the woods were driver, brassie, spoon, and baffy or cleek.

Yips

n: an unfortunate nerve condition which affects the muscles of the hands and wrists on short putts. Golfers with a bad case of the yips have been known to knock a 3~foot putt fifteen feet beyond the hole. Ben Hogan's golf career came to an end primarily because of a bad case of the yips.

NICKNAMES

Severiano (Seve) Ballesteros

This handsome young Spaniard has made a major impact on international golf. He has won the Masters twice, in 1980 and in 1983 and the 1979 and 1984 British Open tournaments. Seve is known for his long and occasionally wild drives along with remarkable ability to recover from impossible spots in the rough.

Miller (Mr. X) Barber

A bachelor for many years who hid behind huge dark sunglasses, he was called "Mr. X" because he fled town quickly after cashing big golf checks. Miller has hit the senior circuit with a bang. He picked up nearly $300,000 in 1984 after making a million and a half for himself on the main tour.

Tommy (The Terrible Tempered Mr. Bang) Bolt

His fiery temperament and inclination to throw clubs when he was angry got him his nickname. He won the 1958 U.S. Open, defeating Gary Player by four strokes.

71

Julius (Moose) Boros

Because he has a wide face and looks a little bit like one, friends called him "Moose." He is also called "Big Julie" and "Old Man River" because of his ambling, easy-going gait and relaxed attitude.

JoAnne (Big Momma) Carner

She is a big woman, 5 feet, 7 inches tall, solidly built, and is the friendly "Momma" to all other women on the LPGA tour. As an amateur she was called "The Great Gundy" when she won five U.S. Amateur championships because her maiden name was Gunderson.

Billy (Buffalo Bill) Casper

Because he had severe allergies to pesticides and to certain foods, his doctors recommended he eat no meat other than buffalo. Billy lost a lot of weight on the diet, which he has regained, and then some, but the nickname stuck. An excellent golfer, he has earned more than one-and-one-half million dollars in prize money by winning 51 tournaments, including U.S. Opens in 1959 and 1966 and the Masters in 1970.

Robert D. (Harpo) Clampett

He looks like Harpo Marx with his shock of curly blond hair. A newcomer to the tour in 1980, Clampett is heralded as a coming star.

Harry (Light Horse) Cooper

Because he had a fast swing and moved quickly, they called him Light Horse Harry. He was a top player in the 1920s and 1930s who almost won several big tournaments.

Fred (Boom Boom) Couples

His drives go off like cannon shots for distances frequently farther than 300 yards, so they call Couples "Boom Boom."

Ben (Gentle Ben) Crenshaw

Crenshaw is called "Gentle Ben" because he is soft-spoken, self-effacing, and always gracious. One of the best putters in modern day golf, he holed a monstrous snake on the 11th at Augusta in 1984 to help him win his first Masters title.

Robert (Wee Bobby) Cruickshank

Called "Wee Bobby" because he was only 5-feet 5-inches tall, Cruickshank was a great player of the 1930s, was twice runner-up for the U.S. Open, once to Jones in 1923 and once to Sarazen in 1932.

Dave (Eagleberger) Eichelberger

In 1980 Dave scored more eagles (16) than anyone

74

(Dave Eichelberger cont'd)

else on the PGA tour. Not only that, but he had two of them at Tallahassee where he won his fourth PGA title.

C.L. (Gibby) Gilbert

Gibby is C.L. Gilbert, Jr. Oddly, he has no first or middle names, just the initials. His father C.L. Gilbert, Sr., also only has initials for a name. The father is known as Gil and the son has been known as Gibby all his life. He's won three championships and nearly a million dollars on the tour.

...But you can call me "GIBBY"

Don (Tex) January

A slim 6-foot Texan who has had 27 tour victories during a long and very successful 28 years of campaigning, Don has won nearly two million dollars. His biggest victory came in the 1967 PGA championship at Columbine Country Club. He was also a member of the 1965 and 1977 Ryder Cup Teams. Since he became a senior player he has been winning more than ever, and has won over a million dollars.

Bernhard (The Red Baron) Langer

Because he comes from Germany and is a golfing ace, Langer has been nicknamed The Red Baron after the first Red Baron, Manfred von Richtofen, World War I German flying ace. Langer wears solid red clothes on the golf tour. Langer (pronounced LAHNGER)

(Bernhard Langer cont'd)
captured the 1985 Masters in sensational fashion, coming from behind to overtake the leaders in the final round.

Gene (The Machine) Littler

Because of his smooth, effortless grooved swing that never varies in its tempo, Gene Littler was called "The Machine." In 1961 he won the U.S. Open at Oakland Hills and became the eighth person to win both the Open and the U.S. Amateur. He has won 28 tour tournaments and more than 2 million dollars in his lifetime.

William (Wild Bill) Mehlhorn

He was a crowd-pleasing regular on the PGA tour in the 1920s and 1930s. Mehlhorn got his nickname because he wore colorful cowboy hats, talked a lot, and behaved unconventionally. One time he perched high in a tree and needled Bobby Cruickshank as Bobby tried to make a thousand dollar putt.

Orville (The Sarge) Moody

Famous for the one and only tour victory in his life, the United States Open of 1969 at the Champions Golf Club in Texas, Moody had been a staff sergeant for 14 years in the army. He is known for his cross-handed putting stroke, which does not work very well, and for his statement, "I never practice golf. All it does is louse up my game."

Greg (The Great White Shark) Norman

His white tow-head, his sharp beak of a nose, and the fact that he used to hunt sharks under the reefs of the Australian coast-

(Greg Norman cont'd)

line led to his nickname. Norman was second in the 1984 U.S. Open to Fuzzy Zoeller, and won two tournaments in 1984.

Edward (Porky) Oliver

A jovial, rotund man, Oliver was never a major tournament winner, but a runner-up in the 1946 PGA and the 1953 Masters. His full nickname was "Pork Chops" because he used to order them for break-fast. Renowned for a score of 16 he made on the 16th hole, a 222-yard par-3 at Cypress Point during the 1954 Crosby Tournament. Porky put four balls into the ocean, went down on the beach to continue the battle, finally sinking a putt on his sixteenth stroke.

Masahi (Jumbo) Ozaki

Tall and muscular, one of the greatest Japanese players of all time, he could hit the ball a country mile. He was called "Jumbo" because he was unusually large for a Japanese.

Barbara (L'il Tiger) Romack

Although she's tiny, not over 5-feet 3-inches, she's a tiger who never let her opponent get away from her. In 1954 she won the U.S. Amateur championship in a final match that took 29½ hours to play because of intermittent thundershowers.

Paul (Little Poison) Runyan

Paul Runyan was called "Little Poison" because although he was physically small, only about 5-feet 6-inches tall, and slight, he was absolute murder to his opponents. He slaughtered Sam Snead in the finals of the

(Paul Runyan cont'd)

1938 PGA championship 8 and 6, consistently putting his 5-wood second shots inside Snead's iron shots to the greens.

Horton (The Joplin Ghost) Smith

Because he is tall, unassuming, inobtrusive, quiet, and born in Joplin, Missouri, Smith was called "The Joplin Ghost," He was the greatest putter of the 1930s and the winner of two Masters titles, 1934 and 1936. They also called him "The Velvet Touch" because of his delicate putting stroke that invariably found the hole.

Hollis (Spacey) Stacy

She won the USGA Girls championship for three consecutive years. As a professional she has won three LPGA Opens. Stacy is one of the tour's most flamboyant performers who loves rock and roll dancing. She is called "Spacey" because she always seems to be somewhere else than the space she's occupying at the moment.

Craig (The Walrus) Stadler

Craig's weight varies between 250 and 190 pounds, but he plays marvelous golf at any weight, ambling along in a bearlike shuffle with his belt anchored several inches below his ample belly. His nickname is obviously appropriate, and to top off the image, he has a big bushy moustache. The 1982 Masters was his first major championship and in that year he was the leading money winner on the PGA tour with a total of $446,442.

Lee (The Merry Mex) Trevino

A genial, talkative Texan of Mexican heritage, Trevino sports a suitable nickname. Trevino's major victories are the U.S. Open in 1968, two British Open championships, and two PGA championships, the most recent in 1984.

Frank Urban (Fuzzy) Zoeller

Zoeller's nickname comes from the initials of his name: F.U.Z. A real character of modern day golf, colorful, talkative, he won the Masters Tournament in 1979 after a playoff with Ed Sneed and Tom Watson. Fuzzy is noted for his unusual swing with hands held low and for placing the clubhead outside his line and then drawing it into the ball before making his swing.

Lee Trevino

HARRY VARDON

One of the best players of all time, Harry Vardon (1870-1937) also was most responsible for making golf popular in its early days. Along with James Braid and John Henry Taylor, Vardon dominated the game in the years between 1896 and 1914. He won six British Open Championships, a record which still stands. He was also runner-up four times and third twice. Most golfers believe he was the originator of the "Vardon Grip" (he was not, J.H. Taylor was), which featured the little finger of the right hand overlapping the forefinger of the left hand for greater compactness.

Vardon was so accurate a wood player that it was said that on his second round of the day, he would find himself in the middle of the fairway hitting out of the divots he had made on his first round.

Vardon came to the United States at the height of his career and won the U.S. Open Championship in 1900. He also came close to winning the U.S. Open again when he tied for the title with young (twenty-year-old) Francis Ouimet of the United States along with Edward "Ted" Ray, long-driving fellow British star. Ouimet won that playoff in dramatic fashion on the demanding Brookline course, The Country Club, outside of Boston in 1913.

Vardon won the last of his opens in 1914, eighteen years after his first which was a tribute to his sound consistent swing. Vardon's style was especially rhythmic and graceful and appeared to be effortless. He played from an open stance, that is, with his left foot drawn back from the line of flight, and oddly, he violated the rule of modern day golf instructions by breaking his left arm in his back swing. Of course, he straightened it on the forward swing. He played with shorter and lighter clubs than the other good players of his era and was considered a long driver by his fellow competitors.

Vardon was 5-feet 9-inches tall and carried ten wooden-shafted

clubs, two of which were spares for his driver and brassie. Shafts broke easily in those days and the heads would fly off at unexpected times.

Vardon was called a golfing genius by Bernard Darwin, the leading golf writer of that era. Vardon was so accurate with his long shots to the green that he rarely had to use his niblick to make his approach. His temperament was serene and he played with "gallant courage" most confidently. He was a true "gentleman golfer", most considerate of his opponent's feelings.

Three of Vardon's six championships were won with the hard "guttie" ball and three were won after the introduction of the rubber-cored Haskell ball. Vardon was considered a good putter but not a great one. It was said that if he had been a great putter he would have been undefeated in major competition for fifteen years.

In January 1900 Vardon toured the United States and played matches nearly every day. It was this tour that brought golf to the attention of the multitude of Americans who, until that time, considered golf a rich man's pastime, an effete sport.

They saw a real he-man striking the golf ball prodigious distances and they began to want to participate in this then novel sport.

JOHN HENRY TAYLOR

The third member, along with Harry Vardon and James Braid, of the "Great Triumvirate" of golf, John Henry Taylor (1871-1963) was a master of the mashie (today's 5-iron) and with this club could make the ball do tricks. The mashie then had deep grooves in its face markings that would be illegal in today's game.

Playing with Englishman Taylor in America one time, Bobby Jones complimented him on a particularly good drive whereupon Taylor barked, "What did you expect?" and finished the round without saying another word.

"J.H.", a dour, shy man won the British Open five times—1894, 1895, 1900, 1909, and 1913. He was runner-up in 1896, 1906, and tied for the runner-up spot in 1904 and 1905. He was also runner-up in the U.S. Open of 1900 losing to his perennial rival Harry Vardon.

Taylor began as a caddie at Westward Ho! in England and at the age of seventeen became an assistant green-keeper. Of course, he could and did play all the golf he wanted to and his skill bought him to the attention of the better golfers. Soon he was challenged by famous Andrew Kirkaldy of St. Andrews. He beat Kirkaldy and later succeeded him as professional at the Winchester Club in Surrey, England. Taylor moved to Royal Mid-Surrey where he stayed for more than forty years.

Taylor was a stern competitor and approached every championship as if it were a battle. He had a strong firm-footed stance and a short punched swing. He could drive the ball low and with great accuracy. Nobody else could match his compact stroke. One of his greatest victories in the Open came at Hoylake in appalling wind and rain. He pulled his cap down tightly over his ears, planted his sturdy hobnailed boots firmly in the ground and drove the ball straight through the wind as if it were not there.

J.H. had no less than ten holes-in-one in his long distinguished career. The most opportune one came at famous old Prestwick in the 1925 British Open Championship, the tournament won by "Long Jim" Barnes of the United States. Taylor's hole-in-one enabled him to tie for fifth in the tournament.

Taylor was a bold player in a day of conservative golf. He was one of the first to challenge the deep bunkers in front of the greens rather than play safe by hitting short and then using his niblick to the green. He was not as long a driver as Vardon, but he was Vardon's equal in steadiness and accuracy.

Taylor was so shy that once, when his club members wanted to give a party for him, to celebrate one of his championships, he deliberately took the train to a stop past the golf club, walked back over the moors to his house so he would not be seen and therefore would not have to go to the party.

In 1957 the Royal North Devon paid him the highest honor of his life by electing him president. He lived to the ripe old age of 92.

JAMES BRAID

The third member of the "Great Triumvirate," James "Big Jim" Braid (1870-1950), was a Scot. Together with Harry Vardon and J.H. Taylor, the three golfers dominated British golf from 1874 to World War I. Among them they shared sixteen British Open championships. Braid won five—1901, 1905, 1906, 1908, and 1910. Braid's record score for the British Open, a 291 in 1908, stood up for nineteen years until Robert T. "Bobby" Jones, Jr., broke it in 1927. Although Big Jim was a tall, slim man, he was not an unusually long hitter for most of his career. Then suddenly, almost overnight, he discovered the secret of long driving and from then on was known as one of the longest drivers of golf. Braid also had thirteen holes-in-one in his long career. Braid later became a renowned golf course designer. He is probably most famous for building the classic Gleneagles Kings Course in Scotland. It is said that he strolled over the hills and through the heather and planted spikes, apparently at random, saying, "We'll have a green here, a tee there." The result was one of the greatest and most picturesque courses in the world.

He came from a humble background—the son of a ploughman. His father, who never played golf, was unsympathetic to James's ambitions on the links and to his desire to become a professional golfer. Braid left school at the age of thirteen and became a journeyman carpenter, but managed to play in amateur golf events in his home area. After he won an amateur title in his early twenties, he was encouraged to turn professional and he went to London as an apprentice club-maker.

All golf clubs were made by hand and there was a growing demand for good clubmakers. His pay at first was eight pence an hour, but later on his salary was raised to a shilling (twelve cents).

Braid played golf in the evenings after work and soon developed

an individual style. He had a full swing "with a very loose knee (the left) when he really went after the ball." It was said that he played with "a divine fury."

By 1895 Braid started to make his mark in golf. He tied J.H. Taylor in an important match at West Drayton. By 1901 Braid had won his first British Open Championship.

By that time J.H. Taylor and Vardon had each won the title three times. Within a few years Braid became the first man to win the Open Championship five times, although Taylor equalled this record later and Vardon surpassed it. To put in perspective the marvelous golfing feats of Braid, Taylor, and Vardon, it is informative to note that in the modern era only Peter Thomson and Tom Watson have won the title five times.

Braid was in great demand as a golf course architect. Many a Scottish course today is proud of a Braid design and, according to the custom of giving holes distinctive names, the most difficult hole on a course will often bear the Braid name—"Braid's Brawest" (toughest). Once in a while a hole may be called, "Braid's Folly," a name that connotes the fact that some club members thought Braid had created a poorly designed hole.

At the age of seventy, James Braid was honored by the Royal and Ancient Golf Club of St. Andrews by being named an honorary member. Braid died at the age of eighty. He was a reserved man, an immensely painstaking man of few words.

WALTER HAGEN

One of the most colorful golfers of all time, Walter "The Haig" Hagen (1892-1969), was the first professional golfer allowed to enter the front door of swank country clubs. Once that happened the standing of all professional golfers improved from "tradesmen" to "gentlemen". He had broken the class barrier, and it stayed broken from then on.

Walter had a slashing swing with a pronounced forward sway, but he could make every shot in the bag. He was noted for his showmanship. He would often pretend that a shot was very difficult and take a great deal of time to survey it. Then he would execute it successfully with a smile and great flair.

Hagen won eleven national championships, four British Opens, two United States Opens, and five PGA championships. The PGA was conducted at match play in the 1920s when The Haig was at the peak of his ability. He won twenty-two straight matches in the PGA tourneys, an unmatchable feat and one that will never be equalled now that the event has become a medal play event.

Hagen played about 1,500 exhibitions all over the world. Before he would start, he would ask some knowledgeable person what the course record was for the links he was about to attack, and then he would bet huge sums of money that he could beat it. In nearly all cases he did.

On one occasion Hagen had bet he would break the course record of 67 at a particular course. A large gallery was following him as he came to the eighteenth green. He needed to sink a twenty-five foot putt to break the record and win the bet.

The crowd was hushed and expectant as he bent over the ball. There wasn't a sound, not even a whisper. Then Hagen suddenly stopped, looked up, and said to the crowd, "Is there anybody here who thinks I'm not going to make this putt?" The tension was broken, of course. Then The Haig did sink the putt and won the bets. Hagen hauled away his winnings and the gate receipts in a suit case.

When Robert T. "Bobby" Jones was in his prime, Hagen played Jones four successive rounds of match play in a challenge match, "the World's Greatest Pro vs. the World's Greatest Amateur." He defeated Jones 12 and 11, the worst trouncing Jones ever took.

Melvin "Chick" Harbert (later PGA Champion himself in 1954) was a boy wonder of golf in Michigan in the 1930s. When Hagen visited the Benton Harbor area, young Harbert, seventeen years old, was invited to play in an exhibition of golf against Hagen. Chick relates the story, "I was nervous at first playing against the great golfer, but finally I settled down and when we came to the 18th hole we were even. We were both on the par-4 green in two strokes. I was a little farther away than the Haig, about fifteen feet to his ten.

"Very carefully I surveyed my putt. I circled to the left, I circled to the right. I got down on my hands and knees behind the ball. Then I stepped up and sank the putt for the birdie I thought would beat Hagen.

"He accepted the situation calmly. He circled to the right, he circled to the left, he even got down on his hands and knees mimicking exactly every move I had made. Then he stepped up to his putt and knocked it into the hole *backhanded*!"

Hagen was a master at the psychology of golf and frequently would attempt to mislead his opponent about his club selection. Al Watrous, great golfer of the 1920s, runner-up to Bobby Jones in the British Open of 1921 at Royal Lytham and St. Anne's, told this story about Hagen. They were playing in the 1925 PGA Championship at Olympia Fields in Chicago, and came to the eighteenth hole, a dangerous par-5 with water in front of the green. The match was tied. Watrous's ball was in the fairway, Hagen's was in the woods to the left. Watrous was away so he had to play first for the green. He could see Walter brandishing a wood club in a practice swing in the rough. That meant that Hagen had a good lie and would be able to go for the green with his second shot. Watrous thought if Hagen was going to use a wood so would he, and when he did he put his ball in the water. Then Hagen pulled out an iron, which he had been intending to use all along, played safely to the fairway and then to the green in three to win the match from Watrous.

Hagen was never known to stoop to pick up a golf tee. After he had driven he would stride off determinedly down the fairway and the gallery would rush to pick up a Hagen souvenir.

Walter loved wine and women, not necessarily in that order. And sometimes in his big touring car he would arrive at a golf course still wearing his tuxedo from the night before. He had been up all night, but that didn't matter. He would change his shoes, put on his fresh white linen knickers and be ready to play in his own good time. He never hurried and was always late. That was "The Haig."

One time Hagen was partying strongly at 2 A.M. when one of his friends told him, "Your opponent for tomorrow has been in bed since ten o'clock." Hagen replied, "Yeah, but he's not sleeping!"

Hagen at one time lived in splendor at the Detroit Athletic Club, a plush men's club famous for its cuisine. The Haig's weight got up to the 300 pound mark. His customary breakfast at 1:00 P.M. was two broiled Maine lobsters (according to one of the DAC waiters who served him).

Hagen dressed in the finest clothes and drove the best of cars. He made a million dollars in his long successful career and he spent most of the money. His motto in life was, "You're only here for a short visit. Don't hurry. Don't worry. And be sure to smell the flowers along the way."

ROBERT T.
JONES, JR.

ROBERT T. JONES, JR.

At the age of 28, Robert T. "Bobby" Jones, Jr. (1902-1971) accomplished "the greatest exhibition of skill and character by any individual athlete, bar none, since the beginning of sports history." He won the British Amateur, the British Open, the United States Open, and the United States Amateur Championships all in the same year—the Grand Slam.

Jones hated the name, Bobby, and was always called Bob by his friends. But the Scots who loved him with a passion dubbed him Bobby and to the rest of the world he remained Bobby all his life. In the 1920s it was Jones who dominated the field in the U.S. Open and U.S. Amateur Championships just as it was Ben Hogan in the 1950s and Jack Nicklaus in the 1960s.

Jones, an attorney-at law by profession, came from a well-to-do family and never played any game but golf. He thought that this focused effort was one of the reasons for his success.

Jones was called the boy wonder of golf. He won the Georgia State Amateur championship when he was only fourteen years old. He also qualified for the U.S. Amateur that year. When he was only seventeen, he was runner-up in three major championships, the Southern Open, the Canadian Open, and the U.S. National Amateur Championship. For a while it appeared that he would be a perpetual runner-up but he broke through in 1920 to win the Southern Amateur. He was medalist in the National Amateur, and played respectably in the U.S. Open, finishing in eighth place.

He moved up to second place in the 1922 U.S. Open and again in the Southern Amateur. At last, in 1923 he won his first U.S. Open, defeating Bobby Cruickshank in a playoff, 76 to 78 at Inwood on Long Island. From then on, there was no stopping him. It was Jones against the field until 1930. He won: the U.S. Open again in 1926,

1929, and 1930; the Amateur in 1924, 1925, 1927, 1928, and 1930; the British Open in 1926, 1927, and 1930; and the British Amateur in 1930. Jones had won thirteen National Championships in only seven years. In the U.S. Amateur he was either winner or runner-up every year from 1924 to 1930 and in the U.S. Open he was either first or second every year, except one from 1922 to 1930.

Jones was only 5-feet 8-inches tall and inclined to be stout. He had a full, fluid, graceful swing that appeared to be so leisurely that the great distances he hit the ball came as a surprise. He was an excellent putter and used an old wooden shafter blade he called "Calamity Jane." It was made for him by master club-maker Tom Stewart in Scotland.

After he won the "Impregnable Quadrilateral" (as the four tournaments were dubbed by sportswriter Grantland Rice), Jones felt that he had accomplished everything he possibly could do in golf. The stress of tournament play took a grievous toll on his nerves and body. He could never keep his breakfast down on the morning of a crucial match. He would lose from seven to ten pounds over the course of a four-day tournament.

A lucrative contract—a million dollars—was offered him by the Spalding Company, premier maker of golf clubs and other sports equipment. It meant that Bobby would have to relinquish his amateur standing and become a professional in the eyes of the United States Golf Association. He accepted the proposal and soon Spalding began to manufacture new Robert T. Jones, Jr. models of golf clubs. The golfing public bought them by the millions. Jones also made some very successful movie shorts that demonstrated his swing, club by club.

Jone's next endeavor was the building of the Augusta National Golf Club at Augusta, Georgia. He envisioned a golf club composed of prominent members from all over the country, from all over the world, an invited group of golf enthusiasts who would play on one of the finest golf courses in the world. Famed Scottish designer, Donald McKenzie worked with Jones and turned a former nursery in the magnificent rolling countryside into the Augusta National Golf Club, one of the most gloriously beautiful courses in the world.

Next, Jones invited a few of his friends to an Invitational Tournament at the club in spring when the azaleas and dogwood were in bloom. From that small group there evolved an annual get-together which came to be called the Masters Tournament, for it was clear that Jones was inviting the masters of golf to play in his tournament every year.

In the meantime Jones had contracted a seriously debilitating spinal disease. Until his death in 1971 he suffered a slow and painful deterioration of his body. His mind remained bright and alert and he was always cheerful, never admitting to anyone that he was in pain.

In the early days of the Masters, Jones would always participate in the tournament, though his golfing skills were no longer good enough to keep up with the stars of those days—Gene Sarazen, Craig Wood, Horton Smith, Ralph Guldahl, and others.

It was the custom each year that Jones would play with the previous year's winner in the first round. So it happened that in 1929 Henry Picard (winner of the Masters in 1938) was playing with Jones as they came to the 9th hole, a 420-yard par-4 with an elevated green that slopes severely from back to front. Jones's second shot went just over the back edge of the green. Picard said to Jones, "I'll bet you the clubhouse you can't keep your chip-shot on the green." Jones scoffed at Picard.

Picard said, "His chip-shot rolled down the green and right off the front of it. The next year the green was flattened out."

In 1958 the first World Amateur Golf Team Championship was, most fittingly, played at the "Old Course" at St. Andrews, Scotland. Jones, then seriously ailing, was named Captain of the American team.

By then he was using a wheel chair, but he determined to make one last pilgrimage to old St. Andrews and the charming Scottish people he loved so well. Shortly before he left for Scotland, he was asked whether he would accept "the Freedom of the City" while he was there. He knew it would be an honor, but did not know precisely what was involved. He accepted the invitation.

The presentation ceremony was held at the Younger Graduation Hall of St. Andrews University and was attended by 1,700 enthusiasts. Jones was driven up the aisle of the Hall in a golf cart (the only one allowed at St. Andrews) and then he climbed the stairs to the stage with the help of a hickory-shafted cane.

In his presentation speech Provost Robert Leonard told Jones, "We welcome you back as an old and dearly loved friend, as an ambassador in the cause of international understanding and good will."

Jones was told that among the privileges he would have in the future were, "the right to cast shells, to take divots, and to dry his washing on the first and last fairways of the Old Course." He was also named a Burgess and Guild Brother of the City of St. Andrews. The last American before Jones to be so honored was Benjamin Franklin, 199 years earlier.

As Jones left the auditorium, the assemblage broke out softly into the old Scottish song, "Will Ye No' Come Back Again?" and there was not a dry eye in the house because Jones knew and everyone else knew, too, that he would never come back again.

GENE SARAZEN

Gene Sarazen is one of golf's all-time leading lights, with one of the longest careers in any sport. He is one of only four players who have won all four of the major professional tournaments, the U.S. Open in 1922 and 1932, the British Open in 1932, the PGA Championship in 1922, 1923, and 1933, and the Masters in 1935.

Gene's father was a carpenter who as a young man in Italy, had studied to be a priest before he came to America. When Gene was young, he worked as an apprentice to his father and also caddied to earn extra money at the nearby Apawamis Club. Gene was only eight years old when he started, so diminutive and so likeable that the members of the club went out of their way to see that he did not have to carry a heavy bag.

As Gene grew older he spent as much time as he could on the golf course. His father frowned on Gene's golf aspirations. When Gene had an attack of pleurisy and the doctor's advice was for him to get out of the dusty carpentry shop and work in the open air, Gene became an assistant professional at Brooklawn Country Club in Connecticut. He had a natural swing and a marvelous sense of rhythm and balance. Although only 5-feet 5½-inches tall, Sarazen had a stocky frame, strong hands and arms, and sturdy legs. He could drive a ball straight and far with the best of them.

When Gene was only eighteen, he was encouraged to enter the 1920 U.S. Open at Inverness in Toledo, Ohio. He played very well, qualified third, and finished thirtieth. Two years later, at twenty, he became the youngest U.S. Open champion of all time when he won at Lakeville in Flushing, Long Island.

Gene is famous for several remarkable golf feats. The one the public remembers most is undoubtedly, "the shot that was heard around the world." It happened in the second Masters tournament in 1935.

Bobby Jones had invited sixty-three of his friends, the best golfers in the world to play in his Invitational Tournament at the Augusta National Golf Course. Not for several more years would the tournament be called the Masters. Sarazen started off with a 68 to Craig Wood's 69. The next day Gene shot 71 to Craig's 72 but on the third round Wood roared back with a 68 to Gene's 73. On the fateful last day Gene started three strokes behind Craig Wood who was playing in front of him.

When Sarazen reached the 485-yard par-5 fifteenth hole, he was still three strokes behind Wood. Gene knew that Wood was in the clubhouse with a last round of 73. Gene had to shoot a score of three-under par on the last four holes in order to tie Wood. It was apparently an impossible task because those last four holes are extremely difficult and demanding.

Gene drove 265 yards on the fifteenth hole and landed in the fairway. The fairway is high on this hole and from where his drive had stopped Gene could look down on the green in the distant shadows.

Sarazen turned away from his ball in the wet fairway grass and peered down the long slope to the green, 220 yards away. A freezing wind disturbed the flag and ripped through his protective sweater. Around him, one thousand eyewitnesses huddled together in a crescent that bulged behind the green and thinned out to a single line on either side of the fairway.

Before the green lay a pond—not much of a pond, really—perhaps forty feet across at its broadest. It protected the green, yet it could be an easy birdie for a player who could put together two excellent wood shots and was willing to gamble.

Gene Sarazen was that gambler. He reached for his favored 4-wood, took another quick glimpse ahead through the mist, and swung.

He watched the ball as well as he could as it sailed up into the haze and over the pond to the fifteenth green. It dropped on the apron, popped up twice on the turf, and rolled relentlessly toward the cup as though homing in on a magnet. A thousand voices in the gallery screamed as the ball disappeared into the cup for a double-eagle-2.

Gene Sarazen strode down the remaining two hundred yards of

fairway between the two lines of shouting fans like a king walking to his throne, the 4-wood held in front of him like a scepter. "It was the greatest thrill I have ever had on a golf course," he said. "I realized all I needed now was par to tie."

Gene parred the last three holes and tied Craig Wood. The next day in a 36-hole playoff, Sarazen beat Wood by five strokes.

The second incredible performance by Sarazen happened in the 1932 U.S. Open, which was held at Fresh Meadow Country Club in New York. Gene had been pro there for six seasons, but he felt superstitious about a home pro trying to win an Open on his own course. He didn't want to be jinxed, so he changed jobs to nearby Lakeville. He won the British Open that year and came physically tired to the U.S. Open two weeks later. In those days, the last thirty-six holes of the U.S. Open were played on the same day, so those holes were consecutive. After the first eight holes of his third round Gene stood seven strokes behind the leader, Phil Perkins. Then Gene got hot. There has never been such a streak of low scoring in golf since he set Fresh Meadow afire that day. Gene played the final twenty-eight holes in 100 strokes. That is an average of 3.6 storkes per hole. When he finished he had won with 286 strokes, three strokes ahead of Perkins and Bobby Cruickshank.

For those last twenty-eight holes Gene had four 2's, seven 3's, fourteen 4's and only three 5's. He had a total of nine birdies! In the early days golfers had great difficulty getting the ball out of sand traps. The club would dig into the sand and lose all its force. Gene had the inspired idea of making a club that would skid under the ball instead of digging in. He experimented and developed the first sand wedge with a flange on its bottom so it could skim under the ball and "explode" it from the sand more easily. With his new golfing tool in hand, it was said that Gene would often deliberately shoot for the sand traps because he knew he could get "up and down" in two strokes.

Gene is called "The Squire" or "The Country Squire" because a number of years ago he took some of his substantial winnings and bought a farm in upper New York and became a gentleman farmer.

Sarazen has always been an advocate of playing golf fast. Like Bobby Cruickshank, he believes in the old adage, "Miss 'em quick." Sarazen and George Fazio played the last round of the 1947 Masters in one hour and fifty-seven minutes. Sarazen's score was 70.

Gene is also well-known for his golfing attire. He always wears knickers on the golf course. He has had hundreds of pairs specially made for him and is partly responsible for current interest in the traditional golf attire of the early 1900s.

In the 1950s Gene was playing with an amateur partner, an automobile dealer, who was using golf clubs that were about ten years old. When Gene saw them, he said, "Would you drive a car that's ten years old? They have improved golf clubs as much as they've improved cars." The amateur went out the next day and bought a new set of Sarazen clubs.

Gene officially retired from tournament golf after playing in the 1973 British Open. He created a sensation there when, with television cameras rolling, he scored a remarkable hole-in-one on Troon's famous 126-yard eighth hole, "The Postage Stamp."

Gene always attends the Masters tournament in early April to renew friendships with all his old golfing rivals, Sam Snead, Byron Nelson, Jerry Barber, Cary Middlecoff, Jack Burke, Jr., and Paul Runyan. Gene can be seen sitting on the porch of the old Georgian clubhouse holding court before his many admirers, undoubtedly retelling the story once again of the double-eagle-2 in 1935.

Gene now lives in southern Florida and still plays golf with great skill several times a week. One of the golf courses at PGA headquarters was recently named, "The Squire" and dedicated to him in recognition of his international reputation and his gentlemanly character.

The plaque at PGA headquarters reads, "Gene Sarazen set standards in golf. He was a true competitor who became the first to win the Professional Grand Slam. He attacked golf courses with an unharnessed fury. His style of golf is legendary. His character, his charisma, and his charges won him a legion of followers throughout the world."

BEN HOGAN

Ben Hogan is regarded as the greatest shot-maker of the modern era, possibly the best golfer of all time. Jack Nicklaus is the only player who has come close to the perfection and dominance of the game that Hogan achieved in his prime.

Gene Sarazen has said, "Nobody covered the flag the way Hogan did." Hogan, not a big man at 5-feet 7-inches, weighed only 138 pounds. He was leading money-winner in 1940, about $13,000 in prize money. Compare that amount with the $436,000 Tom Watson earned in 1984!

Hogan was called "The Hawk" because his grey eyes had the piercing steely look of a hawk. He smiled rarely and was all business when he played. He usually wore a white linen visored cap and smoked incessantly. The Scots admired his marvelous play at Carnoustie in 1953 when he won the Open. They dubbed him, "the Wee Ice Mon", a nickname which fitted Ben even more than The Hawk, for he was a cold man.

Hogan was a ruthless perfectionist. He hit thousands of golf balls day after day on the practice tee trying to find the secret of the perfect swing. Ben hooked badly in his early days, a sudden darting right-to-left duck hook. He said, "When I hook I get nauseated."

Ben figured out a way to avoid any possibility of his dreaded hook. He taught himself never to let the clubface close at impact and developed a gentle, accurate right-to-left fade.

Hogan became so accurate with his swing that he could put the ball down on a bedsheet 250 yards down the fairway twenty times in a row. He was a strong competitor who tried to birdie every hole. Ben once said, "If you can't birdie the first hole how can you birdie them all?"

What makes the Ben Hogan story most incredible is that one

foggy morning in Texas in 1949, when he was at the height of his game, he was nearly killed in a terrible car accident. In a dense fog a Greyhound bus hit the Hogan car head-on. For an hour-and-a-half Ben lay in the wreckage, badly smashed up. Then, he had to endure a 150-mile ride to a hospital in El Paso.

Ben had suffered multiple injuries to his legs and to his hip. It was strongly believed not only would he not play golf again, but that he might not even walk again.

His indomitable will brought him through. Although he was limping badly, he captained the Ryder Cup Team that year in England. Some blood vessels in Hogan's legs had been tied off so that when he walked his legs had that constant feeling of "pins and needles." Although he feared he could not complete the 72 holes required in an Open tournament, he signed up for the Los Angeles Open. All competitors had to walk whether they had injured legs or not and no exception would be made for Ben Hogan.

Ben played anyway and tied for first place, but lost the playoff. A few months later he won the U.S. Open at Merion after tieing with Lloyd Mangrum and George Fazio. A year later he brought "The Monster", the Oakland Hills course at Birmingham, Michigan, to its knees with an unbelievable 69 on his last round.

In 1953 he won the Masters, the U.S. Open at Oakmont, and the British Open at Carnoustie.

In order to acclimate himself to the Scottish golf links and the small 1.64 centimeter ball used in the British Open, Hogan went over to Scotland two weeks ahead of time. He rented a house a few miles away near an old Army firing range. It was said that the casual observer could not tell the difference between the shells being fired on the range and the "bullets" being shot by Hogan.

He analyzed the Carnoustie course hole by hole, walking it backward. At last he was ready to go. The weather was foul—raw and windy. Furthermore, Ben was sick with a heavy cold. He shot 73, 71, 70, and a last round of 68, one of the best he had ever played. He birdied the twelfth hole, a vicious dog-leg par-5 every time he played it, driving a low running shot past a dangerous bunker, and then landing his second shot on the green. Ben won the coveted title by four strokes over the field. The crowds cheered their "Wee Ice Mon," who showed them golf as it should be played.

At last the effect of his injuries caught up with Hogan. He lost his putting touch primarily because he could not get the proper signals of balance from his ravaged legs.

Here is an account of one of Ben's last glorious moments before he finally retired from competition. It was one of the most heart-warming scenes in the history of golf.

It was the third day of the 1967 Masters. Ben was making a token appearance, it was thought. His game was gone. Out in a respectable 36, he gave no sign of the fireworks he intended to show on the second nine.

At the tenth hole he sank a 7-foot putt for a birdie-3. At the eleventh he was one foot from the cup in 2 and had his second birdie in a row. At the short twelfth he put a 6-iron fifteen feet from the cup and made a 2, his third birdie in a row. He reached the par-5 thirteenth hole in 2 strokes and down went the fourth birdie.

He parred the fourteenth and again made the par-5 fifteenth green in 2 and birdied that hole, too. Now he was 5-under par. Pars at the sixteenth and seventeenth holes brought him to the 18th needing a sixth birdie to break the course record.

The eighteenth at Augusta is a long hard walk uphill. Poor Ben's legs were tired. Laboriously, slowly, he made that climb, step by step. His tee shot was good. His second carried the bunker in front of the green and skidded to a stop twenty-five feet above the hole.

As Ben walked those last 160 yards to the green, the gallery came to life. They knew they were seeing a living legend, one of the greatest golfers of all time proving his courage and skill in one last magnificent effort of concentration and perfect execution of the golf swing. The crowd continued its tremendous applause for Ben. He tipped his little white hat and there were tears in his eyes as he was enveloped by the heartfelt, thundering, unending display of admiration.

Of course he rolled that twenty-five-foot putt right into the hole for his sixth birdie and a course record score of 30 strokes. Do you think his guardian angel would have allowed him to miss that last putt?

SAM SNEAD

Sam Snead, a real hillbilly, played his early golf barefooted. He grew up in Hot Springs, Virginia and, as a youth, caddied at the famous Homestead resort golf course. The caddies were allowed to play on Mondays. One day the owner of the Homestead saw Sam drive the ball onto a green more than 300 yards away. From then on, Sam had a sponsor. He gave Sam a job in the Pro Shop and eventually encouraged him to test his golfing skills against other great stars of that time, Ben Hogan and Byron Nelson.

Snead developed a smooth, fluid swing that incorporated a big shoulder turn. "Slammin' Sam" could drive the ball farther than any of the other players of his time with the exception of Jimmy Thomson. When Snead was asked what he did to hit an extra long drive he said, "All I do is make everything move faster."

Although Sam won the Masters three times, the PGA three times, and the British Open once, he never could win the U.S. Open.

In his first U.S. Open at Oakland Hills in Birmingham, Michigan in 1937 Sam came into the tournament a heavy favorite to win. He had been burning up the courses, and Oakland Hills, notoriously long and tough, was well suited to his game. Snead was in the clubhouse with a score of 283 having finished early. He appeared to be the winner. Suddenly he heard a roar from the crowd around the eighth green, 200 yards away. Ralph Guldahl had just sunk a long putt for an eagle-3 that put him in the lead. He would beat Snead if he could par the second nine. Par on the Oakland Hills second nine is extremely difficult to achieve, especially under foot-deep open rough conditions. Guldahl lost a stroke at the tenth hole but got a birdie-2 on the thirteenth. Steady pars and a save from the bunker at the fifteenth brought Guldahl home the winner at 281.

Another terribly disappointing moment in Snead's career came in the 1939 U.S. Open at Philadelphia Country Club. He had only two holes to go, and two pars would give him a total of 282 strokes, which would be two shots ahead of Byron Nelson, Craig Wood, and Denny Shute who each had posted scores of 284. The seventeenth hole is a short easy par-4. Snead hit a good drive followed by a weak second shot to the green. He left his first putt six feet short of the cup, his second a foot shy, and the result was a damaging bogey.

Now all he needed was a bogey-6 on the 558 yard par-5 eighteenth to tie or a par to win the title outright. Sam was very upset with himself over the way he had played the seventeenth hole. But, he looked forward with confidence to the eighteenth hole. In his previous rounds he had been reaching that green easily in two strokes. It was practically a par-4 for him.

Sam was so anxious to hit his tee shot that he brushed aside his playing partner who had the honor, the right to play first. Snead decided to smash a long drive.

Sadly, Sam moved everything too quickly. He hit a duck-hook into the left rough where the gallery had trampled the grass into a matted jungle. In spite of a questionable lie, Snead decided to use his brassie, a wood club without much loft, to get out of the rough and close to the green. He took a mighty swing and smashed the ball into the face of a bunker only a hundred yards ahead. Sad to relate, Sam's next stroke did not get the ball out of the bunker. Snead lay 4 and was not yet on the green.

He hit his fifth shot onto the green. Knowing that he had to sink his long putt in order to tie, he went for it and putted three feet past the hole. Carelessly, he missed that putt, too. He walked away, in a daze. Sam had blown another U.S. Open, an experience he never forgot. Nor was he ever allowed to forget it by the newspapermen or his opponents.

Still haunted by this experience, he came close once more in the 1947 U.S. Open at St. Louis Golf Club. There he had to make a putt of about thirty inches to defeat Lou Worsham. Worsham's ball also lay about thirty inches away. Lou said, "I think I'm away," as Sam stepped up to sink his putt. Sam stepped back, flustered.

The officials measured the putts and determined that Sam was away by a half-inch. Sam putted weakly and pushed the ball to the side of the cup. Worsham made his putt and then won the playoff the next day. Sam never again got as close to winning a U.S. Open.

Sam is notoriously thrifty. Some say he has hundreds of pairs of brand new, never-worn golf shoes in the attic of his house near the Homestead. There are rumors, too, that he has never trusted banks and that all of his money is buried in tin cans in his back yard.

Years ago when Sam took his first train ride, he arrived in New York and was greeted with a newspaper article containing his photograph. Sam asked, "How did they get that? I've never been in New York before in my life!"

There's an interesting story about the way Snead won his second Masters title in 1952. He and Hogan had had a long, continuing rivalry, and in that tournament they completed the third round tied for the lead at 214 strokes apiece.

The two arch rivals went into the final day with the golf world hanging on each stroke. Surely, relentless, machinelike Ben Hogan would beat Sam Snead. Sam would skyrocket again. Hadn't he done it many times before?

Snead was scheduled to start an hour ahead of Hogan. Sam played well for eleven holes and then it appeared that Sam would again blow up. The twelfth hole at Augusta National is a tiny par-3 with a pond in front and on the right side of the green. And there are mean bunkers around its perimeter. The winds, too, are tricky and can blow a golf ball into trouble. Sam dunked his tee shot in the water. He dropped a ball over his shoulder and with the penalty stroke assessed him for going in the water, Sam was shooting his third shot for the green. He still had to cross that dangerous pond.

He swung and almost put the ball in the water again. This time the grass at the edge of the green saved him. But he had a terrible lie. He was playing his fourth shot and looking at the probability of a 6 or worse on the par-3, a loss of three or more strokes of his precious lead.

Sam did his best with a very difficult shot from an awkward stance, one foot higher than the other. He chipped the ball up onto the green, and it rolled and rolled toward the hole, never hesitating at the cup and plunked right in for a sweet bogey-4, one of the best bogeys Sam had ever made in his life. Sam regained his composure, settled down, played the rest of the nine in sound fashion and finished the round with a remarkable 72 under great pressure. At 286 he would beat Ben Hogan provided that Ben did not score 71 or better. Word came that Ben was having putting woes. Five times, Ben Hogan three-putted. He had only a single one-putt that day. The roof had fallen in on "the mechanical man." He finished with a 79, seven over par, when he had needed only a par round to tie. Hogan was not unbeatable that day. Sam Snead was.

Here's a story about another bad hole by Sam Snead. This time it happened in the 1958 Western Open at Plum Hollow Golf Club outside Detroit, Michigan.

The fourth hole at Plum Hollow is a straightaway 445-yard par-4 which runs along 9 Mile Road on its right side. The right rough is only about fifteen yards wide so there is no margin for error on the right, the out-of-bounds side of the hole.

In his second round of the tournament Sam drove his first ball over the fence, out-of-bounds. He teed up another ball, now shooting three, and as he said later, "put it through the same hole in the sky." He was out-of-bounds again and now he was playing his fifth stroke and still was on the tee. This shot found the fairway but his next one, his sixth, went into a bunker on the right side of the green. Then he failed to get out of the bunker on his first attempt. At last he got on the green with his eighth, twenty feet away from the cup. He putted to within three feet and sank his tenth shot. His caddie said later, "He nearly missed the 3-footer, too!"

Sam lost six strokes to the field right there but if he had been able to sink a 6-footer on the 72nd hole on Sunday he would have tied for first place.

Soon afterward the members of Plum Hollow considered his feat noteworthy and placed a bronze plaque on the fourth tee to commemorate the deed. It read, "Duffers take heart! On this, the fourth hole at Plum Hollow on July 14, 1958 Sam Snead took ten strokes. In spite of this horrendous disaster he finished at 283 strokes, only one stroke behind the winner, Doug Ford."

Many of the newspapers and golf magazines carried the story of the "Snead plaque." For a while Snead enjoyed the publicity as golfers from Detroit and around the world would visit the Greenbrier, Sam's home club and tell him, "Sam, I saw your marker the other day at Plum Hollow."

At last he could stand it no longer. The constant reminder of his "horrendous disaster" was getting to him. So he requested, even ordered, Plum Hollow to take it away. "Get that thing out of there!" The marker was removed and today it can be seen in the PGA Golf Museum reminding duffers to "take heart" with the unspoken advice that if Sam Snead can take a ten on a hole, you shouldn't feel too bad if you do, too.

A number of years ago, Snead had such bad putting "yips" that he decided to try putting in croquet style with one hand held high on the shaft of the club and the other down low with the ball positioned between his feet. The style seemed to work better for him than the traditional method which is a miniature golf swing. Then the USGA decided that the new variation was contrary to golf tradition and ruled that the golfer may not straddle the ball when using such a stroke. Sam adapted to the new ruling and now putts in a side-saddle version of the croquet stroke. And he putts extremely well with it.

Sam Snead, one of the greatest golfers of all time and still going strong in his early 70s has won 84 "official" PGA tour victories, more than any other player in history.

MILDRED DIDRIKSON ZAHARIAS

In 1945 Mildred "Babe" Didrikson Zaharias (1913-1956) was named "Woman Athlete of the Year." In 1950 United States sports experts ranked her number one on the list of the greatest female athletes of the first half of the twentieth century. A tomboy in her early years, she went on to star in basketball, baseball, track and field, and finally golf.

In 1932 Babe entered seven events in the National A.A.U. Track and Field championships. She won the javelin throw, the baseball throw, the shot put, the broad jump, the eighty-meter hurdles, and tied for first in the high jump. Now there was a versatile athlete!

Two weeks later in the 1932 Olympics she established a new woman's world record on the javelin. Then she broke the record in the high hurdles. Though tied for first in the high jump, she was disqualified when the judges of that day refused to accept her head-first jump over the bar.

Babe was a great basketball player, too, and once when she missed a foul shot that cost her team the game, she shot 300 fouls a day in practice and atonement for her mistake.

At the urging of sports columnist Grantland Rice, she took up golf. They say that her first drive went over 250 yards down the fairway. Not long afterward, in another round, she was home in two on the 523-yard seventeenth hole at Brentwood Country Club in Santa Monica.

After the Olympics she became a professional golfer and toured the country for a while with Gene Sarazen. Her golf game around the greens was shaky, but she could belt those drives. When she was asked how she did it, she'd say, "I just hitch up my girdle and let 'er fly."

She knew that her short game was weak so she decided to work at becoming a top golfer. To help her attain her goal, the great golf teacher Tommy Armour taught her many of the finer points of the game. Babe worked long hours on the practice tee perfecting her technique. She hit so many balls her hands blistered and broke into raw sores. She bandaged them, soaked them in brine, and went right on practicing. It began to pay off.

About this time she met George Zaharias, a mountain-sized wrestler. It was love at first sight for George and Babe. After they were married, George used to follow her around to the various tournaments admiring his wonderful golfing wife. In those days there was no regular women's golf circuit. A tournament in California might be followed in three weeks by one in Massachusetts, or vice versa.

Once she had strengthened her game, she really attacked golf with a vengeance. Now she wanted to become the best woman golfer in the world. Once again she played in an exhibition match at Brentwood and this time she shot a 65. On another day, with a strong wind behind her, she drove a ball 408 yards.

Babe Didrikson was a professional and of course wanted to play against the best women players. Most of them were in the amateur ranks, so she asked the USGA to allow her to renounce her professional status and become an amateur again. The request was granted in 1944. When World War II was over Babe was ready to play in the U.S. Women's Amateur Championship. Babe won her first two matches by big margins, 4 and 3 each time. Then Maureen Orcutt, a past champion herself, lost to Babe, 6 and 4. Didrikson's semi-final match against Helen Sigel was a little tougher. Babe was nervous and got off to a bad start, but she roared back, winning at the sixteenth hole. In the final she defeated Clara Sherman 11 and 9, the largest margin ever registered in this championship.

Babe went on to win fifteen straight tournaments in 1946 and 1947. She then decided to go after the British Ladies Golf championship, which was to be played on the hilly course at Gullane, Scotland. (The Scots call it "Gillin.")

In the eight rounds she played there she was off the fairway only three times. She visited only three bunkers. On one of those bunker shots she holed out and on the others she had short putts for "gim-mies." She won the title in brilliant fashion.

Having proved she was the best woman golfer in the world, she accepted an offer of $300,000 to make some movie shorts and again turned professional.

In 1953 she found that she had cancer and she underwent radical surgery for its removal. After the operation she practiced hard to regain her strength and vowed that she would best the disease. Once more she won the U.S. Open—the third time in her illustrious career. Her margin of victory was great—twelve strokes over her nearest competitor.

Sadly, the cancer recurred and Babe succumbed at last to the inevitable. She had won more than fifty events—a champion to the end.

JO ANNE CARNER

J ust as Babe Didrikson was called the greatest woman golfer of the 1940s, Jo Anne Carner is considered to be the greatest of the modern era. She joined the LPGA, Ladies Professional Golf Association, after an outstanding career as an amateur. Known then as "The Great Gundy" (her maiden name was Gunderson), she won five U.S. Amateur Championship titles, 1957, 1960, 1962, 1966, and 1968 to tie the record of Glenna Collett Vare who also won five times between 1922 and 1935. Jo Anne even achieved the distinction of winning a Ladies PGA Open, the Burdine's Invitational, as an amateur just before she became a professional.

Since becoming a pro, Carner has won more tournaments, thirty-nine, and earned more money ($1.8 million) than any other woman golfer in history. She was named the tenth member of the LPGA Hall of Fame and was the first woman golfer to earn over $200,000 for three consecutive years.

Jo Anne is 5-feet 7-inches tall. She is outgoing, friendly, and even-tempered, always smiling even when the putts don't go down. She is famous for her short swing that propels the golf ball prodigious distances. It has been said that if all the LPGA tournaments were played on long golf courses Carner might win every time. As it is, with many of the courses shortened to 6,000-yard length, Jo Anne must often play irons from many tees for fear of driving through the fairway.

She is known for the gyrations of her body when she misses a putt and the anguish she conveys in her expressive face.

When Jo Anne Carner came on the tour in 1970 everyone expected her to win immediately, but she started off in a horrible slump. In her first year as a pro she earned a mere $14,000. It was not until 1974, when she earned $87,000, that she truly hit her stride and worked out the problems with her swing. She put herself under the tutelage of Gardner Dickinson, a protegé himself of Ben Hogan. He discovered that Jo Anne was making an improper weight shift and after much practice Jo Anne got it right.

Jo Anne credits the fiery baseball manager Billy Martin for giving her career a great psychological boost just when she needed it.

They met in Florida in 1974 when Billy watched Jo Anne in a couple of early tournaments. After seeing her play, Billy gave Jo Anne a serious lecture that went something like this:

"What are you doing out there? With such a big game why are you just patty-caking it around the golf course? Do you think something lucky is going to happen? You used to make things happen. You used to charge, you used to be very positive and now you're afraid of scoring an 80. Hell, the next day you can score 66 and you are one of the few who are capable of making that kind of a score."

"With his advice ringing in my ears, I decided that Billy was right—I had been playing too cautiously so I stopped patty-caking it around the course and started 'letting 'er fly.' I didn't care where the ball came down. I knew it would hit the ground somewhere. Suddenly I found that the ball was coming down on the fairway and frequently right on the flagstick. It was like recovering from an illness. I could play aggressive golf again—and I did."

Jo Anne also went on a strict diet and managed to lose twenty-two unwanted pounds that seemed to get in the way of her smooth swinging.

She said, "Losing that weight gave me extra stamina especially when I have to play extra holes on a hot humid day on a long demanding course."

In 1979 Jo Anne suffered a serious injury to her wrist when, on a mountain trail, she lost control of her motorbike on loose gravel. Her injury, though severe, might have ended her career but it did not. She stayed off the tour for a few months healing her wounds but came back to play while she was still hurting. The accident probably cost her $100,000 in lost earnings in 1979 for she jumped from $98,000 that year to $185,000 in 1980 and then had the three straight years over $200,000.

Alice Dye, wife of Pete Dye, the excellent golf course designer, relates the story about the way Jo Anne Carner attacks the golf course and her opponent in a golf match. Alice, herself a fine golfer, was playing Jo Anne a head-to-head match on a western course that featured some mean-looking cactus plants. Alice said, "I was in the fairway with an easy shot to the green. Jo Anne had hit the ball into a cactus and I knew there was no way she could get out of it without taking a penalty stroke. I could see her looking the shot over carefully. Then she asked her caddie for her rain-suit. She put on the pants, backed her rear end into the cactus, and while being stabbed by the cactus needles, she played a long iron out of the trouble and put her ball on the green. I couldn't believe it. It was a miraculous shot."

Another time as Jo Anne was about to win a tournament in Orlando, Florida, she hit an errant drive. Her line to the par-5 green was over trees and a big lake, a 240-yard carry. She asked the marshals to clear the gallery from the right side of the fairway and boomed a 3-wood over the trees, over the water onto the green and won the tournament.

Jo Anne and her husband, Don, traveled from tournament to tournament early in her golfing career towing a small trailer behind their car. They lived in the trailer when they came back to home base, Lake Worth, Florida. Jo Anne and Don now travel in a quarter-of-a-million dollar motor home with every possible convenience. They live in a condominium in Palm Beach overlooking the Atlantic ocean when they are not traveling to another tournament. They also have recently bought a sea-going yacht and since both Don and Jo Anne are avid fishermen they are spending more and more time hunting fish rather than Dunlop golf balls.

When Jo Anne was asked recently if she had any intention of giving up the grind of professional golf she said, "I love the game. I love the competition and as long as I can play it I will. It would be nice, though, just to play friendly golf some day."

ARNOLD PALMER

There seems to be a natural law that periodically in sports games a master will arise and set standards of achievement higher than ever before. Such a leader was Arnold Palmer, the symbol of modern professional golf and without doubt the acknowledged hero of the golfing world.

The game of golf underwent a tremendous boom in the late 1950s and early 1960s and a great deal of the credit for the increased public interest in the game must go to Palmer. After winning the U.S. Amateur championship in 1954, Palmer promptly turned professional and soon afterward won the Canadian Open for the first of his 61 victories. He won the Masters every other year from 1958 to 1964, the U.S. Open in 1960, the British Open in 1961 and 1962, and played on six Ryder Cup teams.

One of the most dramatic comebacks in Arnold's career happened in the 1960 U.S. Open at Cherry Hills in Denver, Colorado. The air there, a mile above sea level, is thin, so Arnold was able to drive the ball great distances. In this tournament he played the first three rounds in 72, 71, and 72. Par was 71 so he was two-over par as he started his last round. Mike Souchak was leading the field and was seven shots in front of Arnold, 208 to 215.

Young Jack Nicklaus, then an amateur, was four strokes ahead of Palmer and only three behind Souchak. Arnold told Bob Drum, well-known golf writer, "I may shoot 65 this afternoon. What will that do for me?" Drum told him, "Nothing, you're too far behind."

The first hole at Cherry Hills was a straightaway par-4, 346 yards long. (Since then it has been lengthened and turned into a dogleg.) Arnold, determined to catch Mike Souchak, smashed his drive 340 yards to the center of the first green and two-putted for his birdie. Then he birdied the second hole, a 410-yard par-4, holing a little run-up shot. His third birdie came at the third hole with a wedge second shot one foot from the cup. On the fourth hole Arnold put his wedge eighteen feet from the hole and sank the putt for another birdie. He got a birdie-2 at the sixth and with another wedge stiff to the flag on the seventh hole, he had his sixth birdie in seven holes.

Arnold was out in 30 strokes and had grabbed the lead as the other contenders either fell back or failed to match his incredible burst of great golf. He played the second nine in 35 with eight pars and one birdie. His 65 was the lowest round ever scored by the winner of an Open until Johnny Miller shot 63 on his last round at Oakmont in 1973.

The term "an Arnold Palmer charge" had been born and would follow him through his long illustrious career.

Palmer is known for his daring style of play. No lie is too tough for him, no flagstick so well-guarded that he has to play safe in attacking it. He gave everything he had, or so it seemed, to every shot. His putting touch at the height of his success was nothing less than magical. With a peculiar knock-kneed stance that locked his body into a firm platform, it seemed that Arnie could and did will the ball to the cup.

One of the most famous sport pictures of the 1950s is that of Arnold hurling his visored cap high into the air in a joyous salute to another victory.

No one else, either, ever seemed to be more anguished over a missed putt than Arnie. His personality was so attractive to the crowds of golf fans that soon after he started his remarkably successful career he drew hordes of shoving, pushing fans who adopted him as their own. The crowds came to be called "Arnie's Army" and of course, Arnie himself became known as "The General." Palmer's progress around the courses could easily be tracked by the decibel pitch of the crowds reacting as he sank putts for birdies, eagles, or even for routine pars.

The crowds around the greens often acted as barriers to any Palmer ball that might go too far astray. It was even said that occasionally a Palmer ball would be thrown back onto a green for Arnie. When Jack Nicklaus first came out to challenge Arnie's right as number one, the crowds resented Jack and called him names such as "Fat Jack" or would even applaud a bad shot by Nicklaus. Eventually the crowds accepted Jack for the great golfer and good sportsman he truly is, but in the early days of their competition, a pairing of Nicklaus and Palmer was an explosive one for crowd control.

Arnold has a great sense of humor and does not take himself too seriously. Perhaps that is part of his great appeal to his followers. In the 1961 Masters Gary Player led Palmer by four strokes on the last day of the tournament. Player fell off badly on his last nine to take 40 strokes and was in the clubhouse with a 280. Palmer came to the eighteenth hole after making what appeared to be a true Palmer charge at the lead. Arnie needed only a par-4 to win, a bogey to tie Player.

Arnie drove well to the center of the fairway. Then he put his second shot into the right bunker. The lie was a nasty one, downhill and sidehill. All he had to do now was blast the ball out and two-putt for a tie. Instead, he skimmed the ball over the green down an embankment on the left. He could still have saved his tie with Player with a delicate run-up shot. He elected to putt up the slope. He putted badly and ran the ball twenty feet beyond the hole. He took two more putts and Gary had backed into his first Masters title.

Palmer smiled and said, "I remember thinking before I hit that second shot all I have to do is get it on the green and two-putt for a four. That's where I made my mistake, thinking about something besides the ball. If I'd just kept my mind on swinging the club properly, there wouldn't have been any problem."

In the 1966 U.S. Open at Olympic Country Club at San Francisco Palmer led Billy Casper by three strokes, 207 to 210 as they both started the last round playing together. Casper was wild off the tee on the first nine as Palmer blistered the first nine holes in 32 strokes, three under par. Arnie then led Casper by seven strokes with only nine holes to go.

At the tenth Palmer took three strokes from the edge of the green. He hit a bad iron shot at the thirteenth and another stroke was gone. With five holes to play he still led by five strokes. Then he lost two at the short 150-yard, par-3 fifteenth, taking a four while Casper sank a twenty-footer for a birdie-2.

The sixteenth hole was a par-5, 604 yards long. Arnold hooked his drive into the trees and mucked an iron shot trying to extricate himself from trouble. Then he landed in a bunker. Casper was on his way to a cool birdie-4—Arnold 6, Casper 4, and the lead was down to one stroke.

Arnold drove badly again at the seventeenth and failed to sink a five-and-a-half foot putt for par. The match was tied. Both players parred the last hole, Arnold just managing to sink a tricky four-footer. In the playoff the next day Casper beat Palmer soundly 69 to 73. Casper had accomplished an unbelievable come-from-behind victory in the U.S. Open—a "reverse charge" against the famous Arnold Palmer.

On another occasion Palmer was playing the eighteenth hole in the 1967 Los Angeles Open at the Rancho Park Golf Course in Los Angeles. His score was near the top of the field as he drove into the fairway on the short par-5 hole. On the right side of the hole extending from the clubhouse out about 240 yards is a fenced-in driving range. It is protected by a chain-link fence about thirty feet high. On the left hand side is Patricia Avenue close to the fairway which narrows to a bottleneck at the green.

Palmer hit his second shot into the range, dropped another ball, penalty stroke, hitting four. His next shot went out of bounds onto Patricia Avenue. Another ball, another penalty stroke! Bang! Into the range again. Then, one more shot onto Patricia Avenue. At last, on his tenth shot Arnold was on the green. He made a twelve. Someone asked him how he did it. He laughed and said, "If I hadn't sunk a good-sized putt I would have had thirteen."

Arnold Palmer was not only "The General" but undoubtedly the King and probably the most exciting player of modern-day golf.

JACK NICKLAUS

Jack Nicklaus was winner of the United States Athlete of the Decade (1970-1979) Award. This is awarded to the best athlete in all American sports over a ten-year period. That practically says it all.

Jack's record is unmatched in golf history. He has won seventy tour victories and finished second or third ninety-one times. Eight times between 1964 and 1976 he had the lowest scoring average. He has been named PGA Player of the Year five times.

When he was a youth in the early 1950s, Jack's father, a well-to-do pharmacist in Columbus, Ohio, encouraged Jack to persevere with golf. He even built a special golf driving net in the basement of the Nicklaus residence. To do that, it was necessary to excavate an extra two feet to give Jack swinging room. The Nicklauses were members of a magnificent golf course in Columbus, Scioto Country Club, designed by the world-famous golf architect, Donald Ross, a Scot who specialized in building deep, forbidding sand bunkers, and small, undulating greens.

In the wintertime at Scioto a special Quonset hut open at one end enabled the young Nicklaus to drive his five-hundred practice golf balls a day. Jack's father and his professional teacher, Jack Grout, felt that Jack should learn to hit the ball hard. "Later on, we'll teach him to hit it straight." Jack's game prospered and soon he was driving the ball prodigious distances. At the age of thirteen, Jack won the Ohio State Junior Championship. More remarkable, playing against a field of professionals at the age of sixteen, he won the Ohio State Open. His final rounds were 64 and 72—a sixteen year old!

No wonder the world of golf started to take notice of the young man from the Buckeye State.

At nineteen he won his first major championship, the U.S. Amateur, defeating Charlie Coe who had, himself, won the title twice before in 1949 and 1958. By this time Jack had grown to 5-feet 11-inches, and had developed an unusually strong body and tremendously powerful legs. That enabled him to drive the ball high and extremely far, which meant he had to temper his stroke in the 1961 U.S. Amateur championship held at Pebble Beach, California. There is a chasm on the right-hand side of the eighth hole at Pebble Beach some 285 yards from the tee. Jack found that he had to "lay up" there with a 1-iron because he was hitting his 3-wood over the edge of the cliff. Jack defeated Dudley Wysong 8 and 6 in the final match to win his second amateur title.

At last at the age of twenty-two, Jack decided to become a professional golfer. The lure of the money on the professional tour was proving too great. He left Ohio State University just a few course credits short of getting his degree in business administration. It was there that he got his nickname "The Bear," because he looks somewhat like a bear. Later, on the tour, with his sun-bleached hair, he became "The Golden Bear."

In his first pro tournament he won only $33.33—a disappointing start. Five months later he won his first major tournament, the 1962 U.S. Open, when he defeated Arnold Palmer at Oakmont, Pennsylvania, in a playoff, 71 to 74. He would go on to win nineteen major championships (five Masters, five PGA championships, four U.S. Opens, and three British Opens in addition to the two U.S. Amateur championships he had already won).

In 1965 he took the Augusta National Golf Course apart with a third-round course record score of 64. This enabled him to beat the field by a whopping nine strokes (271 to the 280 scores of Arnold Palmer and Gary Player). Jack had nineteen birdies in the four days, eight of them on his record round. He exhibited his awesome power by using no more than a drive and 6-iron to any par-4 green and he reached the par-5s (the second, eighth, thirteenth, and fifteenth holes) in two strokes each with drives and 3-irons or 5-irons. The eighth hole is 520 yards long. The Golden Bear covered the ground with a drive and a 5-iron that momentous day.

Reminiscing about that round Jack talked about the part pure luck sometimes plays. He was one under par when he reached the 220-yard long par-3 fourth hole. That day the tee was placed between the

back and front tee so it played about 195 yards into the wind. Jack said, "I hit my four-iron 'fat' [meaning behind the ball] and was disgusted with the shot. A photographer took my picture when I made a terrible face. My shot just barely carried the front bunker, hit, and rolled to about ten feet away from the hole. I made the two for another birdie. The putt had a left to right bend."

The film of the 1965 Masters shows, too, that Jack nearly three-putted the thirteenth hole that year. After making the green 455 yards away in two shots with a drive and a 5-iron, his first putt from forty-five feet away from the cup left him eight feet short. He had a slippery downhill, sidehill putt to make. His putt just barely reached the front edge of the cup, hesitated a moment, and then toppled in. Again, Lady Luck was with him.

Another tremendously dramatic Nicklaus victory occurred in 1970 at the Old Course in St. Andrews, Scotland, when Doug Sanders needed only to sink a three-and-a-half-foot putt on the eighteenth green to beat Jack by one stroke. Here's what happened:

One stroke ahead of Jack Nicklaus at the seventy-second tee, Doug Sanders could win the historic British Open championship if he scored a par-4 on the last hole, the eighteenth, with its monstrous green and its forbidding entrance through the treacherous Valley of Sin.

Doug drove carefully and placed his shot to the left, away from the out-of-bounds on the right. He then had to make a pitch-shot of seventy yards to the plateaued green.

His pitch-shot rolled on and on, past the hole, into a very dangerous position above it. The green was very slick. Doug Sanders needed to get down in two strokes to win. The slope was a little to his right and he overestimated the effect it would have on the ball and left himself with a second putt of three-and-a-half feet.

Doug stood up to the putt and then stepped away to pick up what he later said was a pebble near or on his line to the cup. He seemed to have lost his concentration. Sanders then pushed the putt to the right. The ball never touched the hole. Five strokes, a bogey, on the eighteenth, cost sentimental favorite Doug Sanders the outright title and threw him into a tie with formidable Jack Nicklaus.

The next day Nicklaus beat Sanders in the playoff, 72 to 73 for his first British Open championship.

Another highlight of Jack's career happened in the 1975 Masters.

Tom Weiskopf had taken the lead at the end of the third round and the scoreboard looked like this:

Weiskopf	69	72	66	207
Nicklaus	68	67	73	208

That day Nicklaus was playing in the twosome immediately ahead of Weiskopf and Miller. Weiskopf had lost his lead when he dunked his tee-shot into the pond in front of the eleventh green, giving Nicklaus the edge. After Jack three-putted the fourteenth, Tom followed with a birdie-3 to seize the lead once more.

Nicklaus was one stroke behind Weiskopf as he reached the 190-yard sixteenth, the "water-hole," famous to television audiences all over the world because of the breath-taking beauty of its blue lake surrounded by azaleas and dogwood. Nicklaus' tee shot found the green safely, but he faced a nasty forty-foot left-to-right breaking putt.

The cup on the sixteenth hole was cut that day on the far right top corner of the green, in a most awkward place. Jack later said that he "knew he could make the putt" because some years before from the same spot he had had the same putt and had holed it. He struck the putt firmly and "knew" it would be good. He started to dance to his right with his putter raised in the air as the ball made its last necessary veer for the center of the hole. Down it went for the birdie-2. The customarily reticent Nicklaus leaped into the air in elation.

Jack's birdie and the resultant roars of the massed crowd must have affected Tom Weiskopf who was waiting on the sixteenth tee. He had memories of other tee-shots into the water on the left, and, overly cautious, hit a weak iron to the front of the sixteenth green, never really having a chance for his par. He left his first putt woefully short of the cup, eighteen feet away. Jack was once more in the lead and he never lost it, winning by that single stroke over Weiskopf.

Jack Nicklaus, a strong family man, now limits his professional appearances to about fifteen of the most important world tournaments. That way he can spend more time at home, fishing, playing tennis, and cheering his sons on in their own athletic careers. Jack and Barbara Nicklaus have four sons, Jack Jr., Steve, Michael, and Gary (named for Gary Player) and a daughter Nancy. Already Jack, Jr. and Gary are showing great promise as golfers. Young Gary, in a driving contest last year, managed to hit his ball 340 yards. Perhaps one day another Nicklaus may surpass the records of Jack William Nicklaus?

TOM WATSON

Tom Watson is only 5-feet 9-inches tall and weighs 160 pounds. He is one of the greatest golfers in the world and one of the few golfers in the modern age who can drive the ball 300 yards or more.

Tom was born in Kansas Ciy in 1949. His father was his early teacher in golf. Although Tom played college golf for Stanford University he really did not show exceptional promise then. He decided to play professional golf in 1971. In his first start as a pro he finished twenty-eighth and won $1,065 for his efforts. Since then his record has been amazing.

Watson has won 31 PGA tournaments in the United States as well as five British Open Championships. He has won a total of $3,580,163 (not counting the British titles) and in 1980 was the first player to win more than a half-million dollars in one year. He just barely missed doing it again in 1984 with $476,000.

Tom has been named PGA player of the year no less than six times—1977, 1978, 1979, 1980, 1982, and 1984.

It has been said that Watson came onto the golf scene and challenged the reign of Jack Nicklaus and has successfully toppled Jack from his throne. But both golfers are champions and remarkable athletes.

One of Tom's first important victories was the Masters of 1977. In 1976 and early 1977 Tom had appeared to falter several times when he had a chance to win a major title. He would "blow up" on his last round and someone else would waltz in with a good score and seize the victory. In the 1977 Masters, Watson finally overcame this tendency and won his first major title.

On the last day of that tournament, "the Bear", Jack Nicklaus was playing directly in front of Watson. Nicklaus was making great shots as he often does on the last round of a tournament. He birdied six of the first thirteen holes. Watson matched him stroke for stroke and returned a 67 for Nicklaus's 66 to win by two strokes, 276 to 278.

Here is how he did it: Nicklaus had started the day at 212 strokes, three behind Watson, and by the 10th hole Jack had narrowed the gap to two strokes.

Watson began his round at 7-under par and held that red figure as he parred the first four holes. Then he rammed in birdies on the next four holes, the fifth through the eighth. Watson had gained four strokes on par by then and stood at 11-under par after eight holes.

Jack Nicklaus, playing in the twosome ahead of Watson, started at 4-under par and promptly birdied the first two holes to go 6-under par.

Jack got home in 2 on the uphill eighth and finally cashed a birdie there. That put Nicklaus at 7-under par, 4 strokes behind Watson.

The race narrowed minutes later when Nicklaus was able to birdie the tenth just before Watson's bogey-5 there—Nicklaus 8-under, Watson slipping back to 10-under, only two shots ahead.

Jack's confidence was high as he played the nasty little 3-par water hole, the twelfth. He clicked a sweet 7-iron straight at the flag. His ball ended in a nice flat place on the green and moments later it was in the center of the cup for a birdie-2. That moved Jack to within a single shot of Watson, who had watched the birdie stroke from the twelfth tee, where he was waiting to play his next shot.

Nicklaus got his birdie-4 at the thirteenth hole and momentarily was tied for the lead with Watson at 10-under par. Tom was on the thirteenth comfortably in 2, came close to the eagle-3 that really would have set him up in front, but, most importantly, had gone one stroke ahead of Jack again—Watson 11-under par, Nicklaus 10-under.

Then, what did Watson do but three-putt the fourteenth and once more fall back into a tie with Jack at 10-under.

Nicklaus was heading down the fifteenth, the pond-guarded 5-par. After two prodigious shots, a drive and a towering 4-iron to the back edge of the green, the roar of the crowd and the nearby scoreboard told Nicklaus that Watson had lost his precious lead stroke at the fourteenth.

Watson did not weaken. He came right back with his own birdie at the fifteenth—on the green in two strokes and two putts for the 4. Watson and Nicklaus were again tied, at 11 under par.

Both players got their 3s at the sixteenth. Jack had to tackle the seventeenth hole first. He played it beautifully with a long drive to the left center of the fairway and a marvelously controlled 8-iron to twenty feet from the flag. The putt would not drop. Jack headed for the last hole as Watson's second shot at the seventeenth landed on the green about the same distance away from the hole as Jack's had moments before.

The green was icy, the putt was "impossible" to make. But Watson putted that ball into the center of the cup and did a delighted "war dance" when it went in. Watson was now a stroke ahead with one hole to play.

Nicklaus was on the eighteenth fairway when he heard the cheers from Watson's gallery at the seventeenth hole. He had to get his own birdie or lose out. Jack played a poor shot, caught the bunker in front of the green, and although he blasted out well to only twelve feet from the cup, he did not hole the putt to save his par.

With a two-stroke lead now, Watson played a "safe" par, a 3-wood to the center of the fairway and a 7-iron to twenty feet from the hole. He two-putted and had a two-stroke winning margin in the 41st Masters. Watson had decisively beaten Jack Nicklaus in a head-to-head confrontation down the stretch in a major championship.

Another great victory for Watson came in the 1982 U.S. Open at the famed Pebble Beach links in Carmel, California. Watson's win at Pebble Beach must be viewed against the background of Jack Nicklaus's earlier experiences there.

Jack had won one of the U.S. Amateur titles at Pebble Beach in 1961 before he became a professional and also had won the Bing Crosby Invitational there in 1967 and 1972. The final round of the Crosby is always played at Pebble Beach. It might well be considered to be Jack Nicklaus's home course for he seems to know every blade of grass on it. Tom had played the course many times when he was in college at Stanford but could not be considered as knowledgeable about the links as Jack.

On the final day of play of the U.S. Open at Pebble Beach in 1982, Watson had played himself into the lead with scores of 72, 72, and 68 for 212, to stand three strokes ahead of Nicklaus who was at 215 on scores of 74, 70, and 71. So Jack needed to pick up three strokes on Watson, four to beat him. Nicklaus started his last round slowly with a bogey and a par but sank a long putt on the third for a birdie-3. Then he dropped a 20-footer on the fourth for another birdie. On the fifth he was only two feet from the hole for another birdie. The sixth, a par-5, he reached in two strokes and two-putted for another birdie. On the seventh, the 110-yard par-3, he was only eleven feet from the hole and he canned his fifth birdie in a row. He was now tied with Watson who was playing several holes behind him. Ominously on the seventh hole, Watson missed a 2½-foot putt for a birdie and remained at 4-under par where he stood when he started the round.

An important turning point for Watson happened at the tenth hole, a 424-yard par-4 on the cliffside with the ocean on the right. Watson's second shot found a bunker on the right hand side of the green and he barely avoided sending his ball down the cliff. He exploded to twenty-five feet from the cup and then sank the putt for his par. This putt boosted Watson into the lead because Nicklaus had just three-putted the eleventh hole.

At the eleventh Tom sank a difficult sidehill putt for another birdie and now led Nicklaus by two strokes. Then Watson gave back a stroke with a weak 4 at the 204-yard par-3 twelfth where he bunkered his tee shot, then came out fifteen feet short of the cup, and failed to drop the par-saving putt.

As Watson prepared to putt a 35-footer for a birdie on the fourteenth, a tremendous roar went up from the crowd ahead. The scoreboard nearby soon showed a red "4" for Jack. Jack had birdied the fifteenth hole and was now tied with Tom for the lead. Coolly, Tom putted that difficult downhill, sidehill putt squarely into the back of the hole. Tom again was one stroke ahead.

Tom parred the par-4 fifteenth. He was on the green in two and down in two more from twenty feet. But on the par-4 sixteenth that slides downhill to the right, Tom made a driving error and put himself into a deep pit bunker. All he could do was get the ball out sideways onto the fairway with no thought of making the green. He had to settle for a bogey-5 and with two holes to go he was again tied with Nicklaus.

Now Nicklaus was in the clubhouse at 4-under-par 282. Watson was playing the difficult 209-yard par-3 seventeenth into a strong wind. Tom needed two pars on what are considered by the experts to be two of the most difficult holes in the world. One slip and Nicklaus had the title.

The cup on the seventeenth hole that day was cut well to the left of the wide but short from front-to-back green. Watson played boldly for the flag. His ball drew slightly left and ended on the high rough near the left edge of the green.

At this moment the TV sports announcer with Jack Nicklaus back of the eighteenth green practically conceded the tournament to Nicklaus. He thought Watson could never in a million years make par from the lie he had at seventeen. Furthermore the green sloped away from him steeply. He could conceivably lose another stroke there if the ball "got away" from him.

Tom studied the shot carefully and thinking to himself, "I've practiced this shot a thousand times," took his sand wedge and popped that ball out of the rough safely onto the green above the cup. He could see that the ball was rolling toward the hole so, anticipating that it might go in, Tom started a little dance of victory. Bang, the ball hit the flagstick still traveling fast, and down it went for a miraculous birdie-2. Watson was in the lead by one stroke again.

Tom played the oceanside eighteenth in regulation style, driving safely to the right, laid up short in two and pitched to the green about twenty feet above the cup in three strokes. He did not have to make the last birdie but he did. He was U.S. Open Champion of 1982 and once again he had slammed the door in Jack Nicklaus's face.

Fortunately, a sports photographer was there at the seventeenth green and captured the drama of Tom Watson's "impossible" pitch into the cup for what proved to be the winning margin of victory. More than 100,000 copies of that photo sequence have been sold. It will go down in the history of golf as one of the greatest strokes ever made under pressure.

CALVIN PEETE

Can you imagine a black man who never touched a golf club until he was 23, learning the game then and going on to win more than a million dollars in eight years on the professional tour? Then imagine that the man has a stiff, bent and crippled right elbow from a childhood injury. Fiction? No, fact! This incredible success story belongs to Calvin Peete who has a most unimposing physique and an awkward swing to match. All Peete does is drive the ball so straight down the fairway to the hole that he led all his competition on the PGA tour in accuracy. In 1984 he won the Vardon Trophy for the lowest scoring average of all, 70.56 strokes per round.

Calvin Peete came from a large and poor family. He has eighteen brothers and sisters. In his teens he worked on a farm in Florida and then dropped out of school. As with other black families, Peete said, "Most of us kids had to get jobs as soon as we were old enough to work so we could help out with the expenses." He made a buck by selling wigs, watches and jewelry to migrant workers. He would load his station wagon and follow the transient workers from farm to farm where fruit was being picked. Once, in Rochester, New York, some of his friends invited him to play golf with them.

Calvin Peete had always considered the game a silly one but he gave it a shot and he was hooked. At about the same time he happened to see Jack Nicklaus on television and had heard the announcer say that Jack had won $200,000 chasing the golf ball that year.

Calvin decided he would be happy with one-third that amount so he set about learning how to achieve that goal. With practice his game improved rapidly to the point where he decided to try to play on the professional tour.

But first he had to pass the test of a professional golf tour qualifying school. Peete failed. Once more he tried. Again he failed. On his third try he made it and got his playing card.

Calvin had three slim years in 1976, 1977, and 1978 with earnings in the $20,000 range, hardly enough to pay his travel expenses and keep body and soul together, much less support his wife and four children. He was discouraged but he continued on the tour.

At last his game clicked.

In the next six years Calvin won ten tournaments and more than $1,500,000 in prize money. In 1984 he was the best of all in scoring average, in driving accuracy, and finished second in the category called "hitting greens in regulation." That means getting on a par-3 green with his first stroke, on a par-4 green with his second, and on a par-5 green with his third stroke. The closest he came to winning his first major championship was when he finished fourth in the 1984 PGA at Shoal Creek in Alabama, losing to Lee Trevino.

Peete is quiet and self-effacing. He is no "personality kid" by any means. In spite of his impaired right arm he is "sneaky long" with his drives and deadly accurate with his irons. He is not a great putter, but is a good one. If he were a great putter, he would have won a number of other tournaments in which he finished close to the leader.

Calvin Peete takes a business-like approach to his game. He stays away from the party crowd and only occasionally relaxes with a beer.

He explains his seriousness this way, "Since I came from such a large family where it was hard to make ends meet, it was natural that I would adopt a serious attitude about whatever I did whether it was golf or just ordinary life itself. It has paid off for me, too."

Calvin has transformed himself into what amounts to a golfing machine. He has set up a constantly repeating pre-shot routine that practically puts him on "automatic" from the time he selects his club until he releases the club through the ball with a grooved swing that puts the ball down the fairway more frequently that any other golfer on the PGA tour.

The next time Calvin Peete is "on camera" in a televised golf event observe the way he stands directly behind the ball before he makes his shot. He is carefully taking aim and, in his mind, is squaring his

body along that intended line to the green or flagstick. Then he takes exactly two steps forward from behind the ball as he holds his club in his right hand, flexing it a little to keep his hands relaxed.

He steps into his final stance, squares his right foot to the target line, completes his grip, waggles the club a couple of more times, and then fires an extremely straight shot.

Calvin has an interesting style, too, when he wants to curve the ball to the right in a slice, or curve it to the left in a hook. He cocks his head to the right for a slice, to the left for a hook. The next time you watch him, note how he turns his head and you will know in advance the kind of shot he is going to play.

An example of the studiousness of Calvin Peete can be seen in his putting and in his bunker play, both phases of the game that are of utmost importance in saving a par or making a birdie.

At first he was weak in both departments but now, after hundreds of hours of hard practice, he can be considered one of the best in both putting and bunker play.

In his early career as a salesman before he took up golf Calvin had two diamonds of about half-carat size in his front teeth. He said later that he did that to set himself apart from the other peddlers who were selling to the migrant market as well.

When Calvin came out on the PGA tour, he kept his unusually bright smile so the diamonds brought him a certain amount of publicity that ordinarily would not have come to a golfer with a conservative game such as his. When he started to make it big, the diamonds came out. Now Calvin flashes only a very white smile in his very dark face. His excellent golf and remarkable record provide all the sparkle he needs.

Calvin Peete, one of the most successful of today's tournament professionals, once said:

"Starting out in golf, I often thought it would be nice to belong to a country club. Now I just might get to own one."

INDEX

HOW MANY BIRDS IS THAT?

From the Forty-spotted Pardalote on Bruny Island to the White-tailed Tropicbird on Cape York

SUE TAYLOR

HYLAND HOUSE

First published in Australia in 2001 by
Hyland House Publishing Pty Ltd
PO Box 122
Flemington, Victoria 3031

National Library of Australia
Cataloguing-in-publication data:
Taylor, Sue, 1949 June 9.
    How many birds is that? : from the forty-spotted
    pardalote on Bruny Island to the white-tailed tropicbird
    on Cape York.

    Bibliography.
    Includes index.
    ISBN 1 86447 044 5.

1. Taylor, Sue, 1949 June 9 – Journeys. 2. Rare birds –
Australia. 3. Bird watching – Australia. I. Title.

598.0723494092

Edited by Bet Moore
Design and layout by Captured Concepts
Printed by Green Giant Press, Singapore

CONTENTS

INTRODUCTION

I am unashamedly a twitcher. Literally. Every time I see a species of Australian bird I have not seen before, I twitch with excitement, much to my husband's amusement. Perhaps that's why Rog and I are still married after nearly 30 years — he continues to find me laughable.

The Oxford English Dictionary provides four meanings for the word 'twitcher', the last one being 'a bird-watcher whose main aim is to collect sightings of rare birds'. It goes on to provide several quotations illustrating usage, the earliest reference being 1968, so the word is a relatively recent addition to the language. The dictionary quotes from *Birds* magazine in 1977:

> Twitchers are difficult to identify because they are polymorphic. Best clues are behavioural including carrying Zeiss binoculars and *Where to Watch Birds*. . . Known to have nested in Wandsworth and possess a sense of humour.

In the interest of historical accuracy, I should point out that I have never nested in Wandsworth.

The dictionary also quotes from *The Times* in 1982:

> Twitchers are only interested in spotting rarities to claim they have seen them. Ornithologists are serious students, who despise and distrust twitchers.

Far be it from me to question such an authority as *The Times*, but it has been my experience that many ornithologists are themselves twitchers.

Having said that, I am happy to confess that I am interested in spotting rarities. Who isn't? To me twitching means more than just adding another tick to my lifelist, another feather in my cap, so to speak. It's a joy to know that the birds are still there. For me, every new sighting is a symbol of hope for the future.

About a decade ago, after I had spent 30 years bird watching, someone asked me if I was in 'The 600 Club'. It was the first time I'd heard of the club and I was immediately attracted to the idea of notching up 600 species of wild birds in Australia.

I couldn't wait to get home and get out all my birdlists and tot up my total. I had seen a lot of Australia and thought I should have a respectable birdlist to match my travels. Rog and I had driven from Perth to Darwin, we had been to the rainforests of Queensland and the wilderness of Tasmania, and visited the rugged Flinders Ranges. I had seen Noisy Pitta at Bedarra; I had seen Orange Chat at Lake Eyre; I had seen huge flocks of Great Crested Grebes at Rotamah and Lesser Frigatebirds at Broome. Thanks to Phillip Maher, I had even seen the endangered Plains Wanderer. Surely I would have an impressive count. Imagine my disappointment when my total was only 307 — barely half way to 600.

The gauntlet had been flung. I didn't know if I'd ever apply to join 'The 600 Club', but I certainly knew that I wanted to qualify for membership. I had already covered most of the continent looking for birds, but now I would have to do it again, and try harder this time.

In the decade since then, Rog and I have done two pelagic trips (one off Eden and one off Portland), been to Kakadu, King Island and the Kimberleys, Cape York and Calperum Station, Tasmania and Tibooburra, Murray-Sunset and the MacDonnell Ranges, and many places in between. We've also visited Gipsy Point five times and the sewage farm at Werribee on countless occasions.

I've done a lot of twitching and Roger has smiled tolerantly throughout.

At the same time, things have changed a lot in ornithological taxonomy. Subspecies have been reclassified as species and species have been changed to subspecies. It hurt to see my total decline as I crossed off the Western Swamphen (now relegated to a race) and replaced five sorts of sittellas with one (aptly named Varied).

The addition of lots of rare vagrants to the official Australian list is of no help at all. Naturally. By my calculation, there are currently 757 species on the Australian mainland list, including 61 species which have been recorded fewer than 10 times. That is to say, the chances of seeing them are about the same as winning Tattslotto. Leaving these aside, I reckon that there are a possible 696 species to see. Six hundred doesn't sound too hard, does it? Trust me — it is.

Consider that there are 11 birds classified as critically endangered, a further 26 endangered and another 48 vulnerable, as well as 31 near threatened. (These figures come from the Action Plan for Australian Birds 2000 published by the Natural Heritage Trust.) Then consider that some birds are nocturnal, some inhabit very remote terrain (58 are only usually seen far out at sea), and some are exceptionally shy and wary of people, with or without binoculars. Now the magnitude of the task begins to take shape.

One birdo told me that it was impossible to qualify for membership of The 600 Club until you were retired and able to commit yourself to the task completely. Initially I found this thought depressing, but then I realised that it just made the challenge all the more difficult — and therefore all the more compelling.

This is the story of my adventures in attempting to qualify for membership of The 600 Club. Here's the bad news: I'm not there yet. Close, but not quite there. This is after four decades of bird watching and countless kilometres of travelling.

I know that the late Roy Wheeler, a well-known ornithologist, achieved the remarkable feat of seeing 600 species in one year. But then, he was an expert. And true, he was retired at the time. I am not an expert. Nor am I yet retired. When any non-retired, non-expert claims to have qualified for membership of The 600 Club in under a decade, I respond with silent scepticism. They've probably seen Night Parrots too.

Twitching is terrific. But exploring this vast continent, even without twitching, is a wonderful experience that I count myself lucky to have had. Roger says that I am a queer bird, but that I definitely can't count myself — lucky or otherwise.

1

All thanks to a Hooded Robin

BIRDS OF THE
VICTORIAN GOLDFIELDS

A few Yellow Box had escaped the axeman's blow.

It was a Hooded Robin that did it. The Rainbow Bee-eater was pretty persuasive, but it was the Hooded Robin that secured the sale. If only the estate agent had known. He did not have to lie about the rabbits or the neighbours. The property was as good as sold. The full commission should have gone to one female Hooded Robin sitting dutifully on her nest.

I was with my parents that day, 25 years ago, when they bought their property in north-central Victoria. They were like excited kids at Christmas. My father took me aside and told me not to tell the agent how much we liked the place. My dear, darling Daddy couldn't see that one glimpse of his face would give the game away. My parents were quite besotted.

All minor problems like the lack of services, inadequate fencing, the isolation, the summer heat, the rabbits — all this was ignored. All they saw was the bush and the birds. The huge granite boulders weathered into artistic shapes were attractive, it is true. The Grey Box and Red Stringybarks were beautiful, a few Blakely's Red Gum and one or two Long-leaved Bundies had survived the axeman's blow and three magnificent Yellow Box grew tall and proud. But it was the Hooded Robin that clinched the deal.

Sheep had been grazing on the property and at some stage most of the large trees had been felled for firewood. Over the next few years it was wonderful to watch the wildflowers gradually return. Now, every spring there are carpets of purple Fairies Aprons so thick it is impossible to walk through them without treading on flowers. There are two species of insectivorous sundews. There are Everlastings, Rock Isotome, Early Nancies, Candles, several sorts of Riceflower, Running Postman, Sarsparilla and at least seven species of orchids. There are hakea and hop bush and three sorts of wattle. Luckily, there are lots of Yellow

Billy-buttons (*Chrysocephalum apiculatum*) because the Diamond Firetails use them to decorate their nests.

About 15 years ago my parents retired to live on their block in the bush. They built a modest home and two dams. They had the phone connected and we watched the street trees slowly die along the route of the cable. More recently the power has been connected, which, on balance, is probably a good thing, despite the ugly, intrusive pylons. Worst of all, the road has been made, which has inevitably attracted traffic. Lots of it. Big trucks hurtling along at great speed, making the most of the short cut between Bendigo and Horsham.

My parents have planted lots of natives around the house, but most of the block has been left to regenerate itself. Most of the native animals seem as prevalent as ever. The resident population of Black Wallabies and Echidna appear quite stable, and Grey Kangaroos in the nearby State Forest are as numerous as ever. (This despite the dreadful virus a couple of years ago when terrified, blind kangaroos strayed out of the forest and on to the road and hopped headlong into trees and traffic.) Yellow-footed Antechinus have accepted the presence of people and happily share their space with us.

Snakes were never common, although each summer we see one or two Red-bellied Blacks and sometimes a Brown. Legless lizards, which were regularly seen in the past, seem to have vanished completely. I have no explanation for this. The open grassland they inhabited has not been disturbed.

There is no apparent decline in the number of small lizards. There are Shinglebacks, White-lipped Skinks and Barking and Painted Geckos. However, we see fewer Gould's Sand Goannas than previously, and there are no longer any Lace Monitors around.

I confess to mixed feelings about the loss of Lace Monitors. One day we watched from the front verandah as a Lace Monitor climbed a Grey Box where Galahs were nesting in a hollow branch. The Galahs made only token protest while the goanna proceeded to eat their eggs. We told ourselves that this was nature, that the goanna had to eat too, that the Galahs would lay again. And lay again they did. Then, a few weeks later, we were once more sitting on the verandah when the monitor returned. This time we watched horrified while the goanna devoured two half-fledged Galah chicks. My father said enough was enough, and found some corrugated iron too slippery to allow any goanna to gain a toehold, and fastened it

Aggressive New Holland Honeyeaters have taken over the house garden.

around the base of the tree. It's one thing to know that predators kill their prey; it's quite another to watch it happening.

Some bird species have declined, a few have prospered. The Rainbow Bee-eaters still come, but seem to be fewer in number each year, and no longer build

Welcome Swallows have adapted happily to human habitation and nest every year, either on the verandah or in the garage.

When an Eastern Yellow Robin nested right beside the verandah, we were initially delighted.

their nest burrows on my parents' block. Rufous Songlarks, too, are fewer in number nowadays, although the population of White-winged Trillers seems stable. It's been some years since I've seen a Black-eared Cuckoo, and even longer since I've seen a Western Gerygone. There are fewer Sittellas and fewer Jacky Winters.

Perhaps there are too many New Holland Honeyeaters, which have taken over the house garden. We have found their nests every month of the year. They perform one useful function, apart from eating unwanted insects, and providing some colour and character to the garden: they invariably inform us when there is a snake in the garden. Their snake (ground) alarm call is quite different from their raptor (sky) alarm call.

Welcome Swallows have also adapted quite happily to human habitation and nest on the verandah or in the garage. Superb Fairy-wrens nest close to the house, apparently oblivious of people passing by. Sometimes they choose their nesting spot unwisely and White-browed Babblers come and steal their nesting material. Once a pair of Eastern Yellow Robins nested conveniently right beside the verandah, or so we thought, until we awoke one morning to find the nest, with mother and two 12-day-old chicks, gone without trace, leaving her mate confused for days. We considered various theories as to the culprit in this drama. I favoured an owl, partly because it occurred at night, and partly because I had known of a similar scenario once before. A Barking Owl in Broome watched a nest of White-gaped Honeyeater chicks grow to an edible size before making a meal of them. I'm not sure if it was a wise old owl, but I thought this behaviour displayed forethought and patience, attributes not readily ascribed to birds.

Of equal interest are the birds that are not present at my parents' place. Why is the Grey Fantail so rare? Why is the Crested Pigeon not there at all? Drive for five minutes in any direction and you're bound to see one. These birds are encroaching on suburban Melbourne with such determination, I predict I'll soon have them at my home in Kew.

One bird I do have in my backyard that my parents do not, is the Grey Butcherbird. There seems no good reason why these glorious songsters are absent from my parents' place. Only once has a butcherbird taunted me by hanging its prey in my backyard. The dead bird was a female House Sparrow. No doubt, had it been a Silvereye, I would find a different description for Grey Butcherbirds than 'glorious songsters'.

We do share some species, my parents and I, even though we are over 200 kilometres apart and they are in the bush and I am in the city. We both have Galahs, Sulphur-crested Cockatoos, Willie Wagtails, White-plumed Honeyeaters, Eastern Spinebills, Red Wattlebirds, Silvereyes, Magpies and Magpie-larks. While I admire Spotted Pardalotes, they enjoy the Yellow-rumped race of the Spotted as well as Striated Pardalote, and while I am entertained by Brown Thornbills, they have the very common Yellow-rumped as well as the less common Chestnut-rumped. They rarely see Buff-rumped, but there are always Yellow Thornbills foraging busily in the tops of their Deane's Wattles.

While I often see Little Ravens at my home, and only rarely Australian Ravens, for them the situation is reversed. We both have Musk and Little Lorikeets; they also have Purple-crowned, but not Rainbow, which I have in profusion. We both see Wood Duck and Pacific Black Duck flying overhead. Despite the installation of a nest box, my parents have been unable to entice any waterfowl to nest near their dams. In Kew, ducks flying overhead are either destined for the river or looking for a back-yard swimming pool.

Although they have recorded 19 species of honeyeaters, my parents do not see Little Wattlebirds that I have at my home in suburban Melbourne.

I know that I am fortunate to have such an extensive birdlist at my home, only seven kilometres from the Melbourne central business district. I live a long way from the river, yet I have seen Rufous Fantail (which my parents never have), Golden Whistlers (my parents usually see only females passing through in early spring) and (once only) a King Parrot — perhaps an escapee. If only my cat-owning neighbours would practise responsible pet ownership, I'd feel able to take steps to encourage more native birds into my garden.

Both my parents and I see Eastern Rosellas, and I also see Crimson Rosellas which they don't. I don't have to go far from home to see Red-rumped Parrots, which are very common at their place. I have Little Wattlebird which they don't, but to compensate, they have recorded a noteworthy list of 19 honeyeaters. Altogether, there are 54 Australian honeyeaters, of which 35 are listed in the Victorian Atlas. There are 15 listed for Melbourne Water's Western Treatment Plant at Werribee and 18 listed for the whole of East Gippsland, which includes a great variety of habitats from rainforest and woodlands to heaths and coastal plains, so by my reckoning, a total of 19 for one small property in north central Victoria is pretty impressive.

It is true that their total includes two (the Black Honeyeater and the White-fronted Honeyeater) that visited during the drought of 1982 and have not been seen since. It also includes two classified as near threatened, namely the Black-chinned (whose numbers fluctuate from year to year but do not appear to be declining significantly) and the Painted which, I am delighted to say, returns reliably every summer to nest. Now that the trees in my parents' house garden

5

The near threatened Painted Honeyeater returns each summer to breed.

Like the Painted Honeyeater, Mistletoebirds return to nest each year when the mistletoe is in fruit.

have matured, for the last couple of years the Painted has nested very considerately right in front of the house. How many people can sip chablis on their front verandahs while watching Painted Honeyeaters nesting?

Spiny-cheeked Honeyeaters are common and each spring my parents usually find a nest or two. One January, for no discernible reason, they irrupted and every low wattle contained a nest, usually well hidden amongst mistletoe.

Apart from this profusion of honeyeaters, my parents have some other very special birds. There are Red-capped Robins, Gilbert's Whistlers and Southern Whiteface — all resident and breeding. Those captivating little jewels, Mistletoebirds, return to nest each summer. They are always favourites and will put on a wonderful ballet in the early mornings under the sprinkler in the house garden.

One New Year's Day my father and I were strolling along looking for Speckled Warblers when a frighteningly loud mechanical noise came from nowhere. We looked at each other in disbelief. What could it be? Neither of us had ever witnessed such a noise before. Was a home-made gyrocopter about to crash on top of us? The mystery was soon solved, as a huge flock of White Ibis flew over very low, hundreds of wing beats in unison making an extraordinarily loud noise. We've often seen huge skeins of ibis decorating the sky, but never before or since have I witnessed them quite so low or quite so frighteningly loud.

In November 1991, Woodswallows (White-browed and Dusky together) irrupted for no apparent reason. Every scraggly wattle contained a nest of a White-browed Woodswallow and almost every eucalypt accommodated a Dusky's nest, all thoughtfully placed just at my eye-height.

Diamond Doves visit occasionally in summer, making us look twice at the resident Peaceful Doves. Common Bronzewing are frequently seen, Brush Bronzewing infrequently.

Olive-backed Oriole are an uncommon sighting and usually only seen at all because their distinctive call draws our attention to them. Equally unpredictable are Stubble Quail and Painted Button-quail, both rarely seen. We've seen Black Falcon a few times with no pattern to their occurrence. Only once have we seen a White-throated Gerygone, and only once, a pair of Yellow-tailed Black Cockatoos flew over. (Only once, too, I saw a flock of 50 in Kew!) One June a small flock of Swift Parrots paused for a drink at the dam. These endangered parrots breed in Tasmania over summer and return to the mainland in March. Clearance of timber means fewer tree hollows are available for nesting and what hollows remain are sometimes appropriated by Common Starlings. It is estimated that only 1000 breeding pairs of these small parrots remain.

Peregrine Falcons nest in the flora reserve near my parents' place. In Melbourne they nest on high rise city buildings and feed on feral pigeons. The Australian population of this once endangered bird is now considered stable, with something over 5000 breeding pairs. Brown Falcons are my parents' most common raptor. They nest in the state forest behind my parents' property. Wedge-tailed Eagles used to nest there too, but they have not returned to that nest for many years. Wedgies usually have several nests in their territory and rotate breeding between them. I can only assume that this pair has gone forever, which is a dreadful shame. We still see them often and it is always a thrill. Little Eagles are common too, as well as Whistling Kites.

The female Crested Bellbird used to be a familiar sight, but alas, I have not seen one for years.

My parents often see Australian Owlet Nightjars, and Tawny Frogmouths have nested across the road a couple of times. Southern Boobooks usually answer our calls when we sit on the verandah on summer evenings, although it's a long time since I've heard a Barking Owl. These owls are also suffering from loss of tree hollows and the southern race is classified as near threatened.

Seven species seen regularly at my parents' place are classified as near threatened. Of these seven species, four appear to me to be just as numerous as the day my parents bought the block, two have declined and the jury's still out on the last one. It is gratifying to note that Hooded Robins, Black-chinned and Painted Honeyeaters and Diamond Firetails are still common. Sadly, however, the Crested Bellbird has declined noticeably. Crested Bellbirds were common years ago; now they are infrequently heard and rarely seen. Numbers of Brown Treecreepers are also diminishing. It is difficult to assess any decline in populations of Speckled Warblers as they were never common. Every year I search in vain amongst the fallen branches and dead wattles for a Speckled Warbler's nest. One year I may be lucky. Then I will not regret the disappearance of Black-eared Cuckoos.

The major threat to all these species is loss of habitat. Being migratory, the Painted Honeyeater requires protection of habitat over the whole of its range, not just at its summer stopover. The Brown Treecreeper population is affected by a decline in the availability of tree hollows for nesting. The last Brown Treecreeper's nest I found was in an old fence-post, which, no doubt, it considered just as good as a tree stump.

Diamond Firetails suffer from changed habitat. The introduction of exotic grasses provides conditions more suited to the more common Red-browed Finch. Diamond Firetails are the only finches reliably seen at my parents' place.

We often see a Diamond Firetail with a long piece of grass in his beak. This avian equivalent of a box of chocolates is a gift for some fortunate female.

Red-browed Finches are often seen within a kilometre westwards in habitat that, to my eye, looks identical. As far as I can tell, there are no exotic grasses there. Diamond Firetails are also subject to illegal trapping: that is the price they pay for being so cute. They deserve better. These darling little birds are generally uncommon, but at my parents' place they are plentiful.

We often see one with a long piece of grass in his beak. I've seen them with grass up to 60 centimetres long. That's a lot of grass for a little bird — comparable to a person balancing a telegraph pole! This avian equivalent of a box of chocolates is a gift for his chosen mate. Lots of bobbingaccompanies its presentation to the fortunate female and mating often follows.

Zebra Finches are found 10 kilometres to the east in mallee scrub. One year we saw them much closer when they nested in the base of a nearby Brown Falcon's nest — a seemingly strange place to seek security and yet a frequent phenomenon. Goldfinches are common and have nested at my parents' place more than once, usually in a native pine. They are the only introduced bird regularly seen on the block.

Blackbirds visited once and tried to nest near the house. They were not made to feel welcome and have not returned. One lone cock House Sparrow turned up last summer and hung around by himself for a few weeks before he disappeared. On two occasions, disoriented homing pigeons have stopped by and been most reluctant to move on. But, as yet, there are no Starlings, no Spotted Turtle-doves, no Indian Mynahs — although these unwelcome interlopers seem to be getting closer each year.

As soon as the dams were built, Fairy Martins arrived and, using mud from the dam, built their bottle-shaped nests in the rocks. They came every October for several years — and then they stopped. Sometimes their abandoned nests are utilised now by Striated Pardalotes. But what happened to the Fairy Martins? Why don't they return?

There are still so many beautiful birds at my parents' place, it is easy to enjoy what is there and to forget what has been lost. I've done a lot of twitching there, and when I sat down to compile my lifelist, it was the obvious place to start. We've had innumerable exciting sightings there over the years, and it's all down to one little Hooded Robin.

2

Where else but Werribee?

MAINLY WATERBIRDS

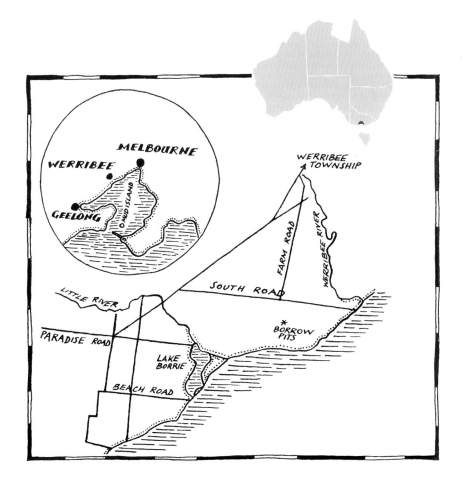

Treatment ponds at Western Treatment Plant, with You Yangs in the background.

'What's on for the weekend?' Bob asked me. It was Friday afternoon and I was packing up my desk, eager to get away. I felt sorry for Bob. His idea of a good time was watching a footy match. He did not know the joy of finding a Willie Wagtail's nest, the excitement of identifying a rare species of wader, the fascination of watching the mating flight of a pipit. He'd never experienced the sheer poetry of watching pelicans soar overhead in perfect formation. I decided to answer him honestly. I can stand ridicule.

'The usual. Shopping. Washing. And I think we'll do a trip to Werribee.'

'Werribee?'

'Yes. Werribee. It's one of my favourite places.'

'Isn't that where the sewage farm is?'

'That's where we go.'

'Doesn't it smell?' Bob's expression was a mixture of incredulity and horror.

I had to concede that sometimes it did smell. 'But that's nothing,' I told him. 'You wind up your windows and drive on. It's the best place in the world for waterbirds.'

Perhaps I'd misjudged him — the ridicule I'd expected never eventuated. Several times since then he's asked me questions about birds, so he's not a completely lost cause. I'll get him to Werribee one day — perhaps when his team's playing interstate.

Roger and I are fortunate to live in Melbourne, with Werribee right on our doorstep. For anyone interested in birds, Werribee is hard to beat, both for the number of birds and the number of species. The sight of a flock of thousands of waders wheeling as if with one mind is a breathtaking experience for anyone. It would even move Bob.

Werribee is a mecca for twitchers and an obvious place for me to visit in order to increase my lifelist. It is worth a visit in any season. Most of the waders breed in the northern hemisphere and visit Werribee from about October to February/March. A few over-winter here, and some are resident (such as Red-necked Avocets, Black-winged Stilts, Pied Oystercatchers and some plovers and dotterels). In summer you never know what rare surprise awaits you. Maybe a Red-necked Phalarope or a Yellow Wagtail.

Werribee is situated about 45 minutes' drive south-west of Melbourne, about 40 kilometres, on excellent roads all the way. The sewage farm, officially known as Melbourne Water's Western Treatment Plant, is on New Farm Road, past the Werribee township. Some of the roads in the farm are open to the public and some areas are off limits. Bird watchers with a permit (and a key) can gain access to some areas. Casual visitors to Melbourne are best advised to contact the Bird Observers Club to discuss access arrangements.

The lagoons on the north side of Paradise Road always provide good birding, as does the mouth of the Little River. In summer the Borrow Pits are worth a visit, as is Beach Road.

Driving along the narrow, sometimes slippery, roads between filtration ponds and deep lagoons is always an adventure. Unexpected presence of sheep or cattle stubbornly blocking the roadway adds occasional interest and the 'Danger Drowning Hazard' sign warns unwary visitors that sludge is 3.5 metres deep. Grass often grows higher than a vehicle, giving no forewarning of oncoming traffic.

Sharp-tailed Sandpipers do not have an obvious sharp tail, but at least they are common and easily seen.

The first time we visited Werribee was with the then World Wildlife Fund (now the World Wide Fund for Nature). The WWF ran a weekend trip under the guidance of its scientific experts who were studying endangered species. We were shown endangered plants: the spiny peppercress on the windy shores of Lake Beeac and the button winklewort in Rokewood Cemetery. We visited the Eastern Barred Bandicoot breeding program in Mooramong. But for me the highlight of the trip was the wonderful Werribee sewage farm. That's how we met Clive Minton, Australia's best known bird bander, and Honorary Vice President of Birds Australia.

I have been interested in birds all my life but had always regarded waders as too hard. To me, they were all LBJs — little brown jobs. They were too small, too far away and all too similar for proper identification. They are all grey or brown or greyish-brown on top, paler underneath and very, very, skittish. I could never get close enough for a proper look.

Clive Minton changed all that. That day in 1990 he taught me to recognise Red-necked Stints and Sharp-tailed and Curlew Sandpipers, and I was hooked. It was easy really — I knew that Curlews had long down-curved bills: so does the Curlew Sandpiper. The Sharp-tailed Sandpiper has a shorter straight bill, a white eyebrow and pointy white edged feathers on its back. Clive didn't say we should look for a sharp tail. As with many birds, this bird's name, while not precisely incorrect, is certainly inappropriate. Apparently Sharp-tailed Sandpipers have pointy tail feathers, which you might be able to see if you held the bird in your hand. Maybe.

Red-necked Stints are much smaller with a shorter neck making them appear more hunched, less elegant. Their necks are only 'red' (russet is a better word) in breeding plumage, either when they've just arrived in Australia or are just about to leave. The thought of these tiny birds flying 17,000 kilometres, all the way from Siberia, is truly amazing. They are only the size of a sparrow and weigh 25 grams. Clive Minton describes them as fitting into a wine glass, but I suspect that Clive has smaller wine glasses than we do. You could fit a Greenshank into one of Roger's wine glasses.

The Common Sandpiper is not common at Werribee.

The three most common waders at Werribee are Red-necked Stints, Curlies and Sharpies. And I could identify all three. I was confident I could get on top of waders then: all I needed was a spotting scope.

Verily, pride cometh before a fall. I was yet to be confronted with the disconcerting differences between breeding, non-breeding and immature plumages and various stages in between! After 10 years of dedicated wader watching, I am still constantly confused.

I give thanks for the few considerate waders who like to stand out in a crowd. The Common Sandpiper (which belies its name in Victoria — it is far from common) proudly bears a white shoulder insignia. It has a long straight bill and a characteristic bob. Terek Sandpipers are the easiest of all to identify. They have a long upturned bill and bright yellow legs. The problem is they're rarely seen at Werribee. Grey-tailed Tattlers, too, are both easy to iden-tify and rare at Werribee. They are a soft grey colour with a long straight bill and yellow legs. They always look fat to me and seem to waddle along the beach.

The Ruddy Turnstone is easily recognised — a chunky little bird with a mot-tled appearance, about the size of a blackbird, with bright orange legs. Of course it isn't ruddy, but it does turn stones. And shells. And seaweed. Common Greenshanks are soon learnt, as long as you don't waste your time looking for green legs — they look a dirty brownish olive to me. Greenshanks are pale, larger than Sandpipers, with an elegant slim stance, a long neck and a long, slightly upturned bill. They are 30-35 centimetres long, somewhere between the size of a Magpie and a Magpie-lark. (Yes, Roger does have a very big wine glass.)

Asian Dowitchers are easily recognised, with their funny-shaped big broad bill. They are on the Werribee list, but they are rare and we've never seen them there. The only place we've seen Asian Dowitchers is at Buffalo Creek in Darwin.

Oystercatchers are also very cooperative. There are only two species and they cannot be confused with each other or with anything else. I always think they get dressed in the dark, because their accessories don't quite match. They have bright red eye-rings, long straight bright red bills and (great fashion gaffe) pink legs. The Sooty Oystercatcher (we call them SOCs) is pure black and prefers rocky coastlines. There's a fair amount of rocky coastline at Werribee, so why it's rare there I do not know. The Pied Oystercatcher (POC) prefers sandy beaches and has a black head and is black above and white below. In flight they are very pretty. Although they are classed as uncommon at Werribee, that is because they are few in number, not because they are difficult to see. We've seen them in every season. If you drive down to the end of Farm Road (this is a public road) and look to the grass area on your right, you are quite likely to see a couple of pairs of POCs at any time of year.

These few birds are the exception that proves the rule. Most waders like to travel incognito. Only the omniscient experts know them by name. They are frustrating, irritating and baffling. And worth every bit of effort.

We had a wonderful weekend with the WWF all those years ago. Despite it being cold and wet, our birdlist included 77 species and I added 12 to my lifelist, including the critically endangered Orange-bellied Parrot. This dear little bird breeds in Tasmania in summer, then migrates north in March and can be found along the mainland coast from Melbourne to the Coorong in South Australia. In 1993, it was estimated that there were fewer than 200 Orange-bellied Parrots left in the wild and a breeding program was started at Melaleuca in the remote south-west of Tasmania. Birds bred in captivity have also been successfully released at Birch's Inlet on the west coast, but numbers are small and the population is fragile. Today there are only 180 mature birds. This little parrot will need all the help we can give it if it is to survive.

We were lucky to see Blue-winged Parrots as well as Orange-bellied and to see the subtle differences between these two easily confused species. They are both small green parrots with blue on their wings. Both have yellow undertail coverts, both have yellow faces with a blue band on their foreheads. The Blue-winged Parrot may even have some orange on its belly! The Orange-bellied Parrot is a greener green, and has less blue on its wings. The Blue-winged Parrot is more an olive colour and has a much more noticeable bright blue wing patch. If you happen to be in the Coorong where the range of both these parrots overlaps with the Elegant Parrot, there is further room for confusion and misidentification. I've never seen these birds together, but my impression of Elegant Parrots is of a slightly larger bird. Like the Orange-bellied, the Elegant Parrot has less blue on

At Werribee we see Black Swans by the thousand.

Australian Shelduck (formerly called Mountain Duck) are abundant in summer.

The Freckled Duck is Australia's rarest waterfowl.

the wing than the Blue-winged, but to be sure of identification, look for the blue band on its forehead, which extends beyond the eye on an Elegant Parrot — at least in an adult male.

As soon as I felt half-confident about sharpies and curlies, I started looking for rarer waders. I'm told that Little Stints are not as rare as previously believed — they're just impossible to identify amongst flocks of Red-necked Stints. Last summer a Hudsonian Godwit visited Werribee. Unfortunately we didn't see it. One uncommon sandpiper we have managed to identify is the Pectoral Sandpiper. After years of looking, we saw one by itself in a shallow pond most cooperatively wandering around. It looked like a sharpie with a slightly longer neck and a slightly longer bill. Rog and I both twitched that day — don't let him tell you otherwise. We've also seen Marsh Sandpiper, which look like small, elegant Greenshank, and the rare vagrant Stilt Sandpiper, which resembles a large curlie.

While Werribee is predominantly thought of as the place to see waders, there are many other waterbirds to be seen there too. There are grebes and pelicans, gulls and terns, herons, egrets, cormorants and ibis. If you're lucky you might see Glossy Ibis — uncommon in Victoria. We've seen them in autumn and winter. There are thousands of coots, and hundreds of moorhen and swamphen and, in summer, lots of crakes. In January Australian Spotted and Spotless Crakes can both be seen. Baillon's Crake is on the list too, but we've never seen one. And ducks. Above all, swans and ducks. You might see 10,000 Black Swans and 50,000 Pink-eared Ducks. There are teal by the tens of thousands, both Chestnut and Grey (look for the paler face to distinguish the Grey Teal from its look-alike, the female Chestnut). There are thousands of Pacific Black Duck and also Australian Shelduck (I confess they will always be Mountain Duck to me) and, in the deeper lagoons, Musk Duck by the hundreds. Blue-billed Duck are common, too, as are Hardheads and Australasian Shovelers. And occasionally there is a handful of Freckled Duck on Lake Borrie. This is Australia's rarest waterfowl, still sometimes shot by duck hunters. It is also an exceptionally boring duck, spending much of its time doing nothing.

Lake Borrie is also where Pied Cormorants nest, perversely in autumn and winter. Elsewhere Pied Cormorants nest in summer. Lake Borrie provides one of

Lake Borrie is a haven for many thousands of waterbirds.

Lake Borrie provides one of only two known Pied Cormorant nesting colonies in Victoria.

only two known Victorian nesting colonies. Little Pied and Little Black Cormorants are very common at Werribee. There are fewer Great Cormorants, and Black-faced Cormorants are rare. We don't always see Darters, although they also breed here.

White-faced Heron are common all year round. Once in winter I saw a flock of over 20, which is unusual as these birds are normally solitary. White-necked

15

Most unusually, these Australasian Grebe didn't see my camera coming.

Heron are not so common, although one winter we had an irruption, and there seemed to be White-necked Herons everywhere.

We've seen all three species of grebes at Werribee, although the Hoary-headed are by far the most common, and Great Crested are quite uncommon — but very amusing. One Great-crested Grebe is funny; the enormous flock we saw once at Rotamah was hugely entertaining. With their clown's orange head ruffs, beady red eyes and silly black crests, they are about as funny-looking as a bird can be. One glimpse of my camera makes most birds fly away. Grebes provide some variety to this scenario. Hoary-headed Grebe run away across the top of the water at great speed. Australasian Grebe dive under the water and swim away. Great-crested Grebe always very cleverly stay well out of range. They come close only when they perceive that I don't have my camera with me. Perhaps I should focus on photographing flowers.

If I thought that waders were difficult to identify it was because I hadn't given sufficient consideration to terns. Terns must be THE most uncooperative birds of the lot. They refuse to sit down and have a spell and give a birdwatcher a fair go. They are constantly hawking over the water — extraordinarily difficult to pick up in binoculars and quite impossible in a scope.

The easiest tern to identify is the biggest — the Caspian with its huge red bill. We don't often see them at Werribee, where they are classified as uncommon. I once watched a Caspian Tern on Mud Island feeding its chick with a fish the size of a sardine. These baby birds must have phenomenal digestive systems.

The only tern at Werribee present all year round is the Crested Tern, the exception that proves the rule — he cooperates by lounging on the beach. Crested Terns have orange-yellow bills and a small black crest on the back of their heads, which simply will not stay in place.

Other terns come and go. Just when you think you have learnt to recognise a Whiskered Tern, you have to look twice and admit that this one's a White-winged Black Tern. Gull-billed Terns are much bigger, but size is hard to assess when they're flying fast a few hundred metres away, and they really do resemble Common Terns, which — you guessed it — are not common.

Little Terns and Fairy Terns are both present but uncommon at Werribee; Fairy Terns breed there. Both these tiny terns have increased in numbers in recent years and are no longer considered vulnerable. I've seen experts baffled trying to identify them. Both can have black or yellow bills; both can have varying amounts of black on their heads and napes. The only useful fact to remember is that if it is winter a small tern at Werribee will be a Fairy Tern. Little Terns visit only in summer.

There are hundreds of Black-winged Stilts, usually accompanied by some immature birds just to confuse the birdwatcher. Sometimes a few Banded Stilts visit from Altona where they breed.

Red-necked Avocets are present all year round. Hundreds of them. Is there a more beautiful bird? Naturally, their heads are not red, but chestnut rather, and their upturned bills are haute couture chic.

Black-winged Stilts also breed at Werribee.

Drive to the end of Beach Road during summer and you may be lucky enough to see some Pacific Golden Plover. Last summer they were loafing mixed in with uncommon Common Terns. Pacific Golden Plover are an absolutely stunning bird when seen in full breeding plumage. Unfortunately we rarely do have this pleasure.

Obviously the big attraction at Werribee is the waterbirds, but it is also a great spot to see raptors and bushbirds. Altogether there are 274 species on the Werribee birdlist: we've seen less than half of them, but since our first visit in 1990, I've added a further 12 species to my lifelist, making a total of 24 new birds for me from Werribee.

White Ibis, a common bird, but nonetheless beautiful.

I don't think we've ever been to Werribee without seeing White-fronted Chats. As a child I was taught to call these birds 'Nun birds', which seems a fair description until you consider that it's the male who's wearing the wimple. They often fly along in front of the car and gain surprising speed. In spring their nesting colonies are easily found low in the bushes by the beach.

The introduced Skylark and Richard's Pipit are both common at Werribee. Both are small, sparrow-coloured groundbirds (between the size of a sparrow and a blackbird) and both have white on the edges of their tails, noticeable in flight. The Skylark has a very slight crest but this isn't always visible. Richard's Pipit has long, pink legs and wags its tail distinctively up and down. The Skylark is often heard before it is seen, hovering at a great height and singing its little heart out.

One very memorable song you are bound to hear if you spend any time at Werribee is the mournful call of the Little Grassbird. It is just three sad notes. It is a beautifully striated little bird, the size of a sparrow. What it's got to be so unhappy about, I can't imagine.

Another little streaked bird about the same size but with a distinctly happier

Seventeen of Australia's 24 raptors have been recorded at Werribee. The Black-shouldered Kite is one of seven species that have been recorded breeding there.

song is the Striated Fieldwren. He is also common at Werribee. He cocks his tail and sings with gusto.

Werribee has a third striated bird, this one smaller and much more common and more friendly and more easily seen. It is the Golden-headed Cisticola (pronounced to rhyme with rib-tickler, and not as if it's a new soft drink). The male in breeding plumage is a bright golden colour — not just his head. He sits on a blade of grass, barely bending it with his insignificant weight, and sings to the world.

Seventeen of Australia's 24 species of raptor have been recorded at Werribee, including the rare Letter-winged Kite. Whistling Kites nest in the gum trees in Farm Road. Brown Falcons nest around the corner in South Road and Black-shouldered Kites nest in the wind-stunted Tuarts planted in Beach Road. I'm told that Brown Goshawks, Nankeen Kestrels and Swamp Harriers breed there too, although I've never found their nests. Swamp Harriers nest on the ground, so I imagine they'd be well hidden in the dense reeds. I've no excuse for not finding the others.

Don't be discouraged by the sludge drowning hazard, don't be put off by the smell or by the preconceptions of the Bobs of this world. When you are in Melbourne and want to boost your bird count, there is only one place to go. Where else but Werribee?

3

The joys of Gipsy Point

BIRDS OF FAR-EAST GIPPSLAND

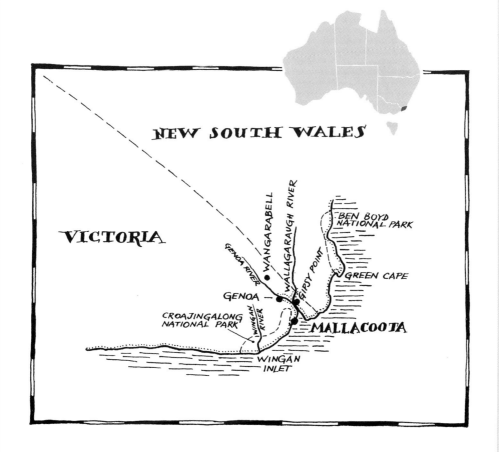

I'll never forget my first sighting of a Glossy Black-Cockatoo. I was sitting by myself in the back of a small bus, which was full of happy, tired birdos. It was approaching dusk and we were being driven back to Gipsy Point Lodge by the proprietor, Alan Robertson, after a day of birding at Wangarabell. Rog had returned to Melbourne for a few days for some work commitments, leaving me at the lodge bird watching. It was October 1990 — our first visit to Gipsy Point. I had prepared a list of about 30 birds I wanted to see and shown it to Alan on arrival. He gave it a cursory glance, then handed it back to me, saying 'Good luck'. Hardly encouraging, I thought!

Although any new bird is exciting, some are very special and I had set my heart on seeing Glossy Black-Cockatoos. They are rare birds, officially classified as near threatened, but according to my pre-holiday reading, spring was the right time for them to appear at Gipsy Point and I was determined to give them my best shot. Now I know that Glossy Blacks are more often seen at Gipsy Point from November to January, but happily I didn't know that then.

As I was at the back of the bus, I was lucky to see them at all — nobody else had. Perhaps this was because I was the only one looking, while everyone else was chatting about the successes of the day. Anyway I saw them. In the fading light they were just black shapes on top of the casuarinas.

I screamed out to Alan above everyone's chatter: 'Stop!' My voice conveyed such a sense of urgency that Alan immediately screeched on the brakes. I scrambled out, oblivious of my fellow passengers. There, in the top of the casuarinas, sitting feeding contentedly on casuarina seeds and ignoring the busload of binoculars now pointing in their direction, quite unmistakably, were three Glossy Black-Cockatoos. Glossy Blacks raise only one chick each year, and they are the only Australian cockatoo to breed exclusively in autumn and winter. Three birds seen in October can safely be assumed to be a pair with this year's youngster.

I didn't twitch on that occasion. I literally jumped with joy. Rog wasn't there to witness my performance, but Alan found it pretty amusing. He still does. He reminds me of it every time he sees me.

I have seen Glossy Black-Cockatoos several times since and it is always a thrill. The Glossy Black-Cockatoo has a humorous grotesquely large bill. In flight its bright red tail patches are conspicuous. Why it is called 'Glossy Black' I can't imagine. It's the least glossy and the least black of all the black cockatoos. It is not properly black at all, more brownish-black. Cayley called it a Casuarina Cockatoo, which is a much better name.

Once I watched a pair feeding a young one. It was fully grown but didn't seem able to crack casuarina seeds without parental aid.

One November morning, we were having breakfast at the lodge when a helpful neighbour rang to say that there were Glossies on the Mallacoota Road. We rushed out straight away, together with Alan's wife, Sue. We saw six birds (two families of three) sitting high up in a eucalypt preening. We couldn't believe our luck when an Australian Raven disturbed them and they flew closer to us. There was a pair of Southern Emu-wren at our feet, but I couldn't take my Zeiss off the Glossy Blacks. We could hear cuckoos, and Sue identified Pallid, Fantailed,

Horsfield's Bronze and Shining Bronze all at once. And the Shining Bronze-Cuckoo was displaying. What is a poor birdo to do? I had to take my eyes off my Glossies to see that. I did the twitchy thing, had a quick look at each bird, then returned to concentrate on my Glossies. When they eventually flew off, the emu-wrens had disappeared. Naturally.

I have many wonderful memories of Gipsy Point Lodge — the friendly people, the delicious food and, of course, the fabulous birds. Gipsy Point is in Far East Gippsland, not far from the well-known tourist town of Mallacoota. It's six hours' drive from Melbourne — a very pleasant trip along the Princes Highway. A friend of ours broke the journey at Sale and photographed Great-crested Grebe on the lake. We usually plan a stop at Stratford Highway Park and feed the Purple Swamphens. Once when we stopped there, we saw swarms of Fork-tailed Swifts.

We've been to Gipsy Point Lodge five times (so far), adding a total of 28 birds to my lifelist. The lodge is located at the junction of the Genoa and Wallagaraugh Rivers at the head of Mallacoota Inlet. Alan and Sue Robertson have moved on and the lodge is now run by

We always stop at Stratford Highway Park to talk to the Swamphens.

Libby and Ian Mitchell. I am assured that there are reasons to visit other than bird watching. They tell me that the fishing is good. I can confirm that the scenery is spectacular, that you can see luminous fungi in autumn, and in spring the wild-flowers are wonderful. I have photographed Flying Duck Orchids (*Caleana major*) in the cemetery in October, the huge and yet delicate orange flowers of the Hairpin Banksia (*Banksia spinulosa*) in May, and the enormous cauliflower heads of cream flowers of the magnificent Red Bloodwoods (*Eucalyptus gummifera*) in April. But for me the overwhelming attraction is the birds. I think it's worth going there just for the Glossy Blacks.

If Glossy Black-Cockatoos are the first birds that spring to mind when I think of Gipsy Point, the second is certainly the Black Bittern, and the third is the Ground Parrot. All special birds; all rare or threatened. The fourth bird that comes to mind is the Southern Emu-wren — not rare or threatened, but a beautiful little bird, Australia's second smallest and always exciting to see. After that, lots of fantastic sightings tumble into my mind together: Satin Bowerbird and bowers decorated with blue treasures; the Wonga Pigeon with its endless call; Spotted Quail-thrush with their subtle beauty; gorgeous Azure Kingfishers and Turquoise Parrots; Eastern Whipbirds with their antiphonal call (the male cracks his whip and she obediently responds 'choo choo' — in my ignorance I used to think it was all the call of one individual bird); pretty Black-faced Monarchs; friendly King Parrots; the black morph of the White-bellied Cuckoo-shrike; Crescent, Tawny-crowned and Scarlet Honeyeaters; and robins! oh, the robins: Eastern Yellow and Flame and Scarlet and Rose and Pink.

We loved Gipsy Point so much on that first visit that we arranged to return six months later for an official bird week run by Graham Pizzey. At last we were going to meet Australia's foremost birdwatcher and nature writer. A couple of years previously we had travelled to the Moira Forest (a distance of some 250 kilometres) for a waterbird weekend because it had been advertised that Graham would be present. He wasn't. But we had some wonderful sightings (including Little Bittern, Australian Spotted Crake, Superb Parrot, Dollarbird, Grey-crowned Babbler and enormous flocks of Nankeen Night-herons), so I forgave them Graham's absence. It wasn't their fault that he had succumbed to the dreaded lurgy at the last moment.

Anyway, we returned to Gipsy Point for the bird week in May 1991 and per-suaded my parents to come along, too. As I recall, they didn't take much per-suasion. They were keen to meet Graham, too.

As always, I had my wishlist with me. I compile my wishlists not by any local knowledge. I go through the *Atlas of Australian Birds* and list all the species I haven't seen that have been recorded at my destination. Then I read everything I can lay my hands on about all the birds on my list.

That's how I had Black Bittern on my list. In Victoria, it is a rare bird. The map for distribution of the Black Bittern in the *Atlas of Australian Birds* shows one tiny pink dot in Victoria, roughly in the vicinity of Mallacoota. The *Atlas of Victorian Birds* records two sightings, one at Mallacoota and one on the Wingan River. That was near enough for me, so I asked Graham about the likelihood of seeing one.

Graham is a polite gentleman and he didn't laugh. With a perfectly straight face, he advised that the best chance of seeing a Black Bittern was from the boat on the river very early in the morning.

It was decidedly cold at six o'clock the next morning. Graham demonstrated his confidence in his advice by staying in bed. Rog and I were both breathing steam like draught horses as we walked down to the jetty. All the kangaroos on the hill were breathing steam, too. Although I wore gloves, my fingers were freez-ing and the seat of the boat was so cold it felt wet. Rog started the engine first go (he's a mechanical genius) and steered us up the river. He'd motor for a while, then turn the engine off and we'd drift, enjoying the quiet. A mist hung over the river. It was eerie, bone-chillingly cold, but extremely beautiful. I decided it was worth the discomfort.

There was very little sign of life, and (when the engine was off) just the sound of the water lapping the boat. No Azure Kingfishers sitting on dead branches beside the river. No Water Dragons posing for my camera. No Masked Lapwing strutting along the tiny sandy beaches. Just me and Rog in a little boat on a river engulfed in fog.

Then through the mist we saw it: a Black Bittern! There was nothing else that big black chunky bird could be. It had been roosting in one of the eucalypts overhanging the water and had seen us before we saw it. I wonder now if it had sat still whether we might have floated underneath unaware of its presence. Anyway, fortunately it flushed and flew a few metres ahead and landed again in a gum tree over the water.

Rog and I saw it simultaneously and strained to watch where it landed. Rog started the engine and we pursued it as quietly as possible with a throbbing diesel engine cutting through the morning mist. The bittern always stayed ahead of us. We never got a good view of it sitting still, but we had several misty glimpses of it in flight.

We rushed back to the lodge and shared our joy with my parents and by the time breakfast came around I had gained sufficient composure to say quite calmly to the famous Mr Pizzey: 'Thank you for your advice about the Black Bittern. We had some lovely sightings.'

The next morning, just about the entire lodge population gathered at the jetty before breakfast, wanting to see our Black Bittern. I felt very smug, very proprietorial. Then, suddenly it occurred to me that if our bittern didn't perform on cue, no one would believe our sighting. And what if they only got a glimpse and said we were mistaken — it wasn't a Black Bittern at all, it was some sort of unusually dark heron. What sort of an idiot was I that I didn't know a heron from a bittern? My mood changed immediately from complacency to anxiety. I was responsible for this lodge full of people abandoning their warm beds to venture onto the freezing foggy river. If the bird didn't appear, I was going to be about as popular as an egg collector.

After that I didn't notice the cold quite so much, or the evocative beauty of the mist over the water. I strained my eyes, peering ahead into the fog, trying to see our bird.

I am delighted to report that the bittern did not let me down. He flushed from the same tree as yesterday when we were at the same spot on the river. So again there were no views of the bird perched in the tree. But everyone saw him fly. And everyone agreed it was unmistakably a Black Bittern. Of course I never doubted it really. Two recorded sightings in Victoria, and we had confirmed a third one with Graham Pizzey to authenticate it. Pretty impressive, hey?

Alan had shown us Ground Parrots on our first visit and I wanted my parents to see them too. These unusual parrots inhabit coastal plains and, true to their name, they walk along the ground in preference to flying. The coastal heath is low but very dense and the parrots hear you coming and walk away unseen long before you have any chance of catching a glimpse.

Although it was freezing on the river before breakfast, it was quite hot by the time we arrived at Green Cape in Ben Boyd National Park in New South Wales, nearly 100 kilometres from the lodge. My first thoughts were not of Ground Parrots but of ground reptiles. I started wondering what might be lurking in the undergrowth: Tiger Snakes, Red-bellied Black Snakes, King Browns. Were we far enough north for Death Adders? I didn't really want to find out.

Graham told us all to form a straight line and to walk through the undergrowth at the same pace. It was madness. The things you do to see a bird. Not even a new species. I wished I'd worn gumboots, despite the heat. The scrub was so dense you couldn't see where you were putting your foot down. Inevitably it was very slow going. I could hear things on the ground and I'm sure they weren't parrots. I had two glimpses of parrots that day, running away from me like little

Dense coastal heathlands are home to the Ground Parrot – and many snakes.

green quail. I had six glimpses of snakes. After the first snake, I'd lost interest in parrots.

The fourth bird that springs to mind when I think of Gipsy Point is the Southern Emu-wren. Is there any more exquisite little bird? Apart from its beauty, the Southern Emu-wren has another great asset: it is best viewed early in the morning before reptiles bestir themselves.

Whenever Rog allowed his warm bed to take preference over a cold boat cruise before breakfast, I'd go looking for emu-wren. They inhabit bushes not far from the lodge, just a few minutes walk towards the Mallacoota-Genoa road. Their wispy little call is like the trill of a Superb Fairy-wren, but lighter. They have bright little intelligent eyes and gossamer-like tails which they proudly hold erect for everyone to see. Emu feathers are unique in having dual shafts. The tail of an emu-wren looks like it's made from emu feathers. Each barb is separate, and the tail has only six feathers. Most birds have from 12-30 feathers in their tails. Could there be a better start to the day than admiring emu-wrens before breakfast?

That bird week with Graham Pizzey and his charming wife, Sue, was very special. Graham has an exceptionally keen ear for bird calls — how he could differentiate the wispy tinkle of a Buff-rumped Thornbill over the noise of the bus engine I'll never know. He taught me how to tell the difference between Brown and Striated Thornbills (more easily differentiated by behaviour than appearance — the Brown is busy in the undergrowth, the Striated hops around in the canopy). He told me to compare the length of the neck with the length of the body to differentiate Great Egrets (neck is longer) from Intermediate Egrets (neck is equal) from Little Egrets (neck is shorter). Behaviour is different too: the Great Egret stands perfectly still then suddenly pounces on its prey, the Intermediate, which prefers taller vegetation, stirs the water with its foot, as does the Little Egret, which is never still. He took us on a boat trip for spectacular views of White-bellied Sea-Eagles catching fish (cleverly floating thanks to some well-placed corks). Every evening after dinner, Graham would miraculously produce a superb slide show, reinforcing what we'd learnt that day.

Some years later we were delighted to go birding with Graham again. He showed us a flock of over a dozen Latham's Snipe at Port Fairy, where we'd gone at dusk to the Pea Soup Short-tailed Shearwater colony to witness these remarkable birds flying back to their burrow nests. This bird is better known as the Muttonbird, as it provided an important part of the diet of early settlers.

The Short-tailed Shearwater is abundant. Huge flocks are reported. There are estimated to be 23 million breeding birds. It is probably Australia's most numerous seabird and is apparently coping with exploitation by humankind. Licensed operators harvest 160,000 chicks each year from Bass Strait Islands, which are used for flesh and feathers, and oil

Great Egret at Mallacoota: neck is longer than body.

for the pharmaceutical industry. The number of nesting burrows on Phillip Island is declining due to dogs, foxes and encroaching housing. It is fair to assume that all mainland colonies face similar difficulties. Apart from various human intrusions, the chicks have to contend with feral cats, Forest Ravens and Pacific Gulls, and burrows are affected by soil erosion.

It was an extraordinary experience visiting this breeding colony in the dark: dozens of squawking birds at our feet and dozens more circling above, some landing very awkwardly beside us and hurrying to their burrows. These birds perform a phenomenal annual migration: a huge figure eight around the Pacific Ocean, travelling up past Japan and on to the West Coast of North America, then, with uncanny precision, tens of millions of Short-tailed shearwaters return home in the last week of September to breed, mainly on Bass Strait islands but also at a few spots on the mainland, such as Port Fairy. All the birds lay their eggs almost simultaneously on 24 November. Visiting a breeding colony is a fascinating, if noisy, experience.

When we left Port Fairy that night, we were accompanied by a Barn Owl that most cooperatively flew beside the car and kept up with us for several minutes, flying surprisingly fast for quite a distance.

But I digress. Back to Gipsy Point. Birding is good in the vicinity of the lodge. I've seen Red-browed Treecreepers on the walk down to the jetty. In the lodge garden we've seen Eastern Whipbird, Satin Bowerbird, King Parrots, Galahs, Red-browed Finches, the ubiquitous New Holland Honeyeater, and (my favourite) Wonga Pigeons. These genteel matronly pigeons seem to me to be wearing old-fashioned silk bloomers that they've carelessly got spattered in mud. In the breeding season (October to January) they call incessantly. Hoo hoo hoo hoo hoo hoo hoo hoo. On and on and on. Alan told me that someone counted 200 calls, then gave up counting before the bird gave up calling. I don't know how the poor pigeons find time to breathe.

Also in the lodge grounds I've seen families of White-winged Choughs — pairs of adults preening each other. The adults have bright red eyes, while the young ones have shiny dark brown eyes. They are very sociable birds with lots of personality. My dad says they look like parties of chattering girls out for a good time.

On several occasions we have had good views of a Nankeen Night Heron roosting by day in the huge conifers in the Gipsy Point township. By craning your neck, you can identify the bird. However, I have had better sightings on the island in the lake at the Melbourne Botanic Gardens, or at the Melbourne zoo, where they are not in captivity but have chosen to breed. Here they have learnt to follow the keeper's food trolley and help themselves to fresh fish when the keeper's back is turned. Very resourceful.

On the road to Mallacoota from Gipsy Point, Double Creek Nature Walk is a good spot for Superb Lyrebirds. We've seen Azure Kingfishers along the creek to the left of the carpark, and Scarlet Honeyeaters near the bridge. A gorgeous sight. This is what makes Mallacoota such a terrific place for birds — so many northern species travel down the coast this far and just make it onto the Victorian list. Birds like Brown Cuckoo-Doves, White-headed Pigeons and Topknot Pigeons.

The Double Creek walking track passes through rainforest and open woodlands, a variety of habitats catering for a variety of birds. Grey Goshawks are sometimes seen here — they nest nearby. Just to be perverse, they are not grey at all: they are a pristine white.

Although there are Lyrebirds at Double Creek, we've never seen a Pilotbird here, and I doubt they are present, despite what you may read elsewhere. Pilotbirds are so named because they are often seen in association with lyrebirds (benefiting from the lyrebirds' scratching which exposes palatable insects). They were said to be piloting the lyrebirds. Having searched unsuccessfully many times at Double Creek, I first saw Pilotbirds at the lower carpark at Tarra Bulga National Park. I'd been told they were there and that was one of the very rare occasions when the birds performed right on cue.

Whenever we go to Mallacoota, we make a point of visiting the airport. Tawny-crowned Honeyeaters are easily found in the scrub. Kangaroos sit on the grass airstrip and watch us looking for (but not finding) Latham's Snipe near the pond.

At this pond once, very bravely, I photographed four beautiful blotched eggs belonging to an angry pair of Masked Lapwing. A hard hat is in order for such activity.

It is not a busy airport. Kangaroos are the only people we've ever seen there. One day we parked by the office for morning coffee. While Roger was momentarily distracted by a New Holland Honeyeater, an impertinent Magpie ate his blueberry muffin. Roger told him quite plainly that worms were better for him, but he was unconvinced.

Mallacoota is a charming little town — except during school holidays. We usually take our scope to Captain Stevenson's Point and look at the waders on the beach below, or look out to sea in the hope of seeing an albatross. We've seen small flocks of Bar-tailed Godwits in the camping ground and families of Wood Ducks usually scatter half-heartedly in front of us.

When we stay at Gipsy Point we usually do a day trip to Wingan Inlet. The turnoff from the Princes Highway is about 30 kilometres past Genoa, back towards Melbourne. This road is narrow and windy and not fit for caravans. Once we arrived to find it shut. The coast here is all part of Croajingalong National Park and on that occasion the ranger had decided that the road was not safe.

I've photographed Kookaburras in the camping area and Hooded Plovers on the beach. These pretty little waders are classified as vulnerable, but we've often seen them at Wingan Inlet and I never tire of watching their twinkling run. Most recently (October 2000) we saw a pair mating at Sandy Point on Waratah Bay in Victoria, where we'd gone to watch Sanderlings running in and out with the waves. Sanderlings must be amongst the most literate of birds: they always behave in textbook fashion — they have studied the field guides assiduously.

There is a walk around Wingan Inlet and on to the beach, incorporating a section of raised board walk. I can vouch heartily that this is excellent habitat for Red-bellied Black Snakes. Black-faced Cormorants and seals can be seen on the rocks out to sea (the Skerries). Pied and Sooty Oystercatchers join the Plovers on the beach and in winter Double-banded Plovers come holidaying from New Zealand.

From our point of view, the other indispensable day trip from Gipsy Point Lodge is the drive to Wangarabell. Wangarabell, such as it is, is some 15 kilometres north of the Princes Highway, but it is the road itself that provides much excellent birding. Once we saw 11 Spotted Quail-thrush along this road and this is where Sue Robertson directed us to the dark morph of the White-bellied Cuckoo-Shrike. On one occasion I attempted to photograph a Spotted Pardalote entering its nest tunnel in the bank beside the road and nearly stepped on a Superb Fairy-wren's nest containing

Nankeen Night Herons often roost in Gipsy Point.

Immature Nankeen Night Herons don't have their parents' beautiful nankeen plumage.

I was very brave to photograph this Masked Lapwing's nest without wearing a hard hat.

27

Hooded Plovers are vulnerable, but are often seen at Wingan Inlet.

three eggs. There is usually a very vocal colony of Yellow-tufted Honeyeaters somewhere along the way. These birds compensate for their gorgeous golden plumage by having an unpleasant harsh call and a rude aggressive manner. Another spectacular bird reliably found along this road is the most colourful Turquoise Parrot. The male is bright green with a bright blue face and a diagnostic red shoulder patch. The only other place I have often seen these parrots is Honeyeater Dam (formerly known as Cyanide Dam) in Chiltern Box Ironbark National Park.

The road to Wangarabell is certainly a very appealing drive. It is, after all, where I saw my first Glossy Black-Cockatoos.

4

The marvellous Mallee

BIRDS OF THE SEMI-ARID COUNTRY

CALPERUM STATION

RENMARK

MILDURA

HATTAH KULKYNE NATIONAL PARK

MURRAY SUNSET NP

MURRAY RIVER

PINAROO

WYPERFELD NATIONAL PARK

COMET BORE

VICTORIA

BORDERTOWN

KIATA

DIMBOOLA

LITTLE DESERT NP

HORSHAM

SOUTH AUSTRALIA

I remember as a kid going with my parents to Kiata to see Malleefowl. We lay on the ground for what seemed like hours, perfectly still, perfectly quiet, pointy sticks miraculously materialising out of nowhere to poke into various parts of our anatomy. After an aeon of discomfort, something moved in the distance. Silently, tentatively, a Malleefowl appeared. The ants invading my private parts were instantly forgotten. A bull ant could have bitten me at that moment and I wouldn't have noticed. I was totally enthralled by the Malleefowl. He was such a magnificent bird, so regal with his head proudly erect and his unhurried, stately walk.

The very beautiful, vulnerable Malleefowl is threatened by loss of habitat.

I remember being surprised at how big he was: the size of a fat, healthy rooster. And so very beautiful. Mottled browns and greys and black and white — perfect camouflage in the dappled light of the bush. A grey head, a pretty white mark under the eye, rich rufous chin, pale underneath with an emphatic black streak down the breast. And huge feet. They are, after all, part of the family called megapodes, literally 'big feet'. I never cease to get a thrill out of seeing these majestic birds, strutting grandly through the mallee.

Although their distribution has reduced significantly over the last 100 years, Malleefowl are found in four states (Western Australia, South Australia, Victoria and New South Wales): wherever there is mallee scrub. Mallees are eucalypts with more than one trunk. They occur below 32 degrees latitude across Australia and normally grow only about six metres in height. There are more than 20 species of mallee in the south-east of the continent, over 200 species in the south-west. The mallee's multiple stems sprout from lignotubers (mallee roots), huge swellings partly or wholly underground, that enable the plant to survive total destruction of its growth above ground. This must help to make harvesting eucalyptus oil a viable industry, as the entire tree can be mercilessly slashed off at ground level. I guiltily remember the wonderful warmth of mallee root fires. How much did I unknowingly contribute to the destruction of this important habitat?

That day nearly 40 years ago, it was Keith Hateley who showed me my first Malleefowl. He is the man responsible for the establishment of the first Victorian sanctuary for the Malleefowl, or Lowan as the local Aborigines call them. (In the south-west, the Aborigines call them Gnow.) The Victorian sanctuary was later expanded into the Little Desert National Park, and Keith became the first ranger. He had taken a close interest in one particular pair of Malleefowl, which he'd named Romeo and Juliet. He took us to wait at their mound, knowing that Romeo would dutifully return to check the temperature. A male Malleefowl maintains the temperature in his mound at a steady 33 degrees centigrade. Rotting vegetation in the bottom produces heat to incubate the eggs. The temperature must be checked regularly and adjusted, either by adding more sand to cool it down or allowing more sun in to warm it up. Mounds can be up to five metres across, a metre and a half high. The male can move 150 tonnes of material in building one. The female saves her energy for egg laying. She lays more than 20, one a week, each one equal to over 10 per cent of her body weight. In one season, the total weight of all the eggs laid by one female can be 270 per cent of her body weight.

Kiata is on the Western Highway about 25 kilometres west of Dimboola, 362 kilometres north-west of Melbourne. Whenever we travel this road we plan to break the drive at the Little Desert National Park south of Kiata. 'Desert' is in fact a misnomer — it receives too much annual rainfall (upwards of 400 mm) to qualify officially as a desert. (A desert receives less than 10 inches, 254 mm.) What it does have to make it desert-like is sand. Pale, infertile, axle-sinking, sand.

The sandy soil supports a surprisingly dense and varied vegetation — banksia, grevillea, melaleuca, baeckea, eutaxia, myrtles, heaths, wattles, and, of course, mallees. In spring the wildflowers display a cacophony of colour — sunny yellow guinea flowers and golden pennants, creamy white candles, pristine white riceflowers and woolly everlastings, pink and white fringe-myrtles and heath-myrtles, and pink velvet bush, pretty purple fringe-lilies, and bright red parrot peas. In November photographers travel to the Little Desert especially to record the Violet Honey-myrtle (*Melaleuca wilsonii*) which, despite its name, is a spectacular, overwhelming, nauseating pink.

And it is sand that attracts the Malleefowl. It is sometimes said that Malleefowls frequent the mallee scrub because they require the mallee leaf-litter for their mounds. But in their New South Wales habitat, acacia is more important than eucalypts, and in the Western Australian wheat belt, hakeas predominate. Sand is the common feature. They could not construct mounds out of clay.

Malleefowl are classified as vulnerable. It is alarming to see how far their territory has contracted since records have been kept. The chicks are on their own when they struggle out of the mound and are easy prey for foxes. Young chicks require low vegetation for protective shelter. The birds won't breed where this understorey has been removed. Feral cats have been known to attack males focused on tending their mounds. But by far the biggest influence on their contracting territory is land clearing.

Malleefowl can be difficult to see — although they are large, they are not common, and they are well camouflaged. The best trick is to find an active mound and wait patiently out of sight. The male will eventually return.

Not all mallee birds are so difficult to see. One of the easiest at the Little Desert is the Mallee Ringneck — a gorgeous brilliant green parrot with a bright yellow mark across the back of its neck, often taken for granted because it is so common. It is the eastern race of the Australian Ringneck and has a green head, unlike his western cousins, the Port Lincoln and Twenty-eight Parrot, which both have black heads. Once, in Hermannsburg, a woman, seeing my binoculars, persuaded me to come and see her rare Hooded Parrot. I accompanied her outside and followed her gaze up a gumtree to see a common Port Lincoln Parrot. There's a nice question of birdo etiquette: whether or not to put her straight. I'm ashamed to say that I did. She did not thank me. In fact, I don't think she believed me. I just spoiled her moment.

Our Australian parrots are enchanting creatures, intelligent and endearing; the Mallee Ringneck is one of the most beautiful (probably much prettier than Hooded Parrots). They nest in tree hollows. Conserving dead trees may prove to be the next big challenge for environmentalists. There is an unfortunately widespread belief that dead trees are no longer an important part of the ecology, whereas in fact the declining number of hollows cannot satisfy demand. Not sufficient attention has yet been paid to the threat posed by feral honeybees in invading tree hollows required by native creatures.

The vulnerable eastern subspecies of the Regent Parrot has declined because of bad forest management. It requires hollows in old river red gums for breeding and mallee woodland for feeding. Trees are not regenerating. The last thing this beautiful big golden parrot needs is a further threat from honeybees. The Regent Parrot is on the birdlist for Little Desert National Park, but I have only ever seen it at Wyperfeld and Hattah.

It was at the Little Desert that I first observed an Australian bird hoarding food. Until then I'd thought that this habit belonged to the jays and woodpeckers of the northern hemisphere. Roger had saved a slice of toast from breakfast. He broke it into little pieces and put it on the ground to see who he might attract. In no time at all a Grey Currawong appeared. The bird proceeded to cache bits of bread in various crannies in the surrounding gumtrees. I've since seen a White-winged Chough burying food, so the behaviour is not unique to currawongs.

This Major Mitchell's Cockatoo had Kodak shares.

Major Mitchell's Cockatoos (sometimes unimaginatively called Pink Cockatoos) are on the Little Desert National Park birdlist, but they are much more easily seen further north. I photographed one sitting in a native cypress pine (*Callitris preissii*) at Hattah/Kulkyne National Park. His immaculate pale pink plumage contrasted exquisitely with the dark green foliage of the callitris. He was eating the cones and posing most cooperatively. Roger said the bird had shares in Kodak.

He was in fact a very welcome consolation prize. We had spent that morning (and indeed every morning and evening for a week) searching in vain for Mallee Emu-wren and Striated Grasswren. The little devils simply would not show themselves.

As soon as we'd arrived at Hattah, we'd called in to see the ranger and seek advice about likely spots for emu-wrens, grasswrens and Chestnut Quail-thrush. The ranger was helpful, if not confident of our chances. We'd seen Spotted Quail-thrush in Far East Gippsland and again on Mt Buffalo, but the Chestnut variety would be a new species for us.

Typical Mallee scrub: this is the road at Hattah where we saw the Chestnut Quail-thrush.

We left the office and saw a pair of Chestnut Quail-thrush on our first attempt. It was on a sandy road, perfectly adequate for 2WD, with stunted mallee scrub all around. The Quail-thrush put on a wonderful display for us, the male uncharacteristically leaving the ground to sit in the low branch of a eucalypt, almost too close for our binoculars, allowing us to get excellent views.

Quail-thrush just might be Australian avifauna's best kept secret. There are five species of Quail-thrush in the world: four in Australia and one in New Guinea, and they are stunningly beautiful. I've heard of people bursting into tears at the beauty of a Turquoise Fairy-wren. I can't imagine what uncontrolled hysteria a Quail-thrush would induce from such souls.

I have never seen a photograph that does justice to the subtle colours of these birds. Their plumage is grey and brown and rich chestnut. The males have bold black and white facial markings. They can be elusive but when sighted they provide a fitting reward that justifies many hours of searching.

This early success filled us with misplaced confidence for our other quarry — the emu-wrens and grasswrens. Their habitat is prickly porcupine grass (*Triodia*), often incorrectly called spinifex. It was November and already very hot in the middle of the day. We had about an hour and a half of good bird watching in the morning between seven-thirty and nine, then again in the evening after six o'clock. The rest of the day was too hot and the birds were too sensible to venture out, or even call. I found nests of Rufous Whistlers and Red-capped Robins, which were pleasant distractions in the absence of emu-wrens and grass-wrens. Another diversion was the truncated call of the Crested Bellbird. It is fascinating to note how calls of one species can vary geographically. Jack Hyett, an outstanding field naturalist, taught me to refer to the very distinctive call of the Crested Bellbird as 'Dick, Dick, the devil'. At Hattah, the Crested Bellbirds have a kinder view of Dick and say instead, 'Dick, Dick, the plonk'.

Looking for emu-wrens and grasswrens was therefore a pleasant occupation, but, in the end, frustratingly unfruitful. Mallee Emu-wrens are classified as vulnerable. Their territory is small, and much of it has been destroyed by clearing. The remaining isolated populations are threatened by bushfire: with such contracted territory there is nowhere for them to escape.

There are three species of emu-wrens in Australia, so called because of their dainty filigreed tails, which look like emu feathers. We'd seen Southern Emu-wren at Gipsy Point and also at Dunkeld, but Mallee Emu-wren would be a new bird for us. They have a very small range in the Victorian Mallee. The third species, the Rufous-crowned Emu-wren is found in *Triodia* in the arid outback of Western Australia, Northern Territory and Queensland.

Grasswrens have long been sought after by Australian birdos, because they are rare and elusive. They are also very delightful. Grasswrens occur only in Australia. Taxonomists have now decided there are 10 species — until recently only eight were recognised. Grasswrens are mainly located in very remote places. They are slightly bigger than fairy-wrens, and have cocked tails and white striations. The Striated Grasswren (the only one found in Victoria) is rare in this state. It may be rare throughout its territory — there is insufficient information available to allow it to be classified.

Both emu-wrens and grasswrens have been recorded at Comet Bore in South Australia and we have gone there several times but never had much luck. Comet Bore is 40 minutes drive north of Bordertown, on the Pinaroo Road. The Bordertown-Pinaroo Road traverses very remote country — the terrain is flat, the soil is sand, all the growth is stunted. The only trees are mallees — mainly *Eucalyptus incrassata*, sometimes called Yellow Mallee, sometimes Ridge-fruited Mallee. A squeaky windmill pumps water into a small dam, the only water for miles around. It is always hot. Once a 4WD pulled in while we were there, otherwise we've always had the place to ourselves. And the kangaroos.

The sandy soil provides an ideal surface for all the little desert creatures to impress their footprints. We've seen prints from lizards and small animals I assumed to be marsupial mice (Ningaui perhaps?), as well as bronzewing and emu. If the mallees are flowering, there are lots of honeyeaters. We've seen Brown-headed, New Holland, Purple-gaped, Spiny-cheeked, Singing, White-eared, White-plumed, Yellow-tufted and Red Wattlebirds.

On one occasion a Collared Sparrowhawk was nesting in the top of a mallee, ensuring that no little birds were present. Sparrowhawks are supposed to build platform-shaped nests 10-30 metres above the ground. At Comet Bore, there are no trees 10 metres high. She'd built as high as she could, about six metres. The nest was an untidy cup shape — probably an old crow's nest.

I always find it difficult to differentiate between Brown Goshawks and Collared Sparrowhawks. There was no doubting this identification from the shape of the tail, which is unambiguous in my photo. The field guides call it a square tail, which it is in flight; at rest it is shaped more like a 'W'. Some uncooperative birds don't show you a good view of their tails. Alec Hawtin (about whom more later) taught me that Lindsay Cupper had coined the saying 'round, frown, brown', meaning if the bird has a round tail and appears to be frowning, then it is a Brown Goshawk. Alternatively, 'square, stare', means if it has a square tail and stares at you rather than frowns, it is a Collared Sparrowhawk. (Lindsay Cupper is well-known for having photographed every Australian raptor for the book he wrote with his father, *Hawks in Focus*.)

This bird must have had eggs because she was reluctant to leave the nest and when she did she skulked around nearby and was never away for

The Collared Sparrowhawk is identified by its stare.

long. She was a magnificent specimen with her glaring ('staring') yellow eyes, soft grey plumage and beautifully barred breast. She almost made up for missing out on emu-wrens and grasswrens. Almost. But not quite.

Perhaps the most sought-after bird in the mallee is Australia's rarest honeyeater, sometimes called Australia's rarest bird, the Black-eared Miner. Its status was classified as critical in 1992, meaning it had a 50 per cent probability of being extinct in five years or two generations, whichever came sooner. It is possible that it is extinct in Victoria. I was told that Black-eared Miners could be seen at Calperum Station, north of Renmark in South Australia, where most maps just show vast expanses of nothing. Calperum is part of the Bookmark Biosphere Reserve run by Environment Australia.

If you wanted to see Black-eared Miners today, you would go to Gluepot Reserve, run by Birds Australia. You can camp there and you will be directed to the nearest colony of Black-eared Miners. Gluepot adjoins Calperum Station and was in the process of being purchased at the time of our trip and was not open to the public. Nor, for that matter, was Calperum Station. I wrote seeking permission to enter the property for the purpose of bird watching. We were given a permit and told to report to the office when we arrived. We arranged to stay in Renmark.

Renmark is named after an Aboriginal word meaning red mud, which is very apt: there's lots of it. We arrived late in the afternoon, and wandered down to the caravan park to watch Purple Swamphen. Totally unafraid of us, they walked quite close plucking young reeds from the water's edge, and eating them holding them with their long toes, displaying as much dexterity as any harpist.

The Magpie-larks in Renmark had a noticeably different call from those in Melbourne. Magpie-larks are known for their antiphonal calls — one bird calls (it can be either the male or the female) and the other answers immediately, so the listener thinks it is the call of one bird. This is how pairs keep in touch with each other. In Renmark, the initiating call was quite different and varied. The response was the same as the response I am used to in Melbourne. I was sorry that I didn't have a tape recorder.

The next morning we set off early for Calperum Station. I knew we'd be better off in a 4WD, but all we had was our trusty Falcon and we were determined to give it a go. In hindsight, we should have hired a 4WD in Renmark, but it did not occur to us at the time.

It took us 50 minutes to drive north to Calperum. It should have been much quicker — on the map it looks like a distance of about 20 kilometres, but the roads are not well signposted, and we took a few wrong turns. I also suspect the map was wrong.

The land is very, very flat. The sand here is ochre-coloured rather than red. The ground looks hard and infertile. We saw lots of porcupine grass, promising lots of little birds, but we had come in search of the Black-eared Miner, and single-mindedly we pursued it.

Over recent years, ornithologists have had difficulty in deciding whether the Black-eared Miner is a race or a species. It interbreeds with Yellow-throated Miners and produces fertile hybrids. Black-eared Miners require very dense mallee. Yellow-throated Miners have more catholic tastes: they will happily inhabit woodlands, scrublands, grasslands, golf courses and gardens. By clearing the habitat, we have expanded the range of the Yellow-throated Miner. (I prefer the old-fashioned name for this bird — the White-rumped Miner, as the white rump is very noticeable in the field.) Yellow-throated Miners now occupy areas formerly the domain of the Black-eared Miner and interbreeding compounds the problem.

With so many hybrids it is virtually impossible to identify pure Black-eared Miners in the field, so don't trust any amateur who reports one! There is not one single point of identification: several points must be present together. I like to be shown such species by an expert, so there can be no doubt of the identification. We'd been told that there was a woman studying Black-eared Miners on Calperum Station and we intended throwing ourselves on her mercy. Her name was Emma.

When we arrived at Calperum, we had to wait for nine o'clock for the office to open, frustratingly wasting the best bird watching time of the day. When someone arrived, we were given maps and instructions and we set off for Oak Bore where we were told we'd be directed to Emma. We were very aware that the best hours of birding were already behind us. It was a very hot day and all the dams were dry. We really were in the outback. The tracks were not designed for 2WD Falcons, with little or no maintenance, the growth down the centre was consistently higher than our undercarriage. The soil was orange, the trees were stunted. Heat haze hovered on the horizon.

There are 10 species of mallee on Calperum. I photographed a flowering myoporum at Cliff Hut Dam. If it hadn't been flowering I might have mistaken it for a wattle because of its long narrow leaves, well adapted for outback heat.

The terrain looked the same for miles in every direction, and there were very few landmarks. Occasionally a man-made structure provided a bearing point, but it would be very easy to get lost in this country. The grids on the maps we'd been given were marked on survey pegs on the ground. It was reassuring to confirm that we really were where we thought we were. As I sat in my air conditioned car, I couldn't help thinking of Edward John Eyre traversing this country in 1839 — little wonder he failed in his attempts at exploring this hot and unfriendly land.

We arrived at Oak Bore just after noon, but there was no one there. We decided to wait. Within five minutes the maintenance man arrived. He looked at our car and said the undercarriage was too low for us to get to where the Black-eared Miners were to be found. The tracks were all overgrown and passable only by 4WD. We listened politely. We hadn't driven this far to be put off that easily.

He said that a woman studying the fauna was

The throat hackles on an Australian Raven are not always visible.

out with her team checking her traps. If we found them, they could direct us to Emma. He suggested we wait for them at Nine Mile Dam, so we set off again.

The land at Nine Mile Dam was very barren, with very few trees. We managed to find some dappled shade under a mallee and sat in wait. An Australian Raven nest was visible through our binoculars some distance away. The young in the nest called constantly the whole time we were there. It didn't do them much good — the parents evidently had to go a fair distance to find food, judging by the infrequency of their visits. Australian Raven can be identified easily if they obligingly call out. The call is reminiscent of Graham Kennedy's notorious imitation. The final syllable dies off very slowly. Once heard it is easily distinguished from all other corvid species. Otherwise they can be hard to identify. Their long throat hackles are not always visible.

Again we did not have to wait too long before a 4WD arrived, carrying the biologist, her assistant and a birdo along for the ride. We followed them as far as they went and watched them check her pits. Earlier that day they had collected

Ningaui and Dunnarts and an unidentified snake. All they collected in the dozen pits they checked in our presence were centipedes, scorpions and various lizards: gheckos, dragons and a two-legged lizard. The birdo pointed out a Malleefowl's footprint in the sand. I was pleased to see that they still survived here.

It was very hot by the time they turned back. Not a good time for birding. Emma was camped on this track a further five kilometres on, they told us. We continued on. We were managing to navigate the undergrowth without too much difficulty, so we were determined to give the Black-eared Miner every chance to show itself. We were confident that if we found Emma, she'd be able to show us this elusive bird.

We were driving along the boundary of the property, with Calperum on our right and Gluepot on our left. We drove much further than five kilometres, the track deteriorated badly. Reluctantly, we had to turn back: no Emma, no Black-eared Miners. It was quicker driving back and we managed to return without getting lost. It was a quarter to five when we arrived back at the office. We'd travelled 160 kilometres through some of the most remote country Australia has to offer. It had been an adventure but, like so many birding expeditions, ultimately unsuccessful in its main objective.

Apart from the Mallee Emu-wren and the Black-eared Miner, there is one other bird that is a 'must see' in this special mallee habitat: that is the Red-lored Whistler, classified as vulnerable, and listed as threatened, by the Victorian Government. Like many birds, this one is badly named: no one pretends it has anything red about it except its eye. The lore of a bird is the area between the eye and the bill, and the so-called Red-lored Whistler has pretty orange-coloured lores. I have a theory that many of the early ornithologists were red/green colour blind. Red seems to be the most commonly misapplied label: Red-necked Stint, Red-necked Avocet, Redthroat, Red-winged Fairy-wren, Red-backed Kingfisher, Red Goshawk, Red-capped Plover, Red-kneed Dotterel, Red Knot, Red-necked Crake, Red-backed and Red-chested Button-quail. They seem to have a ruddy fixation.

Whenever possible I seek expert help in my quest for difficult birds. Not only can this assist in a successful venture, but there can later be no doubt about the sighting. In my search for the Red-lored Whistler, I enlisted assistance from Barry McLean, president of Sunraysia Bird Observers and at that time running 4WD tours through the mallee. I was delighted when Barry brought along another well-known local birdo, Alec Hawtin. With such professional help, I thought we were assured of success.

It was sunny and quite warm the day that Barry and Alec picked us up from our motel in Mildura and took us to Murray-Sunset National Park in search of the Red-lored Whistler. We had a wonderful day. I soon lost count of the number of nests we (or, more accurately, they) found. I remember White-browed Woodswallow chicks in their nest in low branches of a gumtree and Gilbert's Whistlers' nests with eggs and with young in native cypress pines.

Alec found the nest of a Common Bronzewing. It wouldn't have taken long to make, there were so few twigs used. It was about three metres off the ground. Standing underneath, it was possible to look straight through. It contained one white egg. No doubt she would soon return to lay her requisite second egg.

Barry and Alec are not just birdos. They are great field naturalists, too. They showed us as many fascinating insects as birds. They showed us a coconut ants' nest — it looked just like a big coconut, with twigs much bigger than the ants poking out from it in all directions. However do the ants poke them in? Barry showed us the track of crack ants — a ridge in the hard dirt five centimetres wide and 10 centimetres deep. How long did it take ants to make that? Alec showed me the conical pit of an antlion, which I had seen for years in the bush without knowing what it was. It is a trap in the sand: insects fall in, the loose sand prevents escape and the antlion has its prey.

Murray Sunset National Park includes many different habitats, from the wetlands and floodplains of the River Murray to the semi-arid grasslands and heathlands. We spent the day in mallee scrubland, habitat of the Red-lored Whistler, Shy Heathwren and Southern Scrub-robin.

The Southern Scrub-robin is supposed to be shy, but I think it is actually very inquisitive. If you enter its territory it will quickly come and investigate you, then, curiosity satisfied, it will just as quickly disappear. They are ground birds and prefer to run rather than fly. Their lovely subtle warm brown colours provide perfect camouflage in the bush and the black mark through their eye gives them a plaintive look. The textbooks state that the Southern Scrub-robin lays just one egg, which is most unusual for a bushbird. I know of one nest in Inglewood in Victoria that contained two eggs. To the best of my knowledge this has not been reported before.

If the Southern Scrub-robin is inquisitive rather than shy, the Shy Heathwren truly deserves its name. They were called Shy Hylacolas for a while, so Alec named them 'Shy Hys', which is very appropriate because a good sighting is cause for a high five. No wonder this little bird shuns people — it is probably suffering from

Gilbert's Whistler (top) cannot be confused with the Red-lored Whistler (bottom), despite early ornithologists thinking they were the one species.

schizophrenia. It's had so many names it must be suffering an identity crisis. As well as the two names already mentioned, it has been called a Mallee Heathwren, a Shy Ground-wren, a Red-rumped Groundwren (more red!), a Western Groundwren, a Cautious Ground-wren and a Shy Scrub-warbler! It hops around on the ground in pairs or small groups with its tail cocked. Near Bendigo its territory overlaps with the very similar Chestnut-rumped Heathwren. If identification is in doubt, look for the white elbow patch that is worn only by Shy Hys.

We walked for miles searching for the Red-lored Whistler and saw several heathwren and scrub-robins. Thank goodness we were wearing jeans — the porcupine grass was very prickly. Alec is an eremophila enthusiast and he pointed out several different species during the day. Barry was the first person I heard call Yellow-rumped Thornbills, 'Butter Bums'. He didn't claim it was original. I've heard it many times since, attributed to many different people. It's one of those very apt nicknames — once heard, never forgotten.

It was quite late in the day, we had a good bird count and I was trying to persuade myself that I'd had a wonderful time (which was true) and that it didn't really matter that we hadn't seen a Red-lored Whistler (which emphatically wasn't!). Ken Simpson describes Red-lored Whistlers as 'notoriously difficult to see'. I can vouch that he's correct. Note that he doesn't say this about Mallee Emu-wrens or Striated Grasswrens.

Alec had a tape recording of the whistler's song, to attract the bird, and I'm pleased to say that just as were about to give up, there was an answering call to his recording. We tracked it down and had excellent views of this very special bird. I even photographed it. We were lucky: it was a male. The female has much duller colouring. The call is most unusual, with lots of breathy notes as if it has a cold and has trouble breathing.

The Red-lored Whistler is a grey bird, slightly smaller than a Blackbird, with an orange face and an orange wash on its belly. It cannot be confused with Gilbert's Whistler (which has an orange bib and grey belly) despite the fact that for many years early ornithologists believed Red-lored Whistlers to be immature specimens of Gilbert's. It seems that being colour blind was not their only failing.

Seeing this rare bird was a perfect climax to a most enjoyable day. We saw 58 species and heard six others without seeing them. (Our experts saw more, but I only recorded what I saw.) We saw some gorgeous parrots (including Blue Bonnets, Mulgas and Regents) and several honeyeaters, including of course the Mallee Honeyeater, otherwise known as the Yellow-plumed Honeyeater, very similar to our common Greenie (White-plumed Honeyeater) but with a yellow plume and a strongly striated breast. Clearly the highlight was the Red-lored Whistler — truly one of those birds I feel privileged to have seen. Thank you, Barry and Alec! Now how about a Mallee Emu-wren? Or even a Striated Grasswren?

5

Not without the Dramamine!

PELAGIC TRIPS OFF PORTLAND AND EDEN

EDEN

PORTLAND

FURNEAUX
GROUP OF
ISLANDS

POINT NEPEAN

Pelagic trips are not for the faint-hearted. Roger and I have done two such trips — one from Eden in New South Wales and one from Portland in Victoria's south-west. I am pleased to report that on neither occasion were we seasick. Unfortunately, most of the other passengers turned green. One woman on the Eden trip was so ill that she vowed she'd never step foot on a boat again. One woman on the Portland trip was too ill to formulate a vow.

The aim of a pelagic trip is to travel out to sea, preferably as far as the continental shelf, and toss berley into the water to attract seabirds. I hate to think how foul-smelling berley affects people when they're feeling queasy. It's nauseating enough at the best of times.

Like waders and terns and LBJs, seabirds can be very difficult to identify. Out at sea, there's no time to consult a field guide. It's probably far too rough anyway. Seabird enthusiasts study the bird's jizz, meaning its diagnostic demeanour, its flight, its habits, the way it carries its wings, its legs, its head.

Worldwide, there are approximately 9700 recognised bird species, of which about 300 are seabirds. Fewer than half of these can be seen in Australian waters. Seabirds are divided into four groups: Penguins (*Phenisciformes*) having 17 species of which 12 have been recorded in Australia; Tube-noses (*Procellariiformes*) which include an enormous variety of families — albatrosses, petrels, shearwaters, diving-petrels and storm-petrels, 113 species in all, 64 of which are recorded in Australia; birds with four webbed toes (*Pelecaniformes*) — pelicans, gannets, tropicbirds, cormorants and frigatebirds of which there are 50, 19 occurring in Australia; and lastly, the Gull group, comprising skuas, gulls, terns, skimmers and auks, having 107 species, of which 35 have been recorded in Australia.

Our first pelagic trip was arranged by Alan Robertson as part of our bird week at Gipsy Point Lodge. We had a very early breakfast and left in the dark to drive for an hour and a half to Eden, a NSW port on Two Fold Bay, about 50 kilometres north of the Victorian border. Alan had chartered a fishing boat and invited along some pelagic enthusiasts to make up the numbers. Altogether there were about 18 of us. No one mentioned Dramamine.

The boat had a lower and an upper deck, and an awning provided shelter. It had a toilet and a galley where we could help ourselves to tea or coffee. At the time I didn't appreciate what luxuries these were. I spent the day standing in the salt spray at the stern, not wanting to miss a thing. Naturally, by the end of the day I was covered from top to toe with sticky salt.

The weather was kind for May, but the seas were rough as soon as we ventured beyond the bay. There was occasional blue sky, but most of the day was cold, grey and windy. And choppy. Very choppy. Few people ate the seafood salad provided for lunch. Those who had not quite succumbed to the swell were forced to admit defeat at the first whiff of a plate of prawns. Roger ate his with gusto, as did the seabird specialists. I don't remember what vegetarian fare they provided for me, but I'm sure I consumed the lot.

On our first pelagic trip we saw all five Australian species of cormorant: Top left: *Little Pied (with its perpetual frown),* Top right: *Pied (with its orange face) and Black-faced (with a black face!),* Bottom left: *Little Black,* Bottom right: *Great (with its yellow face).*

We saw 17 species of birds in toto that day, including seven new lifers for me. All the experts were disappointed that there were no rare vagrants on the list. I did some twitching, and I wasn't ill, so I was quite happy.

We saw all five Australian species of Cormorant: Little Pied (with its grumpy, perpetual frown), Pied (with its orange face), Little Black (with its black face) and Great (with its yellow face), and my first sighting of the Black-faced Cormorant.

Because it lives on fish, the Black-faced Cormorant is persecuted by fishermen, which is not justified as most of the fish it consumes have no commercial value. In 1977, fishermen shot the last three breeding pairs in Tasmania. The total population of Black-faced Cormorants is estimated at tens of thousands of birds, so it is classified as common, although the Victorian breeding colonies are declining. These birds feed only once a day and its meal can equal one fifth of its body weight. Before flying out to sea, it swallows some small pebbles as ballast, to counteract its natural buoyancy in salt water. It flies with its head held low. All the other cormorants fly with their heads held high.

Australasian Gannets breed on Wedge Light in Port Phillip Bay.

As soon as we left Two Fold Bay, we saw Short-tailed Shearwaters. Muttonbirds have a wingspan of a metre, but at sea, either flying or rafting on the water, they seem much smaller than when they'd landed so awkwardly at our feet at Port Fairy.

We had spectacular sightings of Australasian Gannets diving directly into the sea from a great height. These birds fold their wings into their bodies, turning themselves into avian torpedoes, and splash straight into the middle of a shoal of fish.

Australasian Gannets occur in Australia and New Zealand. The Australian population is something less than 7000, while there are four times this number in New Zealand. There are six breeding colonies in Australia, the biggest at Lawrence Rocks, off Portland. Nearby in Portland Bay, the Australasian Gannet is making the first known attempt at establishing a breeding colony on the Australian mainland. In Port Phillip Bay, it nests on man-made structures — Wedge Light and Pope's Eye, and some birds remain at the breeding colonies all year round.

I twitched in awe when we saw a Great Skua. I could almost hear the theme music from 'Jaws'. It emanated evil. There was an unmistakable pervading feeling of menace. It was similar in size and shape to the Pacific Gull, but dark, with a wingspan of 1.5 metres, and a wicked, hooked beak. These birds are pirates, having learnt that it is easier to frighten other birds into dropping their prey than to catch their own. They also steal eggs.

A complete contrast to the threatening skua was the exquisite Fairy Prion, skimming over the water, very swift and erratic, and very close to the surface. I had always thought of seabirds as being large with ponderous wing beats and was surprised at the delicate beauty of these tiny prions, about the size of a blackbird but much sleeker, more elegant. The Fairy Prion is the smallest prion, blue with a bold black M on its wings, and a large black tip to its tail. It breeds in Australia, including Bass Strait islands, and is threatened by cats and dogs and habitat destruction by rabbits. Like many small seabirds, it feeds mainly at night. After storms, these tiny birds are often found washed up on beaches.

We'd seen Silver Gull and Crested Tern in Two Fold Bay. Later we saw Caspian Tern and when someone identified a White-fronted Tern, I twitched unashamedly. Oblivious of the unhappily green passengers around me, I concentrated on photographing this tern. It cooperated beautifully, hovering over my head for quite a few minutes showing off its lovely plumage. It was pure white, with a deeply forked tail and a fine black bill. It had a black cap with a white forehead band. This is the front of a bird — its forehead. It's called the White-fronted Tern because of an almost invisible white patch between its beak and its cap, not, as might sensibly be thought, because it has an obviously entirely white breast.

This tern is never found inland. It had been regarded as a winter migrant to Australia from New Zealand where it breeds until, in 1979, it was found breeding on the Furneaux Group in Bass Strait, together with Crested Terns. It bred on the Furneaux Group throughout the 1980s, but none were recorded in 1990-91. In 1996 there were just 45 breeding pairs. The worldwide population of White-fronted Terns is estimated at a million birds and most of these are in New Zealand. The Australian breeding population is only 90 breeding birds and is classified as vulnerable.

Albatrosses were following the boat very soon after we left port, eager to feed on the berley. Seeing these regal birds close up was for me the highlight of the trip.

There are nine albatrosses found in Australian waters, divided into three groups. These are the so-called 'great' albatrosses, the largest, with a white back; the mollymawks, not quite so large with a black back; and the sooty albatrosses, which are the smallest and entirely dark grey in colour. On our Eden trip, we saw only albatrosses belonging to the mollymawk group.

We saw many Yellow-nosed Albatrosses, the smallest of the mollymawk group, and many more Black-browed Albatross, both races — Australian (with a dark iris) and New Zealand (with a pale iris). We also saw a few Shy Albatrosses.

When resting on the sea at close quarters, the Yellow-nosed Albatross is easily identified by its black bill with a distinct yellow line along the top. It has a 2.1 metre

Australia's largest Tern, the Caspian, is easily recognised by its large red bill.

The White-fronted Tern hovered obediently above the boat.

Crested Terns are the only ones who give a photographer a fair go.

The Yellow-nosed Albatross is the smallest mollymawk, easily identified at rest.

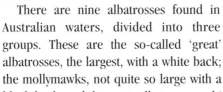

The Black-browed Albatross wears a permanent frown. The New Zealand race is identified by its pale iris.

Up to 10,000 Shy Albatross are killed each year by long line fishing.

wingspan. Being smaller and more slender, it is supposed to be easy to identify in flight, but, believe me, this is not always so.

The Yellow-nosed Albatross breeds on sub-antarctic islands and is common in southern waters from May to September. It prefers shallower waters and so inhabits inshore waters rather than the open ocean. At sea, it associates with other albatrosses. We saw Yellow-nosed and Black-browed together, all scrambling for berley. In this situation, the Yellow-nosed is less aggressive than the Black-browed.

The Black-browed Albatross quite possibly has the largest range of any albatross. It is the most common albatross in Australia, as well as in the North Atlantic. There are up to three million of these birds on the Falkland Islands alone. In southern Australian waters, it is commonly seen from May to November, but it is threatened by long line fishing. It is estimated that the Australian population will decrease by 20 per cent over the next two generations. No wonder it wears a permanent frown.

The third albatross we saw, the Shy Albatross, is the largest of the mollymawks, with a wingspan of 2.6 metres. It is an exceptionally beautiful bird, sometimes having a grey head. I had seen these birds from the shore on many occasions, soaring gracefully on the thermals, but had never imagined that I'd ever get close enough to photograph one.

The Shy Albatross has an effortless flight, more like the flight of the great albatrosses than the other mollymawks, although it flaps more frequently than the larger species and keeps fairly close to the surface of the water. Up to 10,000 birds are killed each year by long line fishing.

We saw several of these birds, but they were individuals, keeping themselves apart from the squawking, clamouring Yellow-nosed and Black-browed fighting over the berley, and made me think that, for once, the ornithologists had got it right: they are reticent and cautious and aptly named.

As we returned to the harbour, all of us exhausted, some of us single-mindedly wanting only to feel terra firma again beneath our feet, we saw two Little Penguins swimming in the water. They looked quite at home at sea, altogether a different perspective from our normal picture of awkward waddling waiters in their smart dinner jackets, hesitantly tottering up the beach.

It was a long day and most of our fellow passengers wished they'd spent it elsewhere. Some felt cheated of special sightings; some were simply suffering from being seasick. I enjoyed the trip. I thought it was worth any minor discomfort if only for the close encounters with albatrosses. I wanted to do another pelagic trip and, as we live in Melbourne, Portland was the nearest opportunity. Pelagic trips from Portland are coordinated once a month by Mike Carter. Trips are often cancelled just prior to departure because of weather conditions. I rang Mike and put our names down for the first available vacancy.

And so it was that, in February 1998, we took off for Portland and our second pelagic adventure. That Saturday was a glorious summer day, filling me with hope that the Eden experience would not be repeated. Surely in February we'd have blue skies and calm seas. But it was not to be. The day had deteriorated by the time we reached Tower Hill. Shortly thereafter we drove into an enormous flock of swifts. The light was dreadful and they were flying exceptionally fast but they were very low and we could easily identify them as White-throated Needletails. At that moment I realised that this meant goodbye to our lovely summer weather.

It is a four-hour drive from Melbourne to Portland, and we arrived late on Saturday afternoon. Before going to bed we took one Dramamine each, as Mike Carter had insisted we should, to guard against seasickness the next day. I had been reluctant to take this drug. I thought my constitution was strong enough to resist seasickness — especially after the Eden experience. But afterwards I was very pleased I had. What a dreadful waste of time and effort (to say nothing of money) to go on a pelagic trip and be so ill that there was no pleasure and, worse! no sightings.

Our alarm woke us on Sunday morning at five-fifteen. It was still quite dark, but we didn't need light to tell us that it was raining. We wondered whether our trip would be cancelled, and I wonder now whether it should have been.

We introduced ourselves to Mike, and drove to the wharf. I was shocked at the size of the boat. We had imagined that it would resemble our Eden fishing vessel, but this tiny dinky toy was less than quarter the size! I reckon it was no more than 10 metres in total from one end to the other.

On this occasion there were 12 passengers and two crew. We recognised one man as one of the pelagic enthusiasts from our Eden trip. He said yes, he remembered that trip, notable because we had not seen anything. That was not my memory. But then it had been my first pelagic trip — my first close-up view of albatrosses, and, unlike him, I was not expecting rare birds. Clearly he judged a trip a failure unless he saw a few rare vagrants.

We spent a very cold 40 minutes waiting for our captain and crew to arrive with the berley. While we waited, we discussed our wishlists. I had a long list of possibilities. As far as I was concerned, any new bird would be welcome, but I did particularly want to see jaegers. And while I knew that albatrosses were more likely in winter, I admitted also that I wanted to see a Wandering Albatross. The truth was that as we'd seen only mollymawks on our Eden trip, any great albatross would do, and a Wandering was more likely than a Royal. Sooty albatrosses are uncommon and I didn't dare hope for one of them.

I was delighted to learn that there was another woman equally keen to see a jaeger. I had feared that all our fellow passengers might all be so experienced that they'd laugh at me wanting to see something as common as a jaeger. My fears were misplaced. Nobody laughed at me. But then they didn't see my thermos.

Unlike the Eden trip, when the organisers thoughtfully provided a seafood salad lunch, on this occasion we were to take our own food and drink. I made sandwiches, but apart from that I did everything wrong. I took a fruit cake which had to be sliced. Wielding a knife on that pitching vessel would have been unwise. Healthy snack bars would have been much better. I took a large bottle of soft drink, when a couple of small bottles would have been easier to manage. And, I cringe to admit it — I didn't admit it on the day — no one on that boat apart from Roger knew that I actually took a thermos. There was absolutely no way that anyone could pour any drink on that moving boat, and attempting to pour boiling water would have been about as wise as wielding a knife. It was then that I began to appreciate the luxury of the galley on our boat from Eden.

As it was February, we had brought sunscreen, sunhats and sunglasses. We did not think of windcheaters. Although the rain had stopped, there was 8/8 cloud cover and the sea was very rough when we eventually left at a quarter to eight. I wondered why we'd dragged ourselves out of bed at five-fifteen.

It got rougher and rougher. The woman who wanted to see a jaeger was very soon lying on the deck with her head on her arms. Evidently she had not obeyed Mike's instructions to take a Dramamine the night before. She remained lying on the deck all day. People wanting to get past just stepped over her. But this did not happen often. It was not safe to move around the boat. I stood up once and immediately fell over, or, more correctly, was thrown off balance. There was nothing to hang on to except some sort of bench for cutting fish, which had a very sharp and dangerous protrusion. I sat down immediately and stayed pretty much in the same spot the whole day. Neither Roger nor I was ill. But then we had taken our Dramamine.

The official record of the trip states:

> Weather. In wake of cold front, SW wind 15 knots moderating to 5 knots by after-noon. Swell 4-5 m moderating to 1-2 m later in day. Cloudy with occasional fil-tered sunlight in middle of day. Light drizzle in harbour, but almost none once at sea. Air temp. Circa 8-15 deg. C, cold for this time of year.

A five-metre swell in such a tiny boat is an unforgettable experience.

As we left the harbour in what I called rain and our official record called light drizzle, we saw a Sacred Kingfisher, a Pacific Gull and both Pied and Sooty Oystercatchers. Good birds, but we could have seen them all from the shore, comfortably from our car.

If the weather didn't improve, the sightings did. No sooner were we out of the harbour than we started seeing Shearwaters. First we saw our old friend the Short-tailed, and then with a twitch, a Flesh-footed and, twitch again, a Hutton's. When we got a good look at the feet, which we often did as they flew very low over the boat eager to get to the berley, the Flesh-Footed were easily identified by their pink feet. This is the second known occurrence of a bird with an appro-priate name. The Hutton's were white underneath.

Most of the petrels and shearwaters were very confusing and difficult to dis-tinguish. Like terns, they have no respect for the amateur birdo. They simply won't stay still.

My field guides tell me that the Flesh-footed Shearwater is bigger than the Short-tailed, which in turn is bigger than the Hutton's. Now if they'd all line up on an identification parade that might be useful information, but while they're swooping overhead taunting you to identify them, it's all pretty academic.

Some of the seabird specialists saw Fluttering Shearwaters that day, but I could not add it to my list. It is almost identical to Hutton's, and for many years they were regarded as the same species. They are so difficult to separate in the field, that the *Atlas of Australian Birds* combines the records. To make matters harder, Hutton's have been known to mix in with flocks of Fluttering. Hutton's Shearwater has a collar, but this is not always visible in the field. Their underwing pattern varies enormously. Anyone who can see the longer more slender bill of Hutton's has superb eyesight — or a vivid imagination. Hutton's Shearwater breeds high up in the mountains of the south island of New Zealand, a fact that was only discovered in 1965. It is an uncommon bird, whereas the Fluttering Shearwater is very common, particularly in winter.

The Great-winged Petrel was on my wishlist and I twitched with gratitude when one of the experts pointed it out. I could not see its white face. It looked to me just like a Shearwater and had I not been surrounded by experts pointing out its distinguishing features, I would have called it a Shearwater and had one fewer tick on my list.

The White-chinned Petrel is bigger that the Great-winged, but this is not obvious when you're following one bird in your binoculars from a heaving boat. The white chin was not conspicuous, but I did see the pale beak. It is common far out to sea. Its black feet distinguish it from the Flesh-footed Shearwater. My field guides tell me that, in flight, the feet of the White-chinned Petrel protrude beyond the tail. I believe them. The White-chinned Petrel is a regular visitor to Australian waters in small numbers, but it is still classified as uncommon.

At about the time we saw the White-chinned Petrel, I decided that, on balance, the trip had been a good idea. We were wet through, freezing cold and unable to use our binoculars a lot of the time as both hands were employed hanging on. Nevertheless, I had four new ticks, and we probably weren't going to drown after all.

Then we saw the jaegers. Someone tried to interest the poor seasick woman lying prostrate on the deck. She did not want to know. To think that she'd gone through all that just to see a jaeger and when they were flying overhead, she was not capable of looking up. I am often amazed at what birdos put themselves through. But I did think that wretched woman was dealt an unfair hand that day. On top of it all, she had to pay for the privilege of being ill, and knowing that a jaeger flew over her head and she didn't see it.

Not just one jaeger either. We saw both the light and dark phase of the Arctic Jaeger, the Pomarine Jaeger and, with great excitement, the rare Long-tailed Jaeger. That alone would have satisfied me. It's hard to twitch when most of your concentration is required in just hanging on, but I managed somehow.

Jaegers are members of the skua family, but these three birds had none of the threat or menace we felt when we'd seen the Great Skua off Eden. The name derives from the German word for hunter. They all engage in piracy ('kleptoparasitism' the biologists call it), but also catch fish, and both the Pomarine and

Long-tailed kill lemmings. In fact the Long-tailed Jaeger doesn't breed unless there is a sufficient supply of lemmings.

Jaegers breed in the northern hemisphere during our winter. Birds we see are not normally in breeding plumage and are therefore more difficult to identify. The long tail feathers, which should be a good guide to identification, are often not present. They do not grow until the bird is three or four years old, and then they are often damaged. Without tail feathers it is difficult to tell the three jaegers apart.

Jaegers vary in size from the size of a Silver Gull to that of a Pacific Gull. Individuals can vary so much that size is not a useful tool in identification. All three jaegers are seen in summer and all three species are polymorphic (have light and dark phases).

The Arctic Jaeger is slim with agile flight and more likely to visit harbours and bays. Roger's seen them at Werribee. The Pomarine Jaeger is the largest of the three, nearly as big as the Great Skua. It is bulkier and has a more ponderous flight. We saw only the dark phase, and could not see any twisted tail feathers, which is diagnostic if present.

The Long-tailed Jaeger was a wonderful bonus, being rare and usually well offshore. It is classified as a vagrant, so we were especially pleased to record it on our list. It is the smallest and slimmest and most tern-like of the Jaegers.

Without a doubt, Roger's favourite birds on that trip were the Storm-Petrels. They flutter across the water like butterflies. They are very small, smaller even than the exquisite Fairy Prion we'd seen off Eden. They are in fact the smallest seabird.

Storm-Petrels feed on the surface of the sea and they appear to dance on the water as their long legs dangle. Even after my infatuation with Fairy Prions, I was unprepared for the beauty of these dainty little birds. I was ready for the magnificence of a great albatross, but not for these tiny fairy-like creatures out in the middle of the ocean.

We saw two sorts of Storm-Petrel: White-faced (mostly) and Wilson's (just a few). Wilson's Storm-Petrels are one of the world's most numerous sea birds, with a global population of many millions. One breeding colony alone (on the South Shetland Islands) has a million pairs. Wilson's Storm-Petrel is reminiscent of a swallow in size and flight and has a distinctive white rump.

White-faced Storm-Petrels are seen only in summer. They nest in colonies on islands in Port Phillip Bay, which they visit at night. It is the only Storm-Petrel that breeds in Australia. In the past it bred on Lord Howe Island, where it was probably exterminated by rats, which were accidentally introduced to the island in 1918.

As soon as we were out to sea, we saw albatrosses, hundreds of them: Yellow-nosed and both the local and New Zealand race of the Black-browed. There were also about a dozen Shy Albatrosses — a very beautiful bird. I had confessed that I had a Wandering Albatross on my wishlist. I hadn't admitted that I also had Royal and Buller's, just as I hadn't admitted I had a thermos in my bag.

I did not have Sooty Albatross on my list. It is so rare I had not bothered writing it down. There was great excitement on the boat when someone first saw a Sooty. Everyone was twitching, except the prostrate female on the deck. The Sooty is a most elegant Albatross, uniformly charcoal in colour with a wedge-shaped tail. Peter Slater states, 'Undoubtedly the two species of Sooty Albatross are the most graceful of all the southern ocean seabirds.' The Australian Atlas refers to rare but regular sightings. The Victorian Atlas records three sightings between 1977-81. We saw two birds on one day!

But that wasn't all. Someone identified a Buller's Albatross, which looks very like the Yellow-nosed. It is a similar size and has similar markings. My notes said 'uncommon autumn-winter'. How lucky we were to see it at all, particularly in February. It breeds in New Zealand at only four known locations. Numbers are declining and it is classified as vulnerable, long line fishing being the major concern.

We saw all these birds as the boat jolted noisily out to sea. Seals cavorted happily around us. It was cold and grey and very bumpy and we were constantly drenched with waves engulfing the entire back half of the boat. Everyone was wet except for the captain, safe in his tiny cabin. I thought we'd never get to the shelf. It was a long, cold, wet — and I have to say often frightening — trip, but in no way could it be described as boring. There was always something happening.

One agile young fellow climbed onto the roof of the cabin. I didn't know he was there until later, when it occurred to me that had he fallen off no one would have known.

When we eventually arrived at the shelf, the captain turned the engine off.

'Isn't it noisy when they turn the engine off!' Roger said.

And he was right. The squawks from the albatrosses and the shearwaters were deafening — when we could hear them. The engine was very loud and had been a constant background noise. It meant conversation was difficult and when someone saw something interesting it sometimes took minutes for word to pass throughout the group, and often whatever it was had gone by the time

The critically endangered Wandering Albatross, with a wingspan up to 3.4 metres, is the world's largest flying bird.

you turned your attention to it. If you were watching the birds at the berley, you could easily miss something flying over the horizon. The birds were like a film without the sound track — until the engine was turned off and we were all suddenly aware of their deafening din.

Almost as soon as the boat stopped, I saw my Wandering Albatross. It came in to give me a good look. I have never seen a Royal Albatross, but the word 'regal' sprang to mind when looking at the Wandering. This bird is one of the three in the group of great albatrosses. It is the largest flying bird alive, with a wingspan up to 3.4 metres. It can travel 15,000 kilometres on a single foraging trip. Fifteen thousand kilometres is roughly the equivalent distance to travelling from Sydney to Perth and back again — twice.

We saw several Wandering Albatrosses: huge white birds with a big pink bill. However, the plumage varies enormously and if you can't see the pink bill they can be difficult to identify. Globally they are classified as endangered with a total population of 55,000, declining at one per cent per annum. They are particularly vulnerable to capture during long line fishing operations, and many thousands are killed each year. The Australian breeding population, on Macquarie and Heard Islands, numbers 35 birds and is critically endangered. The breeding cycle takes 11 months, so birds breed every second year. They lay just one egg. This slow rate of reproduction puts the annual death rate caused by fishermen into perspective. It is seen more often in winter, so we were privileged to see this magnificent bird in February.

Although I hadn't put Sooty Albatross on my wishlist, my list was quite long and included several rare birds. One I had included was the Northern Giant-Petrel. I didn't expect to see it and I wasn't disappointed. We'd seen a Southern Giant-Petrel once at Point Nepean. It had been washed onto the beach during a storm and was recovering from the experience in a quiet back room of the National Parks office. Alas, no Giant-Petrels appeared on our Portland pelagic.

It took us two and a half hours to travel the 48 kilometres back to port from the continental shelf. The trip back was far more comfortable than the trip out, or perhaps it would be more accurate to say that it was less uncomfortable. Mike slept on the way back, lying down on the wet deck. I was too cold to sleep, and too excited by my 11 new ticks.

Mike Carter reported both the Sooty and the Buller's Albatross as rare sightings, as well as the Long-tailed Jaeger.

When we were nearly back into harbour, we stopped near Lawrence Rocks to look at the huge colony of Australasian Gannets. The sea was too rough for the boat to get close enough for photographs, but we did see some Little Penguins sheltering among the rocks, making our bird count for the day 25, not a colossal total, but quite satisfactory even for the enthusiasts, as it included some rarities.

We had a great day. It was cold, wet, exhausting and scary at times. As far as I was concerned it was worth all the discomfort, and good value for $65 each. I suspect that at least one other passenger did not share this view.

I would recommend a pelagic trip to anyone interested in birds. But, whatever you do, for goodness sake, don't forget the Dramamine!

6

Girt by sea

SOME ISLAND EXPERIENCES: BEDARRA,
LORD HOWE, KING, TASMANIA

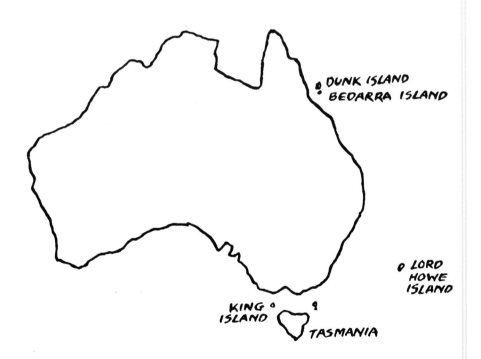

DUNK ISLAND
BEDARRA ISLAND

LORD
HOWE
ISLAND

KING
ISLAND

TASMANIA

I vividly remember scrambling over teetering rocks trying to keep up with the others and at the same time not falling over. High up on the cliffs the views were spectacular. It's a good thing I didn't own a camera in those days — there's no way I could have carried it, let alone taken time to use it. We passed a gorgeous orange orchid, but there was no time to admire it, let alone photograph it. I had to keep up.

There were about a dozen of us, of varying ages and levels of fitness. I was neither the youngest, nor the least fit. But I certainly found the going hardest. It was most disconcerting to step on a large, apparently secure boulder and have it wobble mutinously beneath my feet. And it was infuriating to watch the beautiful bare-footed deckhands (who had joined us for the excursion from a passing luxury yacht) leaping nimbly from rock to rock, joking with each other and laughing in order to show off their perfect white teeth against their flawless brown skin. I stubbed my toes numerous times and had to complete the journey sitting on my backside and sliding along the ground, while one of the young gazelles carried my binoculars for me. I felt very middle aged and overweight and wondered whether the birds were worth it.

They were.

Grey Swiftlets we called them in those days. They've since been reclassified and renamed and are now known as White-rumped Swiftlets. It was September 1983. We were holidaying on Bedarra, a small tropical island near Dunk, off the north Queensland coast. I don't remember who led the expedition or why. We were the only birdos there and the trip wasn't in our honour. A nesting colony of swiftlets was apparently considered rare enough to be of general interest and the excursion was open to everyone on the island, plus the passing yacht.

White-rumped Swiftlets nest in caves — remote ones if this one was any indication. Birds swarmed around the cave entrance like bees around a hive. The tweetering was deafening. Like bats, these swiftlets find their way in the dark using sonar. The nests were tiny, precariously stuck onto the walls of the cave with the birds' saliva and so close together that the birds in adjoining nests touched each other. It was fascinating to see. Some of the nests were empty, others contained just one tiny white egg. I counted about 30 eggs. Not surprisingly, there is a very high mortality rate.

The cave was on private land and access was by invitation only. We were fortunate to have been in the right place at the right time.

We enjoyed our holiday on Bedarra so much that we returned again the following year. We were not invited to visit the swiftlets again. I'm not sure that I would have gone a second time. Not that the arduous climb would put me off now that I know what's at the end of it. But the point is that I do know what's at the end of it. I'd had the experience and I'd hate to think of the birds being disturbed by too many visitors. It would be unforgivable if the birds abandoned the colony because too many people had gone to look at it.

Now, looking back, both our Bedarra holidays merge into one and I don't recall if the pair of Pacific Bazas landing in the palm trees above the diningroom was in 1983 or 1984. The Yellow-bellied Sunbird nesting right in front of our cabin was in 1983, as was the intrepid White-rumped Swiftlet hunt. It was in 1983 that we did a day trip to the Great Barrier Reef and saw, not only spectacular coral and colourful fish, but Black Noddies, Brown Boobies and Black-naped Terns. One lone Brahminy Kite sat in regal splendour at the end of the jetty throughout both holidays. Once it ventured onto the island, only to be relentlessly dive-bombed by White-breasted Woodswallows. Noisy Pitta ran, quite noise-lessly as I recall, under our feet during both holidays, along with equally silent Emerald Dove. A Striated Heron strutted on the sand and Pied Imperial Pigeons flew in each night to roost. Spectacled Monarchs flitted around the cabins and a Sooty Oystercatcher paraded along the beach. An Osprey nested naturally on a cliff top, without the aid of any man-made structure. Orange-footed Scrubfowl scratched the paths each morning before breakfast, and every evening, as we sipped our cocktails by the pool, a Large-tailed Nightjar sat silhouetted in a palm tree and called his monoto-nous 'chop chop chop chop chop' until we accepted it as background noise, like the sea, and no longer heard it.

On one occasion I remember someone spraying a fine mist from a hose and a pair of Yellow-bellied Sunbirds appearing from nowhere to bathe in it.

If my most vivid memory of Bedarra is visiting the White-rumped Swiftlets' cave, then the most memorable bird for me on Lord Howe Island was not the celebrat-ed Woodhen, still teetering on the edge of extinction, nor the spectacular behaviour of the Providence Petrel, wheeling high in the sky above the mountains and then crashing to earth in response to a man's call. No, my most memorable experience on Lord Howe was the unexpected beauty of the fairy-like White Terns.

Brown Boobies flew over when we visited the Great Barrier Reef.

Pied Imperial Pigeons spent the day on the mainland then returned each evening to roost on Bedarra.

These pure white birds with great big black eyes are really most endearing. None of my pre-holiday reading forewarned me of their breath-taking beauty. They are inquisitive and have a fluttering flight that makes them almost phantas-magorical. These exquisite little birds occur throughout the Pacific Ocean and also in the Atlantic and Indian Oceans. Elsewhere they are called Fairy Terns or Love Birds, both of which names are more evocative than our bland 'White Tern'.

If the mortality rate amongst White-rumped Swiftlets is high, for White Terns it must be phenomenal. White Terns build no nest at all. They lay one egg on a bare branch. From my observations, their choice of branch is not always sensi-ble. Eggs and chicks brave weather, wind and predators. The fluffy white chicks are left all alone all day when both parents go out to sea fishing. The introduced

Masked Owls hunt them by night, Pied Currawongs by day. It is a miracle that any survive at all.

Each year White Terns arrive at Lord Howe in September and leave in June. Where they go from June to September is not known. Interestingly, White Terns were not recorded on the island before 1943 and the first breeding record was in 1968.

I wanted to see them of course, they were on my wishlist, but I was not prepared for their ethereal elegance. My notes said: 'WHITE TERN: Present from September to June. Do not build a nest. Observe in spring, summer and autumn on Lagoon Road and Anderson Road on the way to Ned's Beach. Look for droppings.' Cold and scientific. No poetry at all. Just another bird on my list.

I had a list of 19 species I wanted to see on Lord Howe, of which, at the end of the holiday, I had happily ticked 16. I guess I never really had a chance of seeing White-bellied Storm-Petrels, which are usually seen far out at sea. They come to land only to breed and choose Roach Island, a tiny speck to the north of Lord Howe. Had the weather been conducive to a trip in a small boat we would have visited Roach Island, but it was not to be. A distant cyclone produced such strong winds throughout our week on Lord Howe that all scheduled boat trips were cancelled.

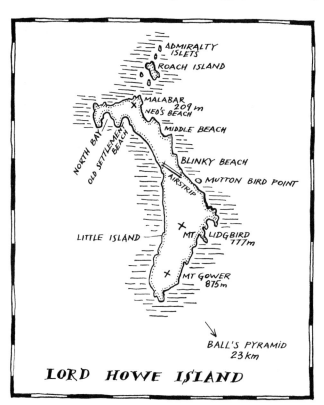

LORD HOWE ISLAND

Because it is an island with no ready means of escape, Lord Howe has suffered more than its fair share from introduced pests. Pigs, goats, cats and rats have all taken their toll on the environment. Thanks to strenuous efforts the first three have been eliminated. Rats remain a problem today. One of the more stupid attempts to control rats was the deliberate introduction of Masked Owls from Tasmania. This owl does prey on mice and rats, but also feeds on White Terns, Black-winged Petrels, Providence Petrel chicks and Woodhen.

Ten Lord Howe bird species are extinct thanks to human intervention and feral introductions. Therefore, it was not with unqualified dismay that I failed to tick Tasmanian Owls on Lord Howe. Not that we didn't try to see it. We did. On three occasions we went spotlighting, looking as instructed at the edge of the forest and on the fenceposts around the airfield. I had decided I would have to go

Lord Howe from the air, showing Mt Lidgbird and Mt Gower.

to Tasmania to pick up this species, where (according to my guide book) they are easily seen on the Freycinet Peninsula, and, better still, they are indigenous. Luckily a trip to Tasmania for this purpose proved unnecessary as, quite unexpectedly, I saw a Masked Owl one fine night on the road to Rutherglen in northern Victoria. This was particularly fortunate as Masked Owls are not common anywhere on the mainland. Indeed only 7000 of the southern race remain and it is classified as near threatened. Sadly, the Tasmanian race is now endangered, with only 1300 birds remaining — a reminder that most guide books become out of date very quickly.

The final bird on my Lord Howe list that I missed was the Kermadec Petrel. My notes read: 'KERMADEC PETREL: Ball's Pyramid, breeds from November to May. Identification difficult. Similar to Providence Petrel. White markings on upper wings. More ponderous flight.'

Ball's Pyramid is a huge rocky outcrop, about 550 metres tall, jutting out of the sea some 23 kilometres south-east of Lord Howe. As all boat trips were cancelled, we took a plane trip over the Pyramid instead. We saw plenty of petrels flying around. They were probably Kermadec Petrels, but I couldn't confirm they had white markings on their upper wings and I certainly wasn't aware that their flight was more ponderous than the flight of the Providence Petrel.

Sixteen out of 19 wasn't bad. If I were compiling my Lord Howe wishlist today it would be different. I would add Canada Goose, Paradise Shelduck, Long-tailed Cuckoo and Common Chaffinch, all vagrants from New Zealand and added to the Lord Howe birdlist since my visit. I would subtract Lord Howe White-eye, which is no longer recognised as a species, but now classified as a subspecies of the Silvereye. I would delete the Lord Howe Golden Whistler too, which is no longer recognised as an endemic subspecies.

These Golden Whistlers were the first birds we saw on the island. One female had taken a fancy to butter and learnt to help herself from the unattended tables in the diningroom of the lodge where we were staying. No one seemed to notice or care. Except me. And I did nothing to discourage her.

Lord Howe Currawongs were the second bird we saw and I regarded them as common. This is a subspecies of the mainland Pied Currawong. However, we are told that the population is small and it is only because they are so conspicuous that they seem to be abundant. They are officially considered to be endangered, as it is estimated that there are only 80 birds left. I reckon we saw all 80 of them. Several times.

The famous Lord Howe Woodhen is also listed as endangered, despite a remarkably successful captive breeding program in the 1980s. Originally, Woodhen occupied forest throughout the island. Humans then intervened with feral pigs and Masked Owls. In 1979 the birds were restricted to Mt Gower and Mt Lidgbird and the total population was estimated at 37 birds. The captive breeding program was accompanied by strenuous efforts to remove feral pests. Only then were Woodhen re-introduced to the lowlands. The population has now stabilised at 200 birds, 130 of which are mature adults. Back-up breeding is conducted at Taronga Park Zoo in Sydney. It is estimated that the island's carrying capacity is 220, although I don't know how this figure has been calculated. Adult birds bond for life and each breeding pair requires a territory of three hectares. The island is 1344 hectares.

Historic reports of huge numbers of Woodhen don't accord with a total population of 220. One zoological collector shot 80 Woodhen between 1912 and 1914. Surely the entire population was greater than 220 at that time. Has human interference with the island reduced its carrying capacity so much?

Woodhen lay four eggs and when the chicks are old enough to fend for themselves they are evicted from the parents' territory. Apparently they die if they can't find a territory of their own.

Woodhen are very curious birds and will respond to any strange noise, for example banging rocks together, shouting or singing. The only other bird I have known to respond to the human voice is the Providence Petrel that can be seen in exactly the same spot, Little Island at the base of Mt Gower. During March, Providence Petrels are seen wheeling around the summits of Mt Gower and Mt

Lidgbird. If you shout at them, they will land — most ungracefully.

Lots of birds are curious, and several respond to sudden loud noises, but Woodhen and Providence Petrel are the only two I know of which respond to the human voice. I'm not talking about mimicry, I'm talking about curiosity. Chestnut Rail are supposed to appear to investigate hand clapping (although they didn't for me) and Rufous Whistlers

White Tern chicks were being hand reared at the bike hire shop.

will call in response to any loud noise, including thunder, chopping wood and hand clapping. If (and only if) there are no Rufous Whistlers in the vicinity, Gilbert's Whistlers will respond to the same loud noises. Singing Honeyeaters reply to hand clapping, with their high pitched 'brrp brrp' call. Why? What do these birds (two rails, one seabird and three songbirds) have in common?

Lord Howe Island is 11 kilometres long and cars are discouraged. Red-tailed Tropicbirds are seen at one end and Woodhens and Providence Petrels at the other. The approved form of transport on this World Heritage island is bicycles. I would like to point out that, contrary to popular belief, It is simply not true that riding a bike is a skill once learnt, never forgotten. I, who once rode a bike to school every day, 35 years

Common Noddy on North Beach, Lord Howe Island.

later wobbled all over the place and was a danger to myself and all other road users. On our first ride, Roger saw some Woodhen which were apparently quite close to the road. I didn't see them. I was too busy hanging on to my handlebars for dear life. The cattlegrids were terrifying, the wind was overpowering and the seat was without doubt the most uncomfortable thing I have ever sat on for more than a nano second. After two days my bottom was so sore I could not sit comfortably on anything and I gave up on bikes for good. I decided if the island's free bus didn't go there, neither did I.

The only good thing about hiring bicycles on Lord Howe was that the woman running the bike hire business was hand rearing two darling fluffy White Tern chicks. If a sore bottom was the price to pay for photographing baby White Terns, I paid it gladly.

We did all the touristy things — except we did not climb Mount Gower, and we did not go snorkelling to admire the world's most southern coral reef. We visited the seabird viewing platform at Muttonbird Point where we saw Masked Boobies with young, lots of Common Noddies, some Red-tailed Tropicbirds and, much to my joy, a Sooty Tern. I had feared we might miss out on this night-feeding bird. Oddly, we did not see any Muttonbirds at Muttonbird Point. We climbed up to Malabar and had superb views of Red-tailed Tropicbirds battling the wind. We saw fluffy tropicbird chicks still

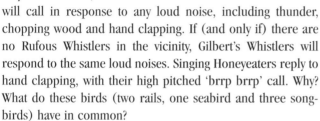

covered with down and larger chicks nearly fully fledged. We walked to Little Island to see Woodhens and Providence Petrels. One morning I got up at quarter to five in the pitch dark and very bravely, with only my torch for company, walked to Blinky Beach, hoping to see Wedge-tailed Shearwaters leaving their burrows. For my trouble I saw one small crab. Later we saw Wedge-tailed Shearwaters on Rabbit Island from Signal Point, Black-winged Petrels and Flesh-footed Shearwaters from the cliff top at Middle Beach, and Little Shearwaters on the Admiralty Islets.

Although the weather precluded boat journeys of any distance, we did two short boat trips that stayed close to shore within the island's natural shelter. This is when we saw Grey Ternlets and Black Noddies. We also saw flying garfish and a giant ray.

Sacred Kingfishers were very common on the island, as were Buff-banded Rail. Pacific Golden Plovers, proud in their gorgeous breeding plumage, strutted around the airstrip.

The first thing most people think of when Lord Howe Island is mentioned, is Kentia Palms. There are in fact five species of palm growing on the island, as well as many other interesting plants. There are Norfolk Island pines, Blackbutt, native rosemary, lignum vitae, and a banyan tree that spreads over an acre.

The things I think of in connection with Lord Howe Island are day lilies (which, although not native, had spread all over the island and were most conspicuous during our stay) and Golden Orb spiders, of which there were millions. And, of course, ethereal White Terns.

The story of our island adventures must include mention of a fleeting trip to King Island in 1990, when we saw many wallabies and several echidna and pademelons, as well as 52 species of birds. And this despite intermittent rain and storms throughout our short visit.

No doubt it was because of the storm that we saw hundreds of White-throated Needletails soaring over our heads. While we admired them through our binoculars, another pair of birdos stopped their car nearby and also enjoyed the spectacle. They identified themselves as birdos not just by their behaviour and their binoculars; the woman had an Audubon bird caller in her hand, just like mine. Feeling mischievous, I turned to face away from her so I couldn't be seen and gave my bird caller a good twiddle. That'll make her take notice, I thought. She'll think there's a rare King Island bird here. But she was three steps ahead of me. Quick as a flash, she twiddled her caller in response. Although she hadn't seen my caller, she'd identified it immediately and hadn't been fooled for an instant.

While at the time I thought 52 was an abysmal bird count and cursed the inclement weather, what I didn't appreciate then was that we had seen two sub-species endemic to King Island now classified as vulnerable (Yellow Wattlebird and Black Currawong) and another one now classified as critically endangered (Scrubtit). We also saw Wild Turkey — hardly a cause for great celebration, but at least another tick. Included in our total too, were three Tasmanian birds: Dusky Robin and Yellow-throated and Strong-billed Honeyeaters.

We did not see the King Island subspecies of Brown Thornbill, which is probably because it was already extinct at the time of our visit. It has not been reported since 1971.

All these vulnerable and endangered birds are suffering from loss of habitat from land clearance and sometimes also from competition from introduced species. Scrubtits are also suffering from tick infestations, as are White-browed Scrubwrens. And the vulnerable King Island subspecies of Green Rosella is threatened by competition from Common Starlings for nest hollows.

Large flocks of starlings are one of my most depressing memories of Tasmania. Common Starlings have the distinction of being the most widespread bird in the world. They were introduced to Melbourne in 1850 and spread quickly throughout Victoria, New South Wales and South Australia. In 1880 they were introduced to Hobart and by 1902 they had made it to Launceston and the West Tamar district. These birds harbour red mites and are a health hazard to humans, a nuisance to farmers and a threat to native species. The Western Australian Agriculture Protection Board shows good sense in patrolling the South Australian border to ensure that starlings don't cross over.

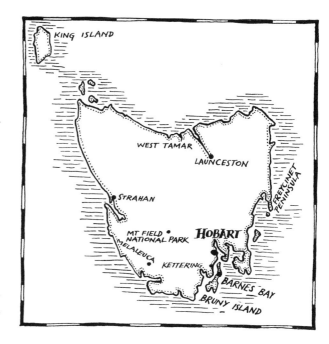

With the addition of the Tasmanian Scrubwren to the Australian birdlist (formerly thought to be a race of the White-browed Scrubwren), Tasmania now boasts 12 endemic species. There are other birds too that, while they do occur on the mainland, are most easily seen in Tasmania. These include Forest Raven, Crescent Honeyeater, Swift and Orange-bellied Parrots (which both breed in Tasmania), Beautiful Firetail (which well deserves its name), and Pink Robin (which deserves a better name).

The Kelp Gull (formerly called the Dominican or Southern Black-backed Gull) eluded me for years in my home state, but I found it was common on the north coast of Tasmania. First recorded in Australia in 1943, its numbers are steadily increasing (I've since seen it in Victoria) and there are fears it may displace our endemic Pacific Gull.

Tasmania has its own race of Grey

Tasmania's endemic Black Currawongs were very tame and very cheeky.

61

Fantail (which is common), Magpie (which is not) and Wedge-tailed Eagle (which is endangered). The Clinking Currawong (the Tasmanian race of the Grey Currawong) is so-called because some imaginative person thought its call sounded like a metallic clink. It is quite common but not in the unavoidable category of the endemic Black Currawong. These birds often sat on the bonnet of our car and fixed us with a beady stare, no doubt trying to intimidate us into providing a free feed. The Black Currawong's call, which I transcribed as 'da-da diddle-ah da', is exactly the same rhythm as the local song of the Flame Robin. Can this be a total coincidence?

We've been to Tasmania twice (or three times if you count our King Island trip). On both occasions we've easily seen eight of the 12 endemics: Tasmanian Native-hen, Green Rosella, Dusky Robin, Yellow Wattlebird, Yellow-throated, Strong-billed and Black-headed Honeyeaters and the aforementioned beady-eyed Black Currawongs. Another two, both LBJs, are not so easily identified: the Scrubtit and the Tasmanian Thornbill (which I confuse with the very similar Brown Thornbill).

We saw the Tasmanian Scrubwren easily enough at Mount Field where we were looking for Scrubtits, but at the time we called it a White-browed Scrubwren. At Mt Field we also saw the refractory Tasmanian Thornbill.

The final endemic, the Forty-spotted Pardalote, must be one of the most easily seen endangered species in the world. The instructions were clear: take the ferry from Kettering to Bruny Island, drive for seven kilometres, then turn left for Barnes Bay. After two kilometres there is a sharp bend and a wooden bridge. Stop here and look in the canopy of the Manna Gums (*Eucalyptus viminalis*). Bingo! Right on cue. These dear little birds even came down from the tree-tops and most cooperatively hopped about on a gate for us.

What a joke. The endangered Forty-spotted Pardalote was quite an exhibitionist, while the common Scrubtit and Tasmanian Thornbill were nothing short of recalcitrant. We twitched, of course, on each occasion, but somehow I didn't feel as if we really earned the pardalote's tick. It was too easy. Not like the White-rumped Swiftlets.

7

A breath of fresh Eyre

BIRDS OF EYRE PENINSULA

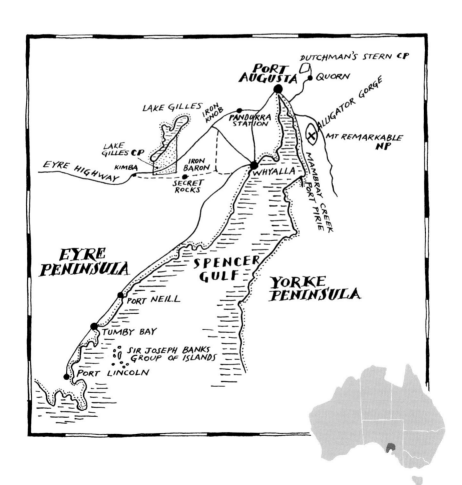

Quite unexpectedly, one evening in August, Rog came home from work and announced that he had applied for, and been granted, three weeks leave starting on his birthday, 24 October. Graciously, he said that now I could organise our holiday. We would go wherever I chose to arrange. He was quite confident that I could get time off work to suit his schedule. By the time his confidence was proved justified, I was more interested in planning the holiday than in expressing anger at his arrogance.

Therefore, instead of remarking that a little more consultation on the timing of our holiday would be appreciated, I reached for my bird list. The most glaring omissions in the passerines were the grasswrens. At that time there were eight species of grasswren recognised in Australia. Recent reclassification has increased this number to 10. We had seen only one — the Dusky Grasswren at King's Canyon. Roger had found them running over the rocks like little mice at the bottom of the canyon early in the morning. We saw them both mornings we were there, quite early, but we did not see them at dusk.

With only three weeks leave available (and our middle-aged predilection for five star hotels and inherent aversion to roughing it) I decided that we would attempt what I hoped would be three relatively easy grasswrens: the White-throated, the Striated and the Thick-billed. The first of these is used in promotional material for Kakadu, so I thought it must be reasonably easy to see it there. We'd spent a week looking unsuccessfully for Striated Grasswren at Hattah in Victoria. This time I thought we'd look in South Australia, where we could also find Thick-billed Grasswren.

I remembered an advertisement in *The Bird Observer* offering to show me Thick-billed Grasswren at Pandurra Station, near Port Augusta in South Australia. I dug it out. It said that Peter Langdon would show me some of the 140+ species recorded on Pandurra Station and specifically mentioned Thick-billed Grasswren, Ground Cuckoo-shrike, Rufous Fieldwren, Turquoise Fairy-wren and Major Mitchell's Cockatoo. I immediately telephoned to request a birdlist and to seek Peter Langdon's assurance that we would be reasonably sure of seeing Thick-billed Grasswren if we came in October. He put the chances at 95 per cent. That was good enough for me.

Our holiday was starting to take shape. We would drive to Port Augusta, then return home to Melbourne and fly to the Top End. I knew that the Top End in November would be uncomfortably sticky, but we could put up with that, for the sake of a White-throated Grasswren. Anyway, there was no option — that was when Roger was taking his holidays.

I devised the itinerary and, since both the South Australian and Northern Territory tourist bureaux in Melbourne have closed, made the bookings through a local travel agency, which, I was assured, specialised in Northern Territory holidays. I requested ground floor, non-smoking rooms. We had 10 days to do the South Australian leg, a day at home, then 11 days for the Top End, arriving home on Saturday evening and leaving all day Sunday free to prepare to return to work on Monday morning. The Northern Territory leg comprised two days travelling, five days in Darwin and four in Kakadu.

The hard work all done, I settled down with my bird books and lists to work out what new birds we could hope to see, in addition to the three grasswrens I had based the trip around.

In no time I had wishlists prepared for both legs of our holiday. There were 16 birds on the South Australian list and a frightening 84 on the Top End list. I wrote off to two birdo contacts I'd never met: one in Port Augusta and one in Darwin, seeking current local knowledge about any of the birds on my lists. Confirming my theory that birdos are the best of people, they both replied. The Port Augusta man told me that we could see the Rock Parrot between Port Neill and Tumby Bay, that the Striated Grasswren inhabited porcupine grass at Secret Rocks, and that the Blue-breasted Fairy-wren was to be found in Lake Gilles Conservation Park. The Darwin contact advised me that my list was absurdly long and that he might be able to help me if I shortened it! There was only one way I wanted to shorten that list — that is by crossing off confirmed sightings!

Rog entered into the spirit of holiday planning by getting details of the route to Secret Rocks from a croweater colleague and pulling some wonderful information on Darwin birds from the internet.

I spent every spare moment with my bird books, jotting down all I could about the habits and habitat of the birds on my wishlists. I had this task almost complete when the day of departure arrived.

Packing must be one of the most boring tasks known to humanity. I usually end up taking far too much, and then curse my stupidity when we get home and I have to unpack all the unused clothes, unread books and untouched essential items I simply couldn't go without. On this occasion, I knew it would be warm where we were going, so I saved a lot of future angst and didn't pack any winter clothes.

The first day of our holiday, 24 October, was a beautiful sunny day. Blue sky and sunshine always lift my spirits. Cholesterol is appropriately ignored on birthdays, so Rog enjoyed his bacon and tomato as he opened his small pile of cards and parcels.

We set off just after eight o'clock. Because of my desire to visit Comet Bore (a possible spot for Striated Grasswren), we were spending the first couple of nights in Bordertown, so we had a very easy drive that first day, with plenty of time for detours. That was probably why Rog suggested that we stop off at Mount Cole. We had previously seen a Powerful Owl roosting in a pine forest there, and a Square-tailed Kite nesting in the nearby forest reserve.

Rog has an excellent locational brain for returning to remote spots visited only once a long time before. Perhaps he was a pigeon in a past life. Or perhaps his geographical ability only seems excellent beside my capacity to get totally lost on routes I have travelled daily for months. In any case, he drove directly to the pine forest where I had previously photographed the Powerful Owl. I was impressed.

We walked up the hill to the owl's favourite roost, and there he was! A great big owl with a half-eaten possum in his talons. He was so large he had to be the male. His huge eyes blinked at us and it was impossible not to attribute human thoughts to that obviously intelligent bird. An excellent start to our birdlist, a truly

Roger drove directly to the pine forest where we'd seen a Powerful Owl years before.

magnificent sight. We looked for the female, but could not find her.

We drove on to the forest reserve for morning tea and to look for the Square-tailed Kite. As I sipped my coffee, I looked up and saw a raptor, right on cue. I only managed a glimpse through the tops of the gum trees, but I was convinced it must be the kite. How lucky could we be! Hastily, we downed our drinks and went in search of the kite's nest. Quite easily we found last year's nest, then, after a little more searching, we found a new, untidy nest about 30 metres high in a *Eucalyptus viminalis*, which we deduced must be this year's. I stood watching the nest while Rog walked further on, in the hope of finding the bird. The terrain was hilly, the bush quite thick, and the track very overgrown. It would have been difficult to set up the scope. I had a good look at the nest through my binoculars, and saw that it was not empty as we had first thought — the bird was sitting on it all the time, almost hidden from below. I yelled at Rog to come back and we both had good glimpses of her white head between the moving leaves.

We returned to the Western Highway, congratulating ourselves on two excellent birds to start our holiday list. Before we reached Horsham, town of my birth, we decided to detour to Murtoa in the hope of seeing Great-crested Grebe on the lake. We had seen them there nesting one year and always hoped to see them again. I have always wanted to photograph this bird — looking as it does like a whimsical joke, an error of creation. However, it has good eyesight and always sees the camera coming. It is one of the laws of nature that you can get much closer to a bird if you're not carrying a camera.

As it was Saturday, and a very pleasant Saturday at that, there was quite a crowd at Lake Murtoa. Luckily, the children were all occupied in the playground,

Musk Ducks are supposed to live on dragonflies and midges, but we saw one hunting ducklings. Musk Duck are usually seen swimming (like this female), not flying or walking. This male at Lake Wendouree in Ballarat has learnt to get out of the water to take bread from tourists.

and the adults were all busy on the tennis courts. No one was paying any attention to the lake. A quick look through our binoculars revealed no grebes of any description, so we settled down to a methodical search of the entire lake, first scanning the perimeter, then the main body of water. No grebes at all. However, we did see a Musk Duck and a Pacific Black Duck with four ducklings. I hoped that the ducklings would be clever enough to keep out of the way of the predator Musk Duck.

We had once watched a male Musk Duck hunting Pacific Black Duck ducklings on the Darling at Wentworth. One parent Black Duck was alone minding the large brood and seemed to be having difficulty protecting them all from the Musk Duck which was diving under water and surfacing amongst the ducklings. A pair of Wood Duck swam over to help guard the ducklings, and we were pleased that the Musk Duck did not kill a duckling while we were watching. I thought it could survive quite well on dragonflies and midges and didn't need to add duckling to its diet.

We left Murtoa without seeing Great-crested Grebe and drove on to Bordertown. We booked into the motel at about five o'clock, and immediately gained half an hour by turning our watches on to South Australian time. There was time to visit Comet Bore before tea.

Comet Bore is about 60 kilometres north of Bordertown, on the Pinaroo Road. We have visited it several times, but have always been disappointed. Still we persist. One day we might see something interesting. On this occasion, our friend the Collared Sparrowhawk was nesting there again, so once again we were disappointed. No chance of grasswren in her presence.

We spent the next day seeing the sights of Bordertown. Bordertown has two main claims to fame — it is the birthplace of Bob Hawke and it has albino kangaroos in its nature park. But Bordertown also has Poocher's Swamp, and swamps are usually worth a visit. We found the swamp easily but the signs were far from welcoming: 'DANGER Runaway Holes Steep Slopes and Deep Water.' Despite the signs, there was not much water in the swamp and we drove through quite safely. We saw Australasian and Hoary-headed, but no Great Crested, Grebes. There were Pacific Black Duck and Grey Teal, Australasian Shovelers and Australian Shelduck, and a flock of white cockies squawked at a Swamp Harrier. We decided it would be an interesting spot to visit in a drought.

We visited Comet Bore again. The drive is always interesting. That morning it did not let us down. After a few kilometres, Roger screeched on the brakes, yelling 'What's that?' In the paddock beside the road, three Magpies were attacking a large male Australian Bustard! It was a new bird for us and one I hadn't even dared to put on my wishlist. He was big and beautiful — I don't know what the Magpies had against him. The paddock was full of green grass, decorated with lots of bright yellow daisies. What a handsome picture that bustard made amongst the yellow flowers.

The bustard looked very stately as he tried to ignore the Magpies. I, on the other hand, did not look at all stately as I fumbled for my camera and twitched at the same time.

The Australian Bustard looked very stately, unlike me as I groped for my camera and twitched at the same time.

As expected, Comet Bore revealed nothing other than the sparrowhawk.

We stopped at Harding Springs, which is a flora reserve maintained by the local field naturalists. In 1911, so the sign informed us, the resident farmer planted two sugar gums to mark his entrance. They have grown so large that their roots soak up any water that might have been left in the spring, which is now quite dry. I suppose it would be heresy to advocate removal of the planted sugar gums, to allow the spring to return to its natural state.

This is the spot to see Buff-rumped Thornbills. That Sunday morning we saw lots of thornbills and pardalotes and sittellas. The air was full of melodious birdsong — Grey Shrike-thrushes, Rufous Whistlers, Grey Butcherbirds and Grey Fantails. We also heard parrots and lorikeets. It is a lovely spot, the only negative note was a tree hollow, which would otherwise have been available for a native creature, occupied by feral honeybees. I hoped the local field naturalists would do the right thing by the hollow-dwelling fauna of Harding Springs, and eradicate this European interloper.

Monday morning was grey. It had rained overnight, and it was too dark to photograph the Willie Wagtail we found on her nest in a red flowering callistemon. I don't like using a flash if it might disturb the bird.

We arrived at Murray Bridge at lunchtime, and it was cold. Why hadn't I packed a jumper? We ate our lunch sitting in the car watching a Magpie-lark feeding two juveniles. A small flock of Silver Gulls was loafing on the grass. Suddenly a bad-tempered swamphen appeared from nowhere, put its head down and charged the flock of seagulls, just for the fun of it. They scattered submissively, so the swamphen turned its attention to the juvenile Magpie-larks. The mother Magpie-lark was not as compliant as the seagulls and turned on the swamphen. The bully quickly gave up on the young mudlarks and returned to attacking the few remaining seagulls. They didn't fight back, but the swamphen was not content until they'd all moved away.

The next morning there was a beautiful rainbow, and occasional rain, as we drove through the Barossa, pausing only at Jim Barry's winery to buy a bottle of 'the Armagh' for Roger's cellar.

At Alligator Gorge in Mount Remarkable National Park, there is an honour system for paying the entry fee at the

At Howard Springs, feral exotic honeybees were occupying a tree hollow that would otherwise be available for a native creature.

boom gate entrance. Mount Remarkable is one of the few places where you can see Sugar Gum (*Eucalyptus cladocalyx*) growing naturally. I was hoping to see Elegant Parrots there, but the nearest we came were Crimson Rosellas. It was warming up when we had lunch at Blue Gum Flat. As he ate his sandwiches, Roger was eaten by vicious ants. Naturally they left me alone — vegetarians aren't nearly as tasty.

After lunch we walked down to the gorge, which is truly spectacular, as good as any of the well-known gorges in the MacDonnell Ranges. Or, on this occasion, better, because there were no tourists. We had the place to ourselves. And a few euros. At the bottom of the gorge, Lilac Hibiscus (*Alyogyne huegelii*) were flowering beautifully, fallen blue petals decorating the ground, and the creek was tinkling happily.

Peter Langdon estimated we had 95% chance of seeing the Thick-billed Grasswren. There was plenty of appropriate habitat.

We were quite warm now and the steep flight of steps back up to our car was daunting. We distracted ourselves by counting the steps. There are 250. A small flock of Inland Thornbills and a pair of Eastern Spinebills provided entertainment for us on the way. We used them as an excuse to stop at each landing to catch our breath, although we daren't linger too long for fear of being locked into the park overnight. We returned to the car just on five o'clock and heaved a sigh of relief when we passed through the still open boom gate.

When we booked into our motel at Port Augusta, the woman at reception was delighted to inform us that we had an excellent first floor room with a wonderful view over the golf course. I made a mental note never again to trust my bookings to a travel agency. Laboriously we carted our luggage up to the first floor, and contemplated the acclaimed view over the golf course. In fairness to the motel management, we had to admit that very few guests would have preferred the rear view over the desert.

The next day we had arranged to spend with Peter Langdon on Pandurra Station. I was looking forward to meeting him. He is a respected ornithologist, field naturalist and artist. But more important than any of this, he had told me that we had a 95 per cent chance of seeing a Thick-billed Grasswren. I had also discussed Rufous Fieldwren with him, and Turquoise and Purple-backed Fairy-wrens. I wanted to add Cinnamon Quail-thrush and Slender-billed Thornbill to this list.

Peter picked us up at our motel at seven-thirty, and without preliminaries I handed him my wishlist. He said we could cross off two straight away — there was no chance of seeing Letter-winged Kites or Scarlet-chested Parrots. The former we knew to be irruptive, following infestation of long-haired rats. The latter was on the Pandurra Station birdlist because he had seen it once, years ago.

He confirmed the advice we had been given that the Rock Parrot could be found on the coast between Port Neill and Tumby Bay and that the Blue-breasted Fairy-wren could be found at the Kimba end of Lake Gilles Conservation Park. He was confident we'd see the Elegant Parrot either at the Arid Lands Botanic Gardens or at the Mambray Creek entrance to Mt Remarkable National Park — the opposite side to where we had been the day before. He made no comment about the likelihood of Striated Grasswrens at Secret Rocks.

He also told us where to see Little Woodswallows in Dutchman's Stern and Gibberbirds east of Lyndhurst and Chestnut-breasted Whiteface on the Strzelecki Track. I made a mental note to try to find time to call in at Dutchman's Stern. Lyndhurst and the Strzelecki Track would have to wait for another occasion.

Before taking us to Pandurra Station, Peter drove us to flats just outside Port Augusta on the Whyalla road. On the way we stopped to admire a Red-backed Kingfisher sitting on a telegraph wire and most obligingly displaying its rufous rump. The flats comprised red clay covered with saltbush and other low vegetation which seemed to extend for miles. White-winged Fairy-wrens played in the scrub. The three of us walked through the saltbush, strung out in a straight line. It was easy walking. The vegetation was sparse and I was confident that any reptiles would be clearly visible at a distance. Very soon Peter's keen eye picked out a Rufous Fieldwren far away. Then another. I was disappointed. I wanted to get a good view of the bird, not a fleeting distant glimpse. We persevered and soon came across a fieldwren sitting atop a bush singing. We approached but he did not flush, just hopped about on top of the bush, clearly visible, totally absorbed in his singing. An excellent sighting of a beautiful little bird, and a great start to the day. I was elated. It wasn't yet eight o'clock. I told Peter that he had earnt his money already, even if we didn't see anything else.

Peter drove us to Pandurra Station, Rog taking the role of gate opener. Each gate has a slightly different closing mechanism, some say because of good old bushman's ingenuity, I say it's a devilish IQ test. One I don't care to take so publicly.

Peter was driving a new Toyota 4WD and I was very comfortable in the front seat. We were lucky that there were no other customers that day and we had Peter and the car to ourselves. The car had lizard-squashing tyres, Peter said, and sure enough, all day he had to take great care to avoid lizards on the track.

We stopped to admire a Black-faced Woodswallow on its nest and a Turquoise Fairy-wren appeared to contemplate us. How lucky can you be? The Turquoise Fairy-wren is a gorgeous creature. Peter told us a story about a woman who burst into tears when she saw her first Turquoise Fairy-wren because it was so beautiful. As a subspecies of the Splendid Fairy-wren, I couldn't count it as a tick, but it was well and truly worth admiring nevertheless.

When we stopped for morning tea we were distracted by a Red-capped Robin with its young. There were lots of Southern Whitefaces and Chestnut-rumped Thornbills and one gorgeous male Mistletoebird. Peter recognised the call of a Redthroat and we tracked it down. A handsome male Crested Bellbird flew past. Then we came across a bush full of Purple-backed Fairy-wrens. They hopped around us curiously, giving us excellent sightings. They are a subspecies of the Variegated Fairy-wren, although I thought they, too, deserved a tick of their own.

Throughout the day we saw many family groups of Emus — dad with the kids. 'Blackheads' Peter called them, as they had grown past being 'stripies'.

After lunch we went looking for the Thick-billed Grasswren. With Peter's earlier telephone assurances, I felt quite confident that we would find it, although it was heating up, quite the wrong time of day to look for birds.

Peter drove us to all his favourite grasswren haunts. We lined up and walked through the scrub, getting warmer all the time. Unlike Striated Grasswren, which inhabit porcupine grass, Thick-billed Grasswren prefer saltbush. After a couple of stops, and what seemed like many hot miles of walking, we detoured to a hill where Peter said we might see Cinnamon Quail-thrush. The terrain all looked the same to me, although sometimes bluebush predominated, sometimes saltbush. There were very few trees and those there were, were gnarled and stunted, and invariably contained at least one nest, old or current.

We did not see quail-thrush, but we did see Slender-billed Thornbills, my second new bird for the day. At last! I had spent many hours looking for this small inconspicuous lookalike of the Buff-rumped Thornbill and I was very pleased to have an expert point it out to me.

Peter suggested we should go to the Redbanks Lookout to look for quail-thrush.

We continued looking for grasswren without success until after six o'clock when we reluctantly persuaded Peter that we should call it a day. Had we not called a halt, I think we'd still be looking. Peter was quite tireless and absolutely determined to find us that bird that he'd said we had a 95 per cent chance of seeing. When we cried enough, as a consolation prize Peter produced a stuffed Thick-billed Grasswren. (Add taxidermy to his many talents!) This specimen had been found outside its known range and he was sending it to the CSIRO for taxonomic identification.

My pleasure at ticking two new lifers moderated my disappointment at not seeing the grasswren I had been told was 95 per cent assured. Peter told us to look at Lake Gilles and Whyalla Conservation Parks, but I knew that if we could not find a grasswren under Peter's expert tuition, we were unlikely to find it on our own. And I was right.

The next day before breakfast, we visited the Arid Lands Botanic Gardens. We arrived at the same time as the man who unlocked the gate — about twenty past seven. He told us that Elegant Parrots were there every morning feeding when he opened up. We followed him to the end of the boardwalk, but there were no parrots. In fact there was nothing much at all. Last time we had visited these gardens there had been an abundance of birds — Chirruping Wedgebills, Redthroats, White-winged Fairy-wrens, White-browed Babblers, and Tawny-crowned, White-fronted, Black and (a first for me then) Pied Honeyeaters. All we saw on this occasion were Little Crows. Disappointed, we went back to our motel for breakfast.

After breakfast, we returned to the Arid Lands Botanic Gardens and there, sitting feeding at the end of the boardwalk, as if they'd never been away, were four Elegant Parrots. The yellow on their tails was a noticeable feature, although this doesn't seem to be highlighted in any of the field guides.

Having achieved success with one parrot, we set off with confidence for Port Neill to locate another. The Rock Parrot is a common bird, so we thought this would be an easy tick. My notes told me that Rock Parrots, the least colourful Australian parrot, nest on islands in Spencer Gulf, feed on grass-seeds, fruit and succulents and can be seen in small groups along the coast, often on pigface. We hoped that we wouldn't need to go further than Port Neill as we had lots of other places to visit and the Rock Parrot was, after all, a common bird.

We drove to Port Neill. The weather was grey and very windy. The habitat was right but there was no sign of our parrots. We were determined to see this common bird, so we drove on to Tumby Bay.

At Tumby Bay we walked the Mangrove and Nature Trail. No parrots. It was still windy, not good birding conditions, and we were beginning to feel dejected. We bought a sandwich and looked for a spot out of the wind to eat our late lunch. South of Tumby Bay, right on the coast, we parked and were about to erect our folding chairs, when a pair of parrots flew over — olive with blue on their wings. Food was instantly forgotten. Where had the parrots landed? If there were two, surely there would be more: they were supposed to be in groups. Or were these parrots illiterate? Hadn't they read the field guides?

We saw two more pairs of Rock Parrots, always flying. We would have liked to get a good look at them perched, but we were confident of our identification, and at that stage we were just pleased to have seen this so-called common bird.

Self-satisfied, we had 'lunch' at four-fifteen at the Sir Joseph Banks Group of Islands Lookout. The wind had not abated and Roger's calves kept reminding him of the 250 steps at Alligator Gorge two days before, so I didn't blame him when he chose not to join me in climbing the steep ladder to the lookout. Very bravely, I ascended the shaky ladder in the gale force winds. At the top there was nothing to see that could not be seen from ground level. The podium marking distances to various points of interest was completely obliterated by bird droppings. Roger, standing safely on terra firma, seemed to think this was funny.

Having spent almost one whole day locating Rock Parrots, we realised we'd have to forego a trip to Dutchman's Stern for Little Woodswallows and concentrate our efforts on grasswren. Accordingly, the next morning we scheduled a trip to Secret Rocks. We stopped at Whyalla to buy a sandwich for lunch and visited the lookout on Hummock Hill. From here we looked down on a hovering Nankeen Kestrel — an unusual viewpoint of a beautiful bird.

Secret Rocks are located between Iron Baron and Kimba. It was very warm and we saw lots of interesting lizards, including a bright orange bearded dragon — appropriate in the red soil. I saw one snake — about a metre long, brown with a very small head it held off the ground. It could have been a Mulga Snake: I did not get a good look.

We found Secret Rocks quite easily and immediately noticed the nearby patches of porcupine grass, but it was hot and the wrong time of day for birding. I was highly conscious of the snake I had seen earlier and was reluctant to walk far off the track. Realistically we knew we had no hope of seeing Striated Grasswren and of course we were right. We hunted dutifully nevertheless.

Then we drove on to Kimba, on the Eyre Highway. Kimba comprises a store emblazoned with the slogan: 'Half Way Across Australia', and an enormous, ridiculous Galah. From Kimba we turned east along the Eyre Highway to Lake Gilles Conservation Park.

At Lake Gilles, we saw sticks flying high in the air for no apparent reason. We deduced it was a willy-willy, without sufficient vegetation to give the usual funnel effect.

Lake Gilles is a large salt lake, so hopefully but, as usual unsuccessfully, we looked for Crimson Chat. We found some shade and ate our lunch, accompanied only by a Spiny-cheeked Honeyeater. We were disappointed at the lack of grasswrens, but we knew we would have been extraordinarily lucky to see them in the heat of the day. Still, with only four days in Port Augusta, we had to try.

The following day, Saturday, was our last in Port Augusta. We decided to make an early start and give the birds every chance to cooperate. We left at seven-thirty for Gilles Conservation Park again. We arrived at eight-forty-five and at eight-forty-six we saw the Blue-breasted Fairy-wren! A pair hopped around in front of us, the proud male displaying his unmistakably deep blue breast in the morning sunshine.

We made only a token gesture looking for grasswren — we had all but given up on them — and soon set off for Whyalla Conservation Park again, looking for Quail-thrush. We had lunch at Wild Dog Hill carpark, trying not to disturb the birds nesting in the Black Oak (*Casuarina paupa*) above our heads — a Yellow-throated Miner, a Magpie and a Tawny Frogmouth. This high density living gives an indication of the scarcity of trees.

Back in Port Augusta, we visited Redbanks Lookout, hoping for Cinnamon Quail-thrush. We had great views of the Flinders Ranges, but no views of quail-thrush.

Frogmouths are masters of disguise. This one (top) realised he'd been sprung, so he grinned at the camera.

We had an uneventful trip home, arriving on Monday in time for lunch and a huge pile of washing. We'd driven 4400 kilometres (not counting what we'd done in Peter Langdon's 4WD) and we'd walked many miles for our six new birds, but they were worth it. We celebrated our success, happy to forget that the whole adventure had been planned around grasswren, which had been spectacularly absent. After all, the day after tomorrow we were off to the Top End to see White-throated Grasswren.

8

Disappointment at Doctor's Gully

BIRDS OF DARWIN AND KAKADU

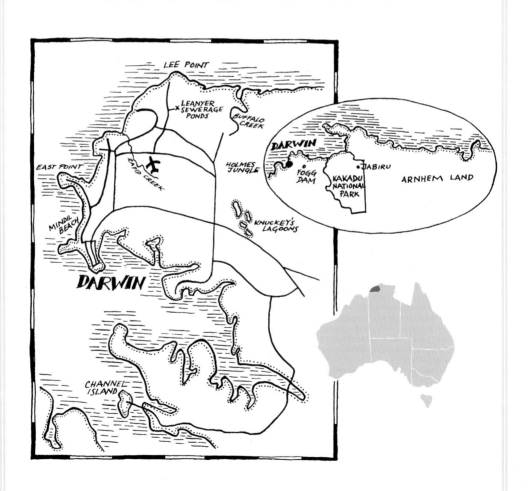

We had only five and a half days in Darwin and a list of 57 possible birds. We'd been to Darwin twice before, but only fleetingly, and there were several common birds we hadn't seen. Birds like the Common Koel, the Mangrove and Green-backed Gerygone and Northern Fantail. On this trip, we planned to rectify this situation. Needless to say any other ticks would be welcome too. We were helped by some wonderful internet notes by Niven McCrie as well as the CSIRO publication 'Finding Birds in Australia's Northern Territory'. We needed all the help we could get. It was November. It was very hot and sticky and unbelievably enervating. It also rained a lot. And I had forgotten to pack raincoats. We have some of those disposable raincoats that fold up to almost the size of a matchbox and I had intended to take them. Of course if we'd been travelling in our own car, there would have been a couple of spare umbrellas in the back. But we were flying. We had plenty of packing space because we had to take two suitcases. The one item we simply could not go without was our spotting scope, and we could not fit it and its tripod into one case. So I filled two cases, which wasn't hard at all, but I could easily have found room for an umbrella or two, as well as our tiny raincoats, if only I'd thought of it.

We left home at six, prepared for a long boring day travelling, and we were not disappointed. At the end of this tiring journey, picking up our hire car in Darwin was a dream. We told them our name, they gave us the car. Magic. The banks should take lessons in service provision from cheap hire car companies.

It rained as soon as we arrived and I immediately realised my oversight in not packing raincoats or umbrellas. I wondered how we'd survive at this time of year without them. In fact we did quite well. We would not have worn raincoats, even if I had taken them — it was far too humid. A brolly would have been useful on a few occasions, but we survived well without one. The rain didn't seem to worry the locals, unless it was torrential, in which case they took shelter and waited for it to stop; people simply ignored the rain and walked about unprotected as if it wasn't happening.

Not only was it raining as we arrived. It was humid and hot and a relief to get into our air conditioned car. Without looking at a map, Rog drove off towards the city, while I frantically searched through my papers for the address of our motel. I found the address and a map just as Rog turned into the street, having driven directly there without one false turn.

Finding the street was one thing; finding our motel was quite another. We drove up and down looking in vain for street numbers. Eventually we located it, more by deduction than good signage. The main entrance was around the corner in a side street. I refused to admit my dismay when I saw that the entire frontage was a construction site. It seemed that our motel was rebuilding its restaurant. I tried to persuade myself that it would be expecting too much of a specialist travel agent to know that one particular motel in the capital city was reconstructing its restaurant. We were to live beside a building site for five days.

The motel had 51 rooms and off-street parking for five cars, one space of which was occupied during our entire stay by a vehicle servicing the swimming pool. On-street parking was restricted to one hour during the day. This parking arrangement was inconvenient to us, but did not seem to bother most guests, who arrived by coach. Only once did we make the mistake of taking advantage of the off-street parking under the banyan tree. The next morning our windscreen was splattered with nauseating green muck! The only birds I had seen in the banyan tree were Peaceful Doves and I couldn't blame them for the mess. Figbirds, perhaps?

Our room was on the first floor, despite my request for a ground floor room. Luckily, I had by now learnt to expect no less of our specialist travel agent, so I took this in my stride. The room smelled dank, a smell which was only dispelled after three days of continuous operation of the air conditioner. The television reception was abominable. After dedicating half an hour to trying to adjust the set, we did not bother to turn it on again.

The rain had stopped by the time we finished unpacking. We hurried to escape from our hot stuffy room to our cool air conditioned car. The list of 'must dos' for Darwin was:

- Botanic Gardens for the Rufous Owl;
- East Point for mangrove birds and the Wandering Tattler; the Wharf for Great-billed Heron;
- Doctor's Gully for Beach Stone-curlew;
- Sewerage Ponds for waders and Garganey;
- Darwin rubbish tip for Barn Swallow;
- Tiger Brennan Drive for Chestnut Rail;
- Knuckey's Lagoon for Garganey, Little Ringed Plover and White-browed Crake;
- Buffalo Creek for waders and Chestnut Rail;
- Casurina Beach and Nightcliff mudflats for waders;
- Holmes Jungle for King Quail, Red-backed and Red-chested Button-quail and Zitting Cisticola; and
- Channel Island for mangrove birds.

Choosing a close, easy-to-find spot, we drove first to the Botanic Gardens to look for the Rufous Owl which, my notes told us, roosts in the big trees along the upper rainforest walk. Rog found the Botanic Gardens without any trouble and we set off to look for the rainforest walk. The signage was good, we found the walk easily; not so the owl. I had thought this would be an easy tick to get us started — a nice, cooperative bird reliably roosting in the Botanic Gardens. No such luck.

We visited the Gardens again on three further occasions, including once at dusk, when the owl should have been active. We were amused to see Magpie Geese roosting high up on branches obviously too insubstantial to take their weight, and, as if not believing they could make such a misjudgement, waiting until the very last moment to flap their wings and prevent the indignity of a fall. The Magpie Geese were amusing but we had come to see an owl. We did not. We were to leave Darwin without adding the Rufous Owl to our lifelist.

After that first unsuccessful owl hunt, hot and sweaty, we sought refuge in the cool car and drove to East Point in search of the Rainbow Pitta. We followed Niven McCrie's excellent directions to a well-used track on the right of the road, and immediately we got out of the car, we heard the pitta's unmistakable 'walk to work' call, but we could not track it down. We saw lots of lizards and plenty of agile wallabies, but very few birds.

Disappointed and uncomfortably hot, we returned to the city for tea. I wondered whether we'd see any birds at all in the rain and the heat. Perhaps it had been foolish to visit the Top End in the wet season.

After a good night's sleep, we were much more positive. At six o'clock the next morning, we left again for East Point and the spot where we had heard pittas the previous evening. An Orange-footed Scrubfowl was tending his mound single-mindedly until he saw my camera, when he instantly disappeared into the rainforest. We walked along the track so well described in our internet instructions and pittas were calling to the left of the track and ahead in the distance. Not wanting to go bush bashing in the rainforest, I chose to believe that the bird calling up ahead would be walking along the track. Rog ventured off to the left.

The track did not go far and opened onto a power line easement, inhabited only by wallabies. A big black bird flew by and I recognised the Common Koel — my first new bird for the trip. I yelled to Rog to come and see it but before he arrived the pitta called again, much closer, on the other side of the easement. I'd had a good look at the Koel, and while it was a new bird for me, it was, after all, common, so I abandoned it in favour of the pitta. I had read that many people leave Darwin without having ticked the pitta and I did not want to be one of them.

As Rog arrived I disappeared into the rainforest on the other side of the easement. There was no track. I had to clamber through creepers (mainly the treacherous wait-a-while), shrubs and branches, trying to make no noise as I stalked the pitta, and pretending that I was not concerned by the ants and spiders. Inevitably, Rog found a better route and was suddenly in front of me, between me and the bird.

'The call's coming from up a tree,' he said.

'Nonsense,' I replied. 'Pittas are ground birds.'

And I kept looking on the ground as far into the short distance as the dense rainforest allowed. The only movement was the constant drip of last night's rain falling from the leaves above. It was already about 30 degrees and the mosies and flies were up and about, joining the spiders and ants. As soon as the pitta stopped calling, I was aware of some creepy-crawly up my back. Defeated, we returned to the clearing of the easement.

The Koel was still sitting on the top of the same tree, so we both had a good look. As Roger started back towards the car, the pitta again called out. I thought it was worth one more try. This time I followed Roger's easier route through the tangle of vines and creepers. Again, Roger found a better way and was soon in front of me once more.

'There's a small black bird up the tree,' he said.

Another wretched bird that hasn't read the field guide, I thought, as I approached as noiselessly as possible. The bird hopped onto a higher branch. The light was not good, but as it hopped up we saw bright red on its undertail coverts and a splash of electric blue on its shoulders. Without a doubt, it was a Rainbow Pitta. Its cap, which is described as chestnut in the field guides, looked more orange to me and extended onto its nape. It called again as we watched. Momentarily, I forgot the spiders and the ants. But I couldn't forget the heat for long, and as soon as the bird hopped further away, we returned to the power line easement.

We felt ridiculously pleased with ourselves, having ticked a bird that we'd been told many people miss out on seeing. The Koel was quite easy (if you can call tolerating that weather for five minutes easy), but we felt that we'd earned the Rainbow Pitta.

Jubilant, we returned to the car, pausing only to admire a Rose-crowned Fruit-dove sitting high on a tree. As if to ensure that we didn't become too elated with success, it started to rain. Rog drove to a beach and parked the car. Notwithstanding the rain, I shoved my binoculars under my tee-shirt and ran to look for Beach Stone-curlews. I scanned the beach quickly: nothing there. But a small bird in the tree beside me caught my attention. It was so close I didn't need binoculars. It was a Green-backed Gerygone! Three ticks before breakfast — this was my sort of birdwatching!

Bush Stone-Curlew are very well camouflaged.

As we drove back towards the city, two Bush Stone-curlews walked proudly across the road in front of the car, demanding our admiration. We returned to the city to explore the wharf, where we were hoping to see Great-billed Heron. Instead we saw seagulls. This was the only place we saw Silver Gulls in Darwin, although we visited many beaches during our stay. We always looked carefully at the gulls to ensure that there were no vagrants in the flock. There never were. We were secretly hoping for a Black-headed Gull, but we saw nothing but seagulls, and we only saw them at the wharf. There was not one sea-gull at the Darwin tip. Why should Territory gulls be so different?

At the wharf we also saw both grey and white phases of the Eastern Reef Egret, and a beautiful Brahminy Kite. We also noted a small cluster of aberrant White-breasted Woodswallows that (my notes told me) remain at the wharf all year, instead of migrating south during the wet season with the rest of their species. Yet another bird that hasn't read the field guides.

Our internet advice was that Chestnut Rail could be seen right beside the road in Tiger Brennan Drive. However, major road works were in progress, so I doubted that any self-respecting rail would venture out of the mangroves. Nevertheless I found what I thought was a likely spot, as far away from the construction noise as possible and stood there clapping stupidly. My applause was rewarded with nothing. We had no luck with any crakes or rails in

Darwin — but nor did we spend any time exploring crocodile-infested creeks.

We drove to Nightcliff where we sat in the car in the rain and pondered what we might have seen had the conditions been more favourable. Then, on to Casuarina Beach. I wondered whether the box jellyfish discouraged the bathers at the nude beach. Or do the nudists simply sunbake during the jellyfish season? I wasn't interested enough to go and look. We concentrated on the beach nearest to the carpark — there was less distance to walk in the heat.

We watched a Rainbow Bee-eater fly into its hole. These gorgeous birds were very common around Darwin. In fact they were one of nine species that we saw every day of our stay. The others were: White Ibis; Common Sandpiper; Masked Lapwing; Peaceful Dove; Bar-shouldered Dove; Red-collared Lorikeet; Magpie-lark; and Figbird. The Pied Imperial-pigeon was also very common, as were Radjah Shelduck and both Yellow and Olive-backed Orioles. We were surprised at how few Black Kites we saw, compared with our previous trips to Darwin, when we remembered them as being the most common bird. This may be explained by the time of the year. The Feral Pigeon was the only introduced bird that we saw during our stay in Darwin.

At Casuarina Beach, the carpark was perhaps 100 metres from the beach and the tide goes a lo-o-o-ong way out. We could see several waders in the far distance, but they were too far away to identify with binoculars. So we returned to the car for the scope and erected it at the top of the beach. There was no shade at all. We identified Pacific Golden Plover, Little Curlew and Ruddy Turnstone before we became unbearably hot and had to give up on the rest. Who knows what we missed out on.

We drove back to Darwin and had lunch in an air conditioned hotel. I tried to make it last as long as possible. Then we hibernated until six o'clock, when we hoped that the atmosphere might again be tolerable. But when I poked my head outside, it didn't seem much cooler. Then, as if to mock the silly southern tourists, it suddenly poured rain.

The rain didn't last long, so we drove to Doctor's Gully, where we were hoping for a Beach Stone-curlew. This is one of the few sites where Beach Stone-curlew may be seen with any regularity, according to my notes. Instead of driving down the steep, windy road to Doctor's Gully, we parked at Bicentennial Park and walked down the steps to the beach. This is where an enterprising entrepreneur takes money daily from tourists who watch him feed the fish. Fish were constantly jumping out of the water every time we visited Doctor's Gully when the tide was in. Why would you pay to watch someone feed them?

We saw a few Peaceful Doves and nothing else. Very soon the rain convinced us we should return to our car. But the tide had come in over the walkway and we could not return by that route without wading through several inches of sea. We walked back to our car up the road we should have driven down.

We visited Doctor's Gully 13 more times during our five and a half days in Darwin, so no one can say that we didn't give the Beach Stone-curlew every chance. We saw Common Sandpiper on every occasion. Once we had great views through the scope of Pacific Golden Plovers. Not until our ninth visit did we find a Striated Heron sitting on its nest with two fluffy little chicks. The birds must have been bemused by our many visits.

At the end of our holiday, after we'd been to Kakadu, on our way to the Darwin airport to fly home we returned to give the Beach Stone-curlew one last chance and to farewell the heron and the chicks — this was our fourteenth visit to Doctor's Gully. The heron's nest was empty. Although the fledging period for Striated Heron is apparently unknown, the chicks were far too young to have left the nest naturally in that time. I was sorry that these dear little chicks hadn't made it to maturity.

We started the next day, Friday, very early at Doctor's Gully. The tide was so far in that there was no beach for a Beach Stone-curlew to frequent. Doctor's Gully has a pleasant but very compact rainforest walk inhabited by Black Flying-foxes, and according to the sign, Green Tree Frogs and Orange-footed Scrubfowl. Judging by the calls the previous evening, there were certainly plenty of frogs, although what sort we could not say. I was disappointed at not seeing a Green Tree Frog. My memory of previous visits to Darwin was that they were very common. We saw a Northern Fantail in this pocket of rainforest, with its distinctive un-fantail-like upright stance, a new bird for us, and when we returned to the beach we saw a White-browed Robin, another tick. This is one of many birds with an inappropriate name. White-winged Robin would be better, as the white on the wing is very obvious and the white brow is difficult to see. Still, what's in a name, a new bird is a new bird. Now we had a total of five new birds before breakfast on day two!

I realised that we would probably only see bush birds before nine o'clock, by which time it is so hot that any sensible creature is hidden for the day. After nine we could only hope to see waterbirds or maybe the Rufous Owl. The greatest difficulty we had with early morning birdwatching was getting our binoculars acclimatised. Every morning we'd express frustration when we raised our binoculars to see nothing but fogged up lenses, until our glasses adapted to the humidity. It was even worse if I tried to take a photograph before the camera had time to adapt. I considered leaving my camera in the boot overnight, but I knew that I would worry about its safety. This was quite irrational, as the scope was in the boot and I didn't worry about that. However, the camera is part of my anatomy, and I wasn't sure that I could survive without it.

Doing our best to ignore the heat, we drove to Holmes Jungle, where we bravely crossed the creek and set off to walk through the grassland. I put the thought of reptiles out of my head and concentrated on looking for King Quail and Red-backed and Red-chested Button-quail. We saw none of these, but we were rewarded with good views of Zitting Cisticolas (another tick). There were lots of kites, both Whistling and Black, as well as a Sea Eagle. There were Brolgas on the swamp as well as Black-necked Stork and all the expected waterbirds — Magpie Geese, Radjah Shelduck, Black-winged Stilt, Pied Heron and Great Egret. Irregular but frequent loud bangs from the adjacent rifle range didn't seem to bother the birds at all. Any farmer considering using gun shots as a bird deterrent should look at such a scene before making any investment.

At the Darwin tip we looked for Barn Swallows, but all we found were Pied Herons.

As we drove out of the carpark, we saw a Collared Kingfisher. Next to Holmes Jungle is the Darwin rubbish tip, which, we had been assured, was well worth a visit. I hoped to see Barn Swallow there. However, all we saw were lots of Pied Herons and a few Black Kites.

Another must do on our Darwin list was the Leanyer Sewerage Ponds, under the control of the Power and Water Authority, affectionately known as PAWA. I had written to them weeks before, seeking access to the ponds and they had sent me a two-page response, setting out the conditions under which they would permit me to enter. First, I had to telephone to arrange to pick up the key, for which I must pay $50 (refundable) deposit. I had to notify the caretaker when I was going to visit, as well as the supervisor. Then access would be granted, subject to my agreement and signature to the other requirements, viz: I must drive only on the sealed causeway; not obstruct the passage of other vehicles; agree to leave if asked to do so by PAWA staff; report any accident on the premises and leave the gate locked at all times. I thought this was all so obvious that it was not worth saying, but I suppose all this bureaucracy keeps someone employed.

We should have known that such instructions are to be obeyed to the letter. But we were in holiday mood and all we remembered was that we must pay $50 to pick up the key, so without telephoning first, we drove to the PAWA head-quarters in Sturt Park. Rog parked and I went in the door marked 'All Enquiries'. It was beautifully cool inside. I explained what I wanted and was told that I must go to 'Accounts Payable', back outside and around the corner. I did so and entered the same building at the rear, looking at the same girl from the other side of the same counter. Another woman took my money, laboriously wrote out a receipt in duplicate, stamped both the receipt and the duplicate, then told me to go to another building to pick up the key. By then, it was five to twelve. In a rush of courtesy, she offered to ring to ensure that the person I was to see was there. Of course, at five to twelve, she had gone to lunch. No, no one else could hand me the key. I must return after one. We drove back to town and had lunch. After one we obediently returned to PAWA, and Rog cautioned me to adopt the appropriate supplicant attitude. In fact this was not necessary, as the woman who gave me the key was very helpful (she'd probably had a good lunch too). She undertook on our behalf to advise the supervisor of the sewerage ponds of our visit. So we had only to ring the caretaker. We did this as soon as we returned to the motel, leaving a message on his answering machine that we would be visiting over the weekend.

Satisfied that we could visit Leanyer the next day, we drove again to East Point, this time to do the mangrove boardwalk, which is well worthwhile, although we couldn't get to the end because the tide was coming in and part of the boardwalk was under water. We visited this boardwalk several times, braving the kamikaze Masked Lapwing who had me in their sights. We had good sightings there, although it was always better in the morning than in the afternoon. This could be partly explained by the fact that the gate is locked at six o'clock and I suspect that there is better birding later than that. We hoped for a Mangrove Robin, a Mangrove Golden Whistler and a Mangrove Grey Fantail. We did not see these. However, we did find a Lemon-bellied Flycatcher sitting on top of her ridiculously tiny nest containing two chicks, extraordinarily well camouflaged, and frustratingly unapproachable in a mangrove in the water 10 metres from the boardwalk. We also had good sightings of the Broad-billed Flycatcher (tick), White-breasted Whistler, Red-headed Honeyeater, Northern Fantail and Yellow White-eye. We had fleeting glimpses of Eastern Curlews and Kingfishers, which might have been either Forest or Collared, we could not tell.

There is a pathway around East Point and I was very impressed with the number of joggers and power walkers using it both morning and night. The humidity forced me to put all thoughts of exercise out of my mind.

It was late afternoon when Rog parked at the end of this pathway near a pleasant secluded beach. When we walked onto the beach, we saw that we were not the first there. A man and a woman sat comfortably on their folding chairs, looking out to sea and sipping champagne, while their teenage son buried himself in the sand up to his neck at the water's edge and waited for the tide to come in.

That evening we dined outside at a beachfront restaurant, with magnificent views over Darwin Harbour. The food was good. But the views were unsurpassable. We watched sunset over the water as the king tide came in, and a lone bat flew in to roost in the palm tree in front of us. We were treated to a spectacular electric storm, with fork lightning inside the pink and white clouds, then sheet lightning as well for good measure. It was a very special experience.

The next morning (after our requisite visits to Doctor's Gully and East Point) we drove to the sewerage farm at Leanyer, a distance of about 10 kilometres. Unlocking the gate was easy, but locking it again was another matter! Rog sat quite patiently in the air conditioned car watching the birds, while I laboured in the heat below, struggling to lock the padlock. When I eventually succeeded, I joined Rog and was rewarded with the spectacle of thousands of Plumed Whistling Ducks. There were also hundreds of Grey Teal, Pacific Black Duck and Pied Heron, dozens of Little Tern and a few Pelican. Unfortunately, over our three

visits to the sewage ponds, the only wader we saw was a
Common Sandpiper. We scanned the enormous flocks of
ducks with our binoculars and were persuaded we had
identified them all. We did not put the scope up, which
we were to learn later was a big mistake. Apparently there
was a Garganey hidden in the flock of whistling ducks.
After going to so much trouble to get into the sewerage
ponds, we missed out on a tick by not troubling to erect
the scope. It served us right really — we should have
known better.

After visiting the sewerage ponds we drove to Buffalo
Creek. Being Saturday, there were too many people for
our liking. Despite the signs warning of crocodiles, this is
a popular fishing spot. No chance of Chestnut Rail today!
I was amazed that people would leave their air conditioned homes to sit in deck chairs in the shade in 35
degree heat at Buffalo Creek for Saturday morning entertainment.

Ignoring the creek entrance, we visited the beach on
the left of the carpark as we drove in. The tide was a long
way out and we were tantalised by many waders too far
away to identify. So, despite the heat, it was out with the
scope. I had read that we could see Beach Stone-curlew
at Buffalo Creek, or even a Great-billed Heron. I wandered about in the shade complaining about the temperature while Rog focused the scope on the waders. After a
very short while, he beckoned me to confirm what he had
found. It was an Asian Dowitcher! Every new lifer deserves
a big tick, but I thought an Asian Dowitcher warranted an
extra large tick. A tick with a capital 'T'. This was a bird I
had never expected to see. For fully five minutes we were
unaware of the temperature.

*Both Plumed (top) and Wandering
Whistling (below) Ducks were common.*

Monday was our last day in Darwin and we still had to visit two spots on our
'must do' list, so we set off early for Channel Island, about 40 kilometres from
Darwin's central city. Our book told us we might see Chestnut Rail, Beach Stone-
curlew, Mangrove Robin, Mangrove Golden Whistler and Mangrove Grey Fantail.
On the way we saw Northern Rosellas — our ninth new bird for the trip.

Darwin's power station is located at Channel Island. The spot we were interested in was a boardwalk, the track to which was located just before the entrance
to the power station. Our book advised us to collect a key from the power
station if the gate were locked. Locked indeed it was, but the man on duty at the
entrance to the power station said we didn't need a key, we should just walk
around the gate — there was no fence!

It took us about 20 sticky minutes to reach the boardwalk. On the way we
heard lots of birdcalls but had few sightings. We did see Mangrove Gerygone

(tick), Spangled Drongo and Helmeted Friarbird. We got lost only once. It was, as promised, extensive and I wondered who would go to the trouble and expense of building a boardwalk through the mangroves, then protecting it with a locked gate (but no fence) and giving it no signage and no publicity in any of the tourist literature. The birdcalls stopped as soon as we reached the boardwalk, and for its entire length we neither heard nor saw any life at all.

When we returned from the walk we looked (at least Roger did, so I suppose I did too) as if we'd just had a shower fully clothed. Our clothes and hair were stuck to our bodies and the effect was not altogether flattering. We had to wonder whether it had been worth it. The only new bird we saw, we had seen along the track before we reached the boardwalk. Although it was very promising terrain, we saw absolutely nothing at all from the boardwalk.

This is a male Black-necked Stork. The female has a yellow iris.

Knuckey's Lagoon was the last remaining spot on our 'must do' list. We knew we were visiting at the wrong time of day for our comfort, but we figured that if there was a Garganey there, we'd see it, whatever time of day it was. We erected the scope and carefully identified every individual bird on the swamp. We saw Green Pygmy-Geese, Glossy Ibis, Black-necked Storks and the inevitable hoards of Wandering Whistling Duck. But there was nothing new. If only we'd been that careful at the sewerage ponds!

On the way back to the motel, Rog turned into a tempting unmade road, not on my map, but heading basically in the right direction. I was very pleased that he did when we saw Little Woodswallows clustering on the telegraph wires. Our eleventh tick for Darwin.

That afternoon we went to the pictures simply for somewhere cool to spend the middle of the day. After we returned the key to the sewerage ponds to the PAWA headquarters, Rog took me back to the motel so I could start thinking about packing while he drove off to buy some beer. He returned shortly afterwards, very excited. He had called in at Doctor's Gully (his twelfth visit) and had seen the Beach Stone-curlew. We hurried back but the bird was nowhere to be seen. I tried hard to be pleased for my spouse that he had seen this extraordinary bird.

That afternoon it rained as if it meant it. A proper tropical torrential downpour, sufficient for the Darwin police to issue a road weather alert over the radio. The radio also informed us that there had been an earthquake at sea and a tsunami was predicted for Darwin! All the emergency services were alerted. Shortly afterwards, this prediction was proved faulty. Someone had miscalculated — a very welcome anticlimax.

On Tuesday morning at seven-forty-five we left Darwin, telling ourselves that we had no right to be disappointed in having achieved 11 new birds (or 12 in Roger's case), especially as one was the Asian Dowitcher and another was the

Rainbow Pitta. But I had expected to see the Rufous Owl, and hoped to see the Great-billed Heron, Chestnut Rail and Mangrove Golden Whistler. I kept thinking of all the birds we might have seen. It's probably just as well we didn't learn about the Garganey at Leanyer Sewerage Ponds until we returned to Melbourne.

So we set off for Kakadu, determined to do better there. White-throated Grasswren, here we come!

First stop, Fogg Dam. We were there in less than an hour, having been stopped once by the fruit fly inspectors. We noticed some improvements since our last visit 16 years previously: boardwalks, lookouts and some wonderfully innovative pillars, providing bird calls at the press of a button. We thought these pillars were a great idea, because the forest was alive with bird calls, and most of the birds were high in the canopy where they were very difficult to identify. A shame they didn't work. No doubt the rangers are more diligent about such things in peak tourist season.

We did the Woodland to Waterlilies walk, a short easy walk through monsoon forest, then along boardwalks beside gorgeous pink waterlillies, with Comb-crested Jacana walking on the lily-pads. We saw a Grey Whistler, Azure and Forest Kingfishers and a Pheasant Coucal, but we heard many more birds than we saw. Golden-headed Cisticola played in the reeds. We saw all the expected waterbirds at Fogg Dam, although the numbers were not as great as we'd seen on our previous visit, or indeed, as we'd seen in Darwin, at the Sewerage Ponds or at Knuckey's Lagoon. We did not see any Garganey or any crakes, but there was some compensation in the excellent views of Crimson Finches and Varied Trillers. I could have spent a lot longer at Fogg Dam. Any birdo visiting Darwin should allow an extra day to devote to exploring this wonderful place.

Rog dragged me away from Fogg Dam and we set off for Kakadu. However, a short time later, when we saw the big new Wetland Visitor Centre, 'Windows on the Wetlands', we had to call in. It is constructed on the top of a hill providing it with panoramic views of the surrounding wetlands — and a hot shadeless uphill walk from the carpark. We decided this centre was built with children in mind. There were several very boring, interactive displays, no doubt designed to be educational rather than entertaining. Why displays can't be both educational and entertaining I do not understand. We enjoyed a cold drink from the iced water fountain, and were surprised that they did not sell any refreshments. My time would have been better spent at Fogg Dam than at the Wetland Visitor Centre.

We entered Kakadu National Park at noon, paying $15 each entry fee. For this we received a very useful visitor guide, which would have been even more useful had it been provided by the Northern Territory Holiday Centre when we were planning the trip. The only fault we found with this guide was the amount of time it recommended should be spent at each attraction, which, in our view, was significantly exaggerated in every case but one. We had three full days in Kakadu, and in the wet season, without a 4WD vehicle, this was quite enough.

At the South Alligator River boat ramp, we looked unsuccessfully for Yellow Chats, then drove on to Mamukala. It was so hot that I left the camera in the car and walked quickly to the bird hide. Long-tailed Finches hopped about Roger's

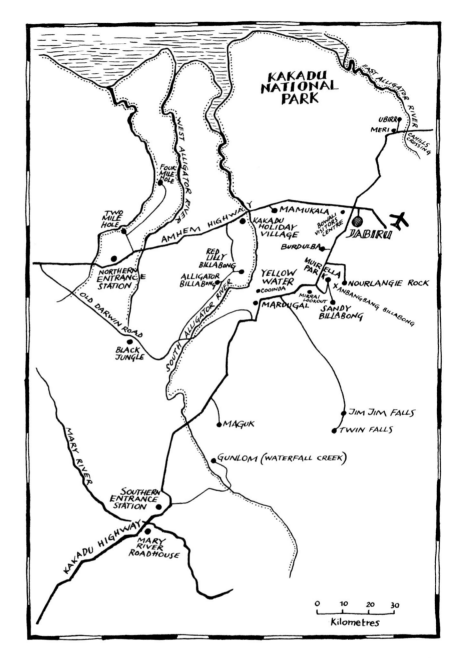

feet in a very friendly fashion, so I returned to get the camera. Predictably, the track was quite finch-less as I walked back to the hide with my camera. A Great Egret posed for me obligingly, so I took its photo and finished the film. So I returned to the car for a new film, taunted all the way by a pair of finches. With a new film loaded, I walked to the hide for the third hot time. Not a finch in sight.

We stayed at the Gagudju Crocodile Hotel at Jabiru. This award-winning hotel is built in the shape of a crocodile. Our room was on the first floor, near the crocodile's back right foot. Blue-faced Honeyeaters hopped around in the

Swamp bloodwood (*Eucalyptus ptychocarpa*) outside our window. This tree had large nuts and the biggest leaves I've ever seen on a gum tree. Our room had everything you would expect in a three and a half star hotel, including excellent television reception, and most important, effective air conditioning, and — what luxury! — a bath.

We had an early meal in the Escarpment Restaurant, which is used as a through route from the pool in the centre of the hotel, to reception in the crocodile's head. Tourists wandered through the diningroom in attire that didn't meet dress standards (clearly spelt out on the Croc-tail Bar by the entrance to the restaurant) on their way to or from reception.

The next morning we had a wake-up call at five-thirty, to be at Cooinda at a quarter to seven for the Yellow Water river cruise we had booked. Cooinda is 40 minutes drive from the hotel. We made it in perfect time and Rog dropped me off at the boat while he parked the car. The boat was smoke-free and one woman was enjoying one last cigarette on the jetty before we left. The boat was chocka — there must have been a hundred people on it — I couldn't see where we'd fit. It was raining a fine misty rain that we could walk around in without getting wet. The smoker confided in me that she hated tour groups. I agreed with her. She said there were two busloads on the boat. Her group had been camping and she wasn't enjoying it. The bus had delivered them to the boat very early and I gathered they had been waiting for us for some time. We were not late, but we were made to feel that we should have been early, as a hundred pairs of eyes accused us of keeping them waiting in the heat.

We had no choice of where to sit. There were only two vacant seats after my smoking friend sat down. They were on each side of the aisle in the second row. The seats were too small. Or was it just that the passengers sitting on both sides of us were too big? Anyway, we were squashed against hot foreign bodies who had been rushed off early before they'd had time for their morning shower. Iced water was provided in the front of the boat (why not the back?) and passengers were continually pushing past us to help themselves — and block our views.

One German woman dressed in blue, with a video camera, took up a position standing in the front of the boat, thus ensuring that she spoilt everyone's view. She moved freely around to guarantee that no one could be sure of a photograph without her in it.

One hundred foreigners became absurdly excited when the first crocodile was sighted. The boat stopped for the woman in blue to film the beast and for everyone else in the boat to attempt to photograph it — only to find out when the film was developed that they had a lovely shot of the woman in blue filming the crocodile. Whenever a crocodile was sighted, everyone rushed to one side of the boat. Rog joked that the boat would capsize. This wasn't so funny when, the week after we returned home, exactly that occurred to a boat full of tourists in Geikie Gorge!

When I thought I saw a Great-billed Heron fly over, the woman in blue was videoing her fourth crocodile and interposed herself between me and my probable new tick.

As well as crocodiles, the pink and blue water lillies were also popular with the crowd, as were Azure Kingfishers. We saw White-breasted Sea-Eagles, Glossy Ibis, Royal Spoonbill, all the usual waterfowl you expect at the Top End as well as Willie Wagtails, Restless and Shining Flycatchers, Bar-breasted Honeyeaters and Red-winged Parrots. The tour guide did not approve of the tourists' admiration for two cute little black piglets with their mother, and explained the damage done by wild boars. He had no objection to the interest in wild brumbies, which he evidently perceived as relatively harmless.

The cruise took precisely an hour and a half, which was about 85 minutes too long for me. Then we had breakfast at Cooinda Lodge, just five minutes drive up the road from the jetty. After breakfast, we drove to Mardugal and walked to the billabong. All we saw were White-throated Honeyeaters, which are pretty little birds, but not worth the hot walk!

We drove back to Yellow Water, hoping to catch another glimpse of the Great-billed Heron. Sadly, we did not, so this magnificent bird did not make it onto our list on this occasion.

We enjoyed our air conditioned car and stopped at every attraction along the road back to Jabiru. We noted the difficult walk to Mirrai Lookout and did not for an instant contemplate doing it. At Muirella Park we saw the 4WD track to Sandy Billabong and were content to stay in our vehicle.

From Muriella Park, we turned back onto the main road and a couple of Partridge Pigeon walked across in front of the car. Twitching, I reached for my camera. They were most obliging and we had a good look at their red faces. Our first new bird in Kakadu was most cooperative. This augured well.

The next stop was Nourlangie Rock, a very pretty spot. The major tourist attraction is the Aboriginal art, which is very well sign-posted and explained. The rock itself is huge — rugged and photogenic. In front of it lies the picturesque Anbangbang Billabong, surrounded by many pleasant picnic spots, which were teeming with bush birds. We walked 250 metres through an area which had been recently burnt and saw several large lizards disappearing into holes high up in the trees. Even such a short walk as this was too much in the heat.

Back at the hotel, we checked the road conditions. The road to Jim Jim falls was closed, which was of no concern to us, as it was designated as 4WD only on our map and we had not included it on our proposed itinerary. However, we were very disappointed to learn that the road to Gunlom (Waterfall Creek) had been declared accessible only by 4WD. This is the only spot where White-throated Grasswren can be seen. We were thwarted in our quest for grasswren before we even began to look. The grasswren live on the escarpment, running between the spinifex with head and tail lowered. Frustratingly, its status is described as locally common.

By way of consolation we booked ourselves on a helicopter tour the next day, first making sure that we would be the only passengers!

On Thursday morning, we returned to Nourlangie Rock and were rewarded with a Black-tailed Treecreeper (tick). This was cause for special celebration as we now had a full hand of treecreepers. A busload of tourists admired the rock art; we admired the Black-tailed Treecreeper.

By nine-fifteen the birds were silenced for the day, and they didn't seem to have an evensong. This gave a very small window of opportunity to see anything at all, let alone anything new.

We dutifully inspected the Bowali Visitor Centre. The guide book instructed us to 'allow a few hours' for this. We found that a few minutes sufficed.

The helicopter flight was the experience of a lifetime. We were shocked to see that the aircraft had no doors! The pilot had a secure looking harness to strap himself into; we were held in by insubstantial lap seat belts. When Roger moved, the whole seat moved, which was quite alarming. The motor was very loud and the machine took a long time to warm up and cool down. We each wore head phones, and had to press a switch to communicate with each other. There was a constant background of very loud static in the head phones, making conversation quite impossible. The tour took an hour and a half to fly to Jim Jim and Twin Falls and back. After about an hour, Rog overcame his terror and began to enjoy it, too. We had spectacular views of the escarpment and the waterfalls, and all the surrounding terrain. This really must be the best way to see Kakadu.

The Ranger Uranium mine seems quite discreet and contained from the air, although the very notion of any sort of mine within a national park is, to say the least, a little odd — let alone the notion of mining in a world heritage area.

No sooner had we taken off than I saw what had to be a Red Goshawk. I looked at Roger hanging on for dear life and decided that there was no point in trying to communicate with him. Nor could I inform the pilot that I wanted a better look at that big red bird. So yet another bird eluded my tick.

The next morning we set off north to Ubirr, which is located on the boundary between the national park and Arnhem Land. This is a popular spot to visit at sunset. We went early in the morning.

We stopped at East Alligator River and walked to Cahills Crossing, where there are some graphic pictures showing when it is, and is not, safe to ford the river in a 4WD. Then we did the Manngarre walk. The thousands of bats don't seem to be mentioned in the brochures. They are very cute with their pretty fox-like faces, and I would far rather look at them than at a crocodile. In this I must be alone. Rog found a Pacific Baza on its nest. The guide book said that this walk took an hour. We hurried and it took 50 minutes. This is the only time I thought the brochure underestimated the time for an attraction. Had the weather been bearable we would have stopped to admire the river and the views and the birdlife and the bats and it would have taken significantly longer than an hour.

We left Kakadu having gained only two new ticks. Most disappointing. I suspect we'd have seen more if we'd stayed in Darwin. I'd hate to calculate what it cost to tick those two Kakadu birds. Worse, we hadn't even been able to start looking for our grasswren. Am I always to be thwarted in my quest for grasswren? Or will it be easier in future, now that there are 10 species to look for, not eight?

9

Only raptors like bushfires

BIRDS OF BROOME

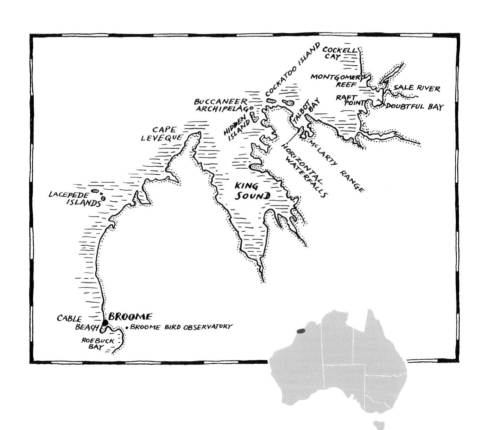

Roger saw the ad. A boat cruise in the Kimberleys catering for bird lovers. Ten days sailing around some of Australia's most remote coastline. A total of eight passengers. 'Good food and wine supplied.'

Tempting, hey? We could escape Melbourne's winter and spend 10 days cruising off the Kimberley coast. It sounded wonderful. It was expensive, but what the hell? We'd see Chestnut Rail and Black Grasswren for sure. And Flock Bronzewing. And, probably, the yellow-faced form of the Partridge Pigeon. We'd seen the red-faced form at Kakadu, and even though it wouldn't constitute a proper tick, I wanted to add the yellow-faced form to my repertoire.

We contacted the tour leader who didn't have a detailed itinerary prepared yet. He said it was important to work around the tides. That part of the Australian coast has some of the largest tides in the world, and of course we wanted to explore the mangroves at low tide in order to see as many as possible of the special local birds.

I had a couple of lengthy phone calls with the tour guide. We joked, I remember, about the remote possibility of seeing a Red Goshawk, we discussed my vegetarian diet and we talked about Aboriginal rock art. Yes, he assured me, the boat was air conditioned. As soon as I started to compile my wishlist, we were hooked: we were definitely going.

We'd been to Broome twice before — we fell in love with the place during our 1982 Perth-Darwin epic and visited again a decade later, in February 1992, when we spent a week at Lord McAlpine's folly at Cable Beach. In fact the folly was ours for visiting Broome in February — a daft decision. Weather is lovely in Broome from April to December. January to March is suitable only for mad dogs and Englishmen.

Broome is one of Australia's most romantic towns: a tropical paradise with a colourful history; the apparently harmonious mingling of many cultures, and, some of Australia's most spectacular scenery, rugged red and white cliffs with freshwater creeks tinkling down into the turquoise sea below. And Cable Beach. Before the tourists found it (and found it they have!) I classed Cable Beach as Australia's most beautiful. When I first discovered it in 1982, it was better than Tidal River at Wilson's Promontory, because there were no people there. Over 20 kilometres of wide white sand, turquoise water, ineluctable picturesque palmtrees, a gentle sea breeze and No People. You'd be lucky to have Tidal River to yourself mid-week in winter during a hurricane. And I fear the same is now true of Cable Beach.

Now it is as commercial as the Gold Coast. Cars drive onto the beach. You can buy every sort of takeaway food known to man or woman, and you can hire anything from beach umbrellas to lockers, from surfboards to jet skis. The last time we were there (and it probably will be the last time) a large-screen television set was propped up on the grassed area near the kiosk broadcasting the WA parachuting championships. Very loudly.

Cable Beach is supposed to be a safe swimming beach, but with the possibility of box jellyfish from November-April and the availability of jet skis for the rest of the year, it doesn't conform to my concept of safe swimming.

I can't see the attraction of riding a camel along the beach at sunset, but luckily for the tour operators I seem to be in the minority. Camels are ugly, smelly, wilful beasts that do not belong in Australia. Where is the attraction in riding one? Cable Beach at sunset is sufficient pleasure in itself. Or it used to be.

Because we'd been to Broome twice before, we'd seen the easy birds and done the touristy things. We'd visited Gantheaume Point, seen Anastasia's Pool, seen the dinosaur's footprints (before they were stolen), seen Chinatown and the Japanese cemetery, learnt all we ever wanted to know about the pearling industry and inspected the world's oldest open air picture theatre. More importantly, we had visited the bird observatory, been gob-smacked by the waders, and sunk in mangrove mud up to our thighs in Little Crab Creek while looking (unsuccessfully) for the elusive Mangrove Golden Whistler.

As I say, we'd seen the easy birds. I didn't mind seeing them again, especially the Lesser Frigatebirds, Oriental Pratincoles and the eye-catching White-breasted Whistlers, but I particularly wanted to tick new ones. My list of expected ticks was quite short; my list of possibles (improbables) was a lot longer.

I thought a Chestnut Rail would be easy, after all they are the size of a chook. They're found in the mangroves at low tide, and while they are classified as rare and are often described as shy, I had high expectations. Chestnut Rails, so we are told, respond to hand clapping. This makes me think that 'inquisitive' might be a better description than 'shy'. I had tried hand clapping in Darwin, where Chestnut Rails are said to inhabit the mangroves quite close to town, but I'd had no luck at all. I stood warily by the crocodile-infested swamps and applauded all Chestnut Rails within hearing. But there were no curtain calls that day. The adjacent noisy road works might have had something to do with it. Or perhaps the birds were all clapped out.

I did not really expect to see a Red Goshawk in the Kimberley, although of course it was on my list of possibles. As was the Letter-winged Kite and Broad-billed Sandpiper. But I did expect to see a Roseate Tern, Red-browed Pardalote, Sandstone Shrike-thrush, Great-billed Heron, Beach Stone-curlew, Mangrove Grey Fantail and that elusive Mangrove Golden Whistler. I had hopes for a Common Redshank, an Oriental Cuckoo and a Pictorella Mannikin. And I really did think that we'd see a Black Grasswren. That would be essential for any bird lover's tour of the Kimberleys.

I'd studied all the books and compiled all my lists — my wishlist, my expected list, my Broome list, my cruise list. My hairdresser said he knew three other people doing the same trip. This struck me as highly unlikely as there were only eight passengers on the boat.

At last the appointed day arrived, all preparations concluded, everything packed. We set off with great expectations.

Flying is never fun. Best I don't recollect that particular flight to Broome. Suffice it to say it was a Saturday, the beginning of school holidays. At eight-thirty that night, we arrived at Broome, exhausted, capable only of booking ourselves into our hotel. In our room, we couldn't find the radio, because we didn't think to look under the phone handset. Rog fell asleep and didn't hear the party downstairs.

It was a very nice hotel: boasting the well-deserved slogan: 'Broome with a view'. Our hotel had a large open terrace overlooking Roebuck Bay. This is a favourite spot for watching the 'Staircase to the Moon', an optical phenomenon which occurs when a full moon coincides with very low tides. The light reflects on the mudflats, revealing a virtual staircase to the moon.

Below the terrace was an inviting expanse of mangroves. I spent as much time amongst these mangroves as the tides allowed, looking for Mangrove Golden Whistlers and Mangrove Grey Fantails. All I saw for my trouble were Black Kites, White Ibis and Torresian Crows.

Sunday was ours (the cruise didn't start until Monday) so we hired a car (from a firm with the slogan 'Broome, Broome') and drove to the port and walked out on the wharf. An Osprey had built its huge, untidy nest on the top of a light pole at the end of the wharf. I don't know why I felt so pleased with myself for finding it — I could hardly have missed it.

At the tourist information centre, I noticed a brochure about fire danger. Rog and I remembered the fires in the Northern Territory from our 1982 trip: lots of them, burning uncontrolled over vast areas of land. There was always a Black Kite in front of the fire, watching for some little terrified creature to try to escape the flames. Only raptors like bushfires.

We drove out to the Bird Observatory which is situated on Roebuck Bay, half an hour's drive from Broome. There were more buildings than on our previous visit. And more people. All of them young, brown, skinny and bare-footed. No one spoke to us, which was quite a change from our previous visit, when the few people there were exceptionally friendly, especially the young wardens, who were extremely enthusiastic. I remember we came across an injured Oriental Pratincole and they tried to catch some grasshoppers to feed it. It didn't take long before they realised that there was no way that two healthy young adults could catch enough insects to provide nourishment for one small bird.

It didn't take long to realise that two fit young adults could not gather enough grasshoppers to feed one Oriental Pratincole.

On this occasion, there were several 4WD in the carpark. I had the impression that a visit to the Bird Observatory was just something tourists do in Broome, an interest in birds was optional. I was pleased I had my Zeiss around my neck to differentiate me from the riffraff.

We did one of the nature walks through the pindan scrub, but it was the wrong time of day to see bushbirds. (Bird score 3: Tawny Frogmouth; Peaceful Dove; Mistletoebird.) So we walked to the beach looking for waders, but the tide was a long way out, so there was no luck there either. (Score 4: White-faced Heron; Little Egret; Pied Oystercatcher; Pelican.)

The big adventure started on Monday morning. We rendezvoused in a downtown carpark and met our guide and our fellow passengers. There were two women from Perth, a couple from Sydney and another couple of birdos from Melbourne, whom we knew by repute. Eight passengers, our guide, the captain, a deckhand and the cook. On a 16-metre ketch, that's plenty!

We stood around in holiday mood laughing and joking while we waited for our transport to the boat. It turned out that six of us had been staying in the same hotel. What are the chances of that in a tourist town with at least 35 places to stay? I was disappointed to see that we had a smoker among us.

Our guide called us all together and gave us each a box of matches. These, he instructed, were to be carried with us at all times. We were going into some very wild places, he warned us, and if we got lost we were to light a fire so that we could be rescued. It was important that we stoked our fire with green leaves during daylight hours to make black smoke. We all remained politely silent. One of us, anyway, had a use for the matches.

We waited for our bus. And waited. And waited. I was happy chatting about Broome and birds. Someone mentioned the wharf. I couldn't help myself. Did you notice the Ospreys' nest? I asked, doing a fair job of smothering my pride. Yes, of course they had. The Melbourne birdo pointed out quietly that there was a bigger one, with a visible chick, on a communication tower right outside our hotel. What a smarty!

The bus eventually came. It was a mini bus — not large enough for nine people plus the two pieces of hand luggage we'd each been restricted to, so our guide went ahead with the luggage and three of the passengers. After a bit more waiting, the bus returned for the second instalment. I noticed we didn't head towards the port. Odd, thought I. Our pleasant young driver explained that we were picking up his grandmother, who was to be our cook. Grandma clambered on board and we all introduced ourselves. Roger said, this is my wife, Sue, the vegetarian. The cook told him not to joke and it was apparent that she had not been informed about my dietary requirement. Half expecting this, I had made space for a tin of vegetarian sausages in my Lilliputian luggage allowance. I made light of the situation outwardly, while inwardly wondering how I'd survive for 10 days on one tin of sausages. Grandma did not greet the news philosophically. She seemed to think that the situation should not have arisen; that our guide was remiss. I had the distinct impression that she couldn't wait to tell him so. In spades. Which she duly did, the instant we arrived on board, while I cringed, embarrassed, in my cabin. Why did I feel guilty? I should have been on deck watching the Lesser Frigatebirds fly over.

'Cabin' is a generous description of our quarters. There were two narrow bunks, a port hole with instructions not to open the window, a fan that didn't work, a light that emitted about half a candlepower and enough room for one person to stand up — as long as the door was closed. Roger said that it wasn't misleading to say that the boat was air conditioned: there was an air conditioner installed, it's just that it was never turned on!

Twelve people on board and only 11 bunks. This was an intriguing puzzle. It turned out that Grandma slept in the wheelhouse, so in the morning you either had to wait in your unbearably stuffy cabin for her to get up, or if you wanted to go on deck, you had to clamber through her bedroom trying not to disturb the sleeping cook. We all soon learned it was best not to disturb Grandma.

But I'm jumping ahead of myself. The reason the bus didn't head towards the port was that our ketch was moored in the bay. There were some scornful words about extortionate berthing fees at the wharf. We had to take off our shoes and wade into the water and clamber aboard the tender while it heaved in the waves — not an especially elegant activity in my particular case. All I could think was, (Providence be praised!) I wasn't wearing pantyhose.

The Captain welcomed us aboard. He was married to Grandma, our formidable cook. He was tanned a dark brown and his skin looked as thick as a crocodile's. Unquestionably master of his tiny domain, he wore a constant sneer against anyone in authority and all city slickers. I had a niggling suspicion that we were all included in the latter category. I doubt he'd ever owned a pair of shoes. We all gathered around and, with the aid of a chart a couple of people in front could see, he showed us generally where we'd be going: past Cape Leveque, into the Buccaneer Archipelago, stop at Hidden Island, then past Cockatoo Island, and into Talbot Bay at the base of the McLarty Range. Here we'd experience the Horizontal Waterfalls. We'd stop at Raft Point and then go into Doubtful Bay, where we'd visit Ruby Falls. We might visit Montgomery Reef, we might go up the Sale River. We'd stop off at the Lacepedes on the way home. The most important rule, the Captain stressed, was the preservation of water. We could flush the toilet as often as we liked (that used sea water) but showers must be kept to an absolute minimum. He seemed quite oblivious to the heat.

I asked our guide if we might see whales, but he said it was the wrong time of year. I'd been so busy reading up on birds, I hadn't thought to read up on whales.

The boat travelled nonstop that first night, passed Cape Leveque and into the Buccaneer Archipelago. Two passengers had some difficulty adjusting to the motion of the boat, but Rog and I were fine. Our cabin was hot and stuffy, but the movement of the boat was quite relaxing. We soon learnt to curb our tongues as every word could be heard between cabins. The worst aspect of our cramped living conditions was that there was nowhere to write up my journal, nowhere to spread out my bird books and tick off my birdlists. Not that there was much to tick off.

The next day we visited Hidden Island. This was a sand island which, our guide informed us, he had selected for its non-arduous walks. Sounded good to me.

I found clambering out of the ketch into the bobbing tender difficult and undignified, and scrambling out of the rollicking tender usually directly into the sea, but sometimes onto slippery rocks, even more laborious and awkward. For this reason, I usually left my camera behind. I missed out on some marvellous shots. Or, as Roger said, I saved a lot of money on film.

On Hidden Island, the sand was as white as my grandmother's sheets. It looked as if we were the first people ever to step foot on that beach.

Unfortunately a squashed beercan soon destroyed this whimsy. It was a beautiful little beach, surrounded by large boulders. At first glance, the rocky hills did not fit my definition of 'non-arduous walking'.

There were lots of footprints across the white sand. Big ones out in the open and small ones around the boulders. The big ones were 18 centimetres long, 15 centimetres wide and about 30 centimetres apart. I was wondering who had made them, when a Black-necked Stork flew off not far away. The small footprints were more difficult to identify. They were in pairs, about 10 centimetres apart. Some sort of hopping mouse perhaps?

Our guide led us all single file bush bashing up the non-arduous hill. My first glance proved pretty accurate. It was too hot to see any birds. I was sweating like the winner of the Caulfield Stakes. At the top of the second hill, Rog and I decided that the beach was more attractive than the walk. We're quick like that.

On the way back we did see Lavender-flanked Fairy-wrens (the Kimberley form of Variegated Fairy-wrens), which was more than the others had to report when they joined us on the beach some half an hour later, their legs all scratched from the undergrowth. We heard a Sandstone Shrike-thrush call in the distance, but didn't see it.

I had my heart set on a Red-browed Pardalote, having searched for them diligently and unsuccessfully on more than one occasion. Our guide assured me that if I saw a pardalote here, it would be Red-browed. Imagine my glee then when I saw a tiny bird fly into a hole in a bank. It must be! I stood quite still and my pardalote soon emerged. It was so beautiful I instantly forgave it for not being Red-browed. It was the Kimberley form of the Striated. Why was my camera back on the boat? The supposedly common Red-browed Pardalote was proving as elusive as any grasswren.

That afternoon we visited Silver Gull Creek. While everyone else was swimming in a huge concrete tank fed by a creek and inhabited by some very friendly little brown frogs, I had a good look at a Northern Fantail. I had seen them before in Darwin, but this was a much better view. The bird's stance is nothing like the can't-stay-still dance of our well-known Grey Fantail, the cheeky Cranky Fan of my childhood. The Northern Fantail sits erect and self-important, with its tail pointing down, quite still.

I also saw a flycatcher and tried hard to convince myself that it was a Broad-billed. Our guide told me it was a female Leaden and, as I couldn't tell the difference between a female Leaden and a female Broad-billed (or a female Satin for that matter, if one had strayed as far as the Kimberley), I couldn't possibly argue with him.

We were starting to get quite friendly with the other couples on the trip, and no longer felt quite as inhibited as we had when we'd each been presented with our very own box of matches. We dared to give voice to our thoughts — at least to each other.

We remained perfectly polite, although one of us who had been assured that he could purchase beer on board was plainly provoked when, hot and bothered, he was told that this was not the case. We did not mutiny. Then.

It became clear that the Captain was making all the decisions — where to go, where and more importantly, when, to stop, where to moor overnight. We were doing his standard tour and the requirements of birdwatching didn't enter into it. Good night, Chestnut Rail!

Birdos like early mornings and late afternoons. I'd hoped we'd be in the tender at low tide silently slipping amongst the mangroves looking for Mangrove Golden Whistlers and Mangrove Grey Fantails, the ones that behave properly, like a fantail should.

It was spectacular scenery. The weather was fine and warm — a little too warm sometimes for our beer-less, shower-less state. We were there to enjoy ourselves with a friendly group of like-minded people. At this stage, I think, we each separately made a personal decision to make the most of the situation. Shame about the photos I wasn't going to take; pity about the birds I'd looked forward to seeing for almost a year. It was a lot of money to spend if we weren't going to see a Black Grasswren.

It was a good thing I'd reconciled myself to few birds and no photos because that night we moored in Talbot Bay, not far from a much larger boat, *The True North*. I warmed to it immediately. It was sleek and beautiful; it had its own dear little helicopter, but above all, it was more than four times our size. I'll bet two people could stand up in its two-berth cabins AND open the door! We could hear *The True North* passengers partying. Our deckhand made some supercilious remarks about the ridiculous number of staff on board. The Captain scoffed at the helicopter. I knew immediately where all my hairdresser's clients were.

Rog squeezed my hand. 'Next time,' he whispered.

'I'll bet we see more birds than them,' I said unconvincingly.

All regrets were forgotten the next day when we saw the whales! Humpback Whales up close — closer than I ever imagined they'd be. An exhilarating experience. When we returned home I took the trouble to read what I should have read before we left. I learnt that each April, Humpback Whales travel north-wards up the coast of Western Australia from Albany, arriving to calve off the Kimberley coast in June. In September, they start the return journey and arrive back in Antarctica in December, to gorge on krill and prepare for next year's migration. We were in the right spot at the right time for calving! This should have been an advertised highlight of the trip. We all felt privileged to witness sightings of these huge peaceful creatures. I think it's their sheer size that makes a close-up encounter so moving.

We saw several pods of Dolphins. Rog and I caught one fleeting glimpse of a Dugong. The deckhand showed us great views of a Great-billed Heron, which made up for my failure to tick it on the Yellow Water cruise. Early one morning when we were moored at Raft Point, one of the Melbourne birdos found a pair of Beach Stone-curlews. Brilliant spotting! How she ever recognised them at such a distance, I'll never know. Even when we got much closer, they were extremely well-camouflaged. Rog was genuinely pleased that I had at last seen these rare and unusual birds that he'd ticked at Doctor's Gully. I felt very guilty that I hadn't felt as pleased for him at the time.

Singing Honeyeaters were the most common bird in Broome on our 1992 trip.

One morning we were in the tender amongst the mangroves and the other Melbourne birdo found us a beautiful Mangrove Robin — an unexpected bonus. All four of us twitched then. I have no doubt that we would have missed out on both these sightings if those Melbourne birdos hadn't been with us.

We did see Sandstone Shrike-thrush and eventually both Mangrove Golden Whistlers and Mangrove Grey Fantails. We also saw Silver-backed Butcherbirds (the Kimberley form of the Grey Butcherbird) and Golden-backed Honeyeaters (the Kimberley form of the Black-chinned). We saw Singing Honeyeaters and Yellow-throated Miners, two of Australia's most widely distributed honeyeaters. I remember the Singing as being the most common bird in Broome on our previous trip. We saw Grey-crowned Babblers and Pheasant Coucal and Peregrine Falcons. We had excellent sightings of White-quilled Rock-pigeons.

Brown Boobies were the only birds we saw every day of the cruise. One curious Booby landed on our boat to check us out. What can you expect from a Booby? They are, after all, so named because they're so stupid they have no fear of people. How stupid can you be? Apart from them, I was surprised at how few birds we saw at sea. We were pretty much hugging the coastline, but you'd see a greater number and variety of birds in Port Phillip Bay. We saw several Sooty Oystercatchers, the northern form, although I can't say I noticed their longer bills. The most common land birds were Brown Honeyeaters and Great Bowerbirds, which were both abundant everywhere we went.

The Beach Stone-curlews and the Mangrove Robin were hard to beat, but for me, the bird highlight of the trip was in Samson Inlet. We were admiring a majestic White-bellied Sea Eagle, when a Brahminy Kite flew into view. Almost immediately a Whistling Kite and a Little Eagle came along. It is very considerate for these two birds to appear together, as incompetent fools like me often confuse them — or they confuse me! Then, as if four raptors together wasn't enough, a

Boobies are called Boobies because they are so stupid that they have no fear of humans.

Square-tailed Kite came into view! My neck was sore from looking up. Another raptor appeared above, very high in the sky. What was it? We all craned our necks, but only one of us was brave enough to attempt identification. It was our tour guide who identified a Red Goshawk — the subject of my jokes months before. Such a rare bird, I hadn't dared hope to see one. There it was, the sixth raptor in our ballet. This is as good as it gets.

Apart from Brown Boobies, blue sky, and spectacular scenery, the other thing that we saw every day was bushfire. It was just as Rog and I had remembered it from 17 years before. Wild, raging, uncontrolled fires, with huge fireballs falling down cliffs and establishing subsidiary fires below, and sombre glowing coals plotting a new eruption as soon as a breath of breeze provided the medium. There were so many fires, it seemed to me that if I were lost, nobody would know which particular fire was my plea for help. I'd be more likely to accidentally self-immolate anyway. We passengers agreed: we would die in the bush rather than deliberately light one of these satanic infernos. Luckily, this reckless pledge was not put to the test.

On the day we saw the six raptors, one of our fellow passengers calculated that we would be returning to Broome on Thursday, not Wednesday, as we had been told. Quietly, he chose his moment when our guide was chatting to the Captain. Innocently he asked which day we returned. Simultaneously they reassured him. 'We return Wednesday,' said our guide confidently. 'We get back Thursday,' said the Captain categorically. We were one step closer to mutiny.

The deckhand was heavily into fish. He didn't know a Pelican from a Pardalote, but he was a piscatorial encyclopaedia. He had a line dangling over the back of the boat all the time and every day he caught several pretty impressive tropical fish. They were tasty too, so I'm told.

On the subject of food, Grandma managed to do a loaves and fishes trick with my one tin of vegetarian sausages. She barbequed a couple, made a curry, a stew and fried rice. No haute cuisine chef could have been more inventive in the circumstances. Well done, Grandma. The food was generally good, although we all missed fresh fruit and vegetables. Whenever some fruit appeared it was quickly scoffed. I could quibble about the quality of the wine. Can cask wine be described as 'good'? Or did the ad mean 'good food', and 'wine', not 'good food and wine'?

The others were more interested in feasting on mud crabs, or on Black-lipped Oysters freshly prised off the rocks. Barramundi jumped out of the water tantalisingly, as if to jeer 'can't catch me!' And they were right. Sparkling metallic blue garfish danced on their tails across the water and huge schools of mackerel made the water boil as they hunted bait fish, and were hunted themselves by White-bellied Sea Eagles.

Naturally we saw several crocodiles, which were much more interesting when seen from the ketch than from the tender. We saw lots of Short-eared Rock-wallabies and once, at night, the deckhand picked out a sea snake by torchlight. One day when we were following a creek up to a waterhole, so we'd have a swim in lieu of a shower, I saw a very attractive snake. Our tour guide, who hadn't seen it, assured me it was a Children's Python. I don't know much about snakes, but as soon as we returned to Broome I looked it up and I'm pretty sure it was a Gwardar — classified as dangerous.

There are some very pretty shells to be found along this coast. Trochus, huge dippers, cowries, cone shells. On one beach, every whelk I picked up without exception was home to a hermit crab. I did find room in my luggage to take home a pure white trumpet shell, fully a foot (30 cm) long.

The Horizontal Waterfalls in Talbot Bay are a phenomenon caused by the huge tides. As the tide turns, massive volumes of water are syphoned through a narrow gorge causing a terrifying amount of turbulence. There have been several proposals to harvest this tidal power to generate electricity. The Captain's trick is to pack the city slickers into the tender and let it lurch violently at great speed from eddy to eddy, spinning without control, preferably not crashing into the sides of the canyon. Everybody gets wet to the skin. Lots of fun.

Even more exciting than this sodden adventure was going rock climbing. Of course it wasn't actually called rock climbing, but that's exactly what it was: a sheer rock face, adjacent to a pretty cascading waterfall, called Ruby Falls. In the heat of the day, we were led up to the escarpment, in search of what?

I saw a Little Pied Cormorant flying overhead, which I could just as easily have seen from the base of the waterfall. Now I have nothing against Little Pied Cormorants *per se*, but I venture to suggest that no birdo would risk life and limb in the Kimberley heat (or anywhere else for that matter) in order to score one Little Pied Cormorant.

Coming back down was worse because the rocks had become slippery by so many people's wet boots. The nearby freshwater crocodiles added to the thrill. It was perfectly safe for anyone as fit and athletic as our guide and the deckhand, but for me it was an experience I care never to repeat — not even if there were Black Grasswrens on the escarpment!

We didn't get up the Sale River — conditions weren't right. Nor did we get out to Montgomery Reef — more of a disappointment to those who had made room in their meagre luggage to transport flippers and snorkels and goggles across the continent.

Instead we visited Cockell Cay where there was an interesting discussion about the identification of some small terns — were they Little Terns or Fairy Terns or both? I will never know.

I looked forward to visiting the Lacepedes. This, we were told, was to be our consolation prize for missing out on Montgomery Reef.

Although it was very hot on those treeless islands, visiting the Lacepedes was for me an experience of a lifetime. There are three islands, named with great originality — Eastern, Middle and Western. Surely I would see Roseate Terns there.

It was our guide's plan to visit Eastern Island in the morning and Western in the afternoon. We set off in the tender at nine — classified as an early start on this trip! It was already heating up. As we passed Middle Island, we saw a Green Turtle lumbering back to the sea having laid her eggs. Plans were instantly altered unilaterally by the deckhand and he took us to Middle Island. The poor Turtle was hot and exhausted. She should have been back in the cool of the sea by now.

Our guide instructed us not to go too close. Dutifully, we all circumnavigated the turtle at a great distance, except our guide who walked carefully up to it with his camera and tripod. (The tripod alone exceeded our luggage allowance.) The deckhand was about to take the tender back to the boat, but yelled out to ask what time we'd like to be collected. Standing right beside the poor exhausted turtle he'd urged us not to disturb, without thinking our guide shouted back that we'd like a couple of hours on the island. It was then that we mutinied.

Spontaneously, with one mind, we all stomped up the beach — and it is difficult to stomp in loose sand. At the top of the beach we were distracted by fluffy white Brown Booby chicks, curiously peering over the tussocks of grass. They were so cute they soothed our wrath.

We each took a deep breath and wandered away in different directions, admiring the boobies.

After a while, I looked back at the turtle. Her tracks were clearly visible; as she returned to the sea from laying her eggs, she'd come across an outcrop of rocks and been diverted, making her trek a couple of hundred metres further than it would otherwise have been. And the tide was going out. The tide was going out faster than her painfully slow lumber down the beach. She'd make one lurch forward, then have to rest for several minutes before trying again.

Our guide saw it too. He asked us to help and hurried back down to the turtle. But the rebellious ranks had not elected a leader and we divided into two schools: one wanted to help the turtle, the other thought it wrong to interfere with nature. She'd be all right if only we left her alone. I was torn between the two, and stood considering the merits of the case. I decided that it was appropriate for us to intervene. I left my camera at the top of the beach, thus foregoing some potentially superb shots, and raced to help. Five of us tried to save the turtle. Two remained fixed to the view that nature should be left undisturbed. Another was conveniently collecting shells some distance away.

The turtle had given up. Her head was lying on the sand. It was all too much effort. We threw water over her to cool her down. Four people tried to pick her up and drag her towards a channel. She was very heavy. I was no use dragging so I kept bailing cool water over her. Eventually we got her to the channel where she lay for a long time. I'm pleased to say that after an hour or so, she did swim into the sea.

That afternoon when we landed on Western Island, it was covered with nesting Brown Boobies. There were chicks of every size and stage of development. So many that they overflowed onto the beach. They were quite fearless and very funny. Unfortunately there was little else on the island. There was no sign of Roseate Terns. I saw Pied Cormorants and Ruddy Turnstones. The intrepid Melbourne birdos walked halfway around the island and saw some waders. I was relieved they didn't report Broad-billed Sandpipers or a Common Redshank.

In the tender on the way back to the boat, our guide tried to count the tracks

Ruddy Turnstone on the Broome jetty.

of turtles returning to the sea after having laid their eggs, but gave up when he reached 300. As soon as the females return to the sea exhausted, they are pounced on by waiting males with only one thing on their minds. Quite often two males jump onto the one poor exhausted female. They don't care if she's got a headache.

That was our last night. Because we were a day later than we'd expected, three people had to leave very early the next morning in order to make hastily revised transport connections. Much was made of farewelling these people the night before, exchanging addresses, promising to send photos.

Imagine our surprise, when we gathered for breakfast the next morning, to realise that our guide had gone too. Our tour leader had departed without saying goodbye! We were unable to thank him for one of the most memorable holidays we have ever had.

Let's face it, even if he wasn't personally responsible for all seven of our new ticks, he did show us a Red Goshawk.

10

More kangaroos than cattle

BIRDS OF DRY COUNTRY

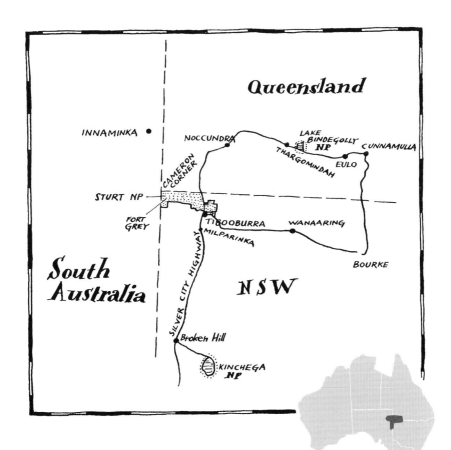

Chats are lovely little birds. They walk instead of hopping. We were familiar with White-fronted chats which are common at Werribee. We'd seen Orange Chats at Lake Eyre and at Mungo National Park. But we'd never seen Crimson Chats or Yellow Chats or Gibberbirds (formerly called Desert Chats).

Yellow Chats and Gibberbirds are rare but Crimson Chats are common, and, more important, they're seen in my home state, Victoria. We had looked for them at Lake Tyrrell in Victoria, Kinchega National Park in New South Wales, at Lake Gilles in South Australia and in the MacDonnell Ranges in the Northern Territory. I was embarrassed that they weren't on my lifelist.

So I planned a trip to Tibooburra — the hottest town in New South Wales and a place I'd always wanted to visit. The very name sounds romantic. Apparently it means large granite boulders in the local Aboriginal language. The trip had an element of adventure too. If it rained sufficiently the road would be closed and we wouldn't be able to get there at all, but, even more exciting, if it rained while we were there, we'd be stranded.

I read everything about Tibooburra I could find and was convinced that, as long as it didn't rain, we could safely do the trip in our Commodore — a standard 2WD. I thought that we should even be able to make it to Pyampa Station to see Grey Grasswren and Grey Falcon. Check on road conditions and take lots of water, cautioned the literature. So we did.

The tiny township of Tibooburra (population 150) is surrounded by Sturt National Park. I had a list of nine birds I wanted to see there. I thought the Crimson Chat should be easy but the others were all going to be difficult. Erratic seems the best word to describe them. They were: Letter-winged Kite, Grey Falcon (very rare), Flock Bronzewing (numbers decreasing), Grey Grasswren, Red-browed Pardalote (proving impossible), Banded Whiteface, Gibberbird, and Cinnamon Quail-thrush.

From Tibooburra, we planned to drive east to Bourke to look for Bourke's Parrot (naturally), another unreliable species.

Our trip was planned for September. It was an exceptionally wet year, which I thought was propitious for two reasons: first, all the rain would have fallen by the time September came around and second, nature would be in its prime, the wildflowers would be blooming and the birds would be in the right frame of mind for mating and nesting and being visible. I was right about the wildflowers.

It took us two days to drive from Melbourne to Tibooburra. We left home very early (four o'clock), breakfasted at Mildura (ten) and arrived at Broken Hill at two-thirty. As instructed, we checked on road conditions at the Information Centre. All roads were open. Tibooburra is 338 kilometres north of Broken Hill. We were shocked to learn that it takes five hours to drive this 338 kilometres, so we decided to spend the night at Broken Hill. A wise decision, because the drive took us much longer than five hours. This is fascinating country; it's a shame to whizz through it without appreciating it properly. The road is laughingly called the Silver City Highway but it is mainly unsealed and unloved, although (at least when we were on it) quite heavily trafficked. Luckily, we had to ford only one creek and that was no more than 15 centimetres deep.

Finding ourselves with some spare time in Broken Hill, we drove out to Menindee Lakes in Kinchega National Park, a distance of some 112 kilometres of good sealed road, and along the way we saw dozens of Emu, but only one car. By contrast, the road north from Broken Hill was unmade, poorly maintained and in constant use. And there were no Emus. It was evident that a decent shower of rain would make the road unpassable.

We spent a very pleasant couple of hours at the Menindee Lakes, recording 26 bird species, all our familiar friends, several waterbirds and raptors, also Mallee Ringneck and Variegated Fairy-wren.

The next morning we left Broken Hill at a quarter past nine, and arrived at Tibooburra at five-forty, our journey having been interrupted by many tantalising diversions. Once we stopped to investigate a movement in some saltbush and I flushed a Little Button-quail. We paused for morning coffee in a dry creek bed and were joined by Apostlebirds and Yellow-throated Miners. Most small birds that waylaid us turned out to be Chirruping Wedgebills, easily recognised by

There were many emus (but no cars) on the road to Menindee Lakes.

their call. My father says that they say 'thirty-two', and that Chiming Wedgebills say 'Did you get drunk?' He might be right about Chiming Wedgebills. I don't think Chirruping Wedgebills speak English at all. I think they say, 'Da, diddley-dum', with the diddley-dum going down the scale. At least the ones in northwestern New South Wales do.

We saw Red-backed Kingfisher, Australian Pratincole, Zebra Finch and Blue Bonnet. Flocks of Cockatiel were common, with their distinctive silhouette and white wing pattern in flight.

I looked carefully at every Black-shouldered Kite we saw, checking the amount of black under its wings. Although I knew that Letter-winged Kites are predominantly nocturnal, they are sometimes seen by day, and they were as likely to be seen here as anywhere. Populations of Letter-winged Kites irrupt following explosions of populations of long-haired rats. I thought the recent wet conditions would surely have encouraged rats to breed.

We followed the tourists to inspect James Poole's grave — he was second in

Apostlebirds often shared our morning tea.

command to Charles Sturt on his 1844 expedition inland looking for good pasture. Harsh temperatures and inadequate supplies took their toll and Poole died of scurvy. He was buried underneath a grevillea near a waterhole at Milparinka. There are worse places to be buried.

It was well after five o'clock when we arrived in Tibooburra, but we went directly to the National Parks office nevertheless. It was closed of course, but a notice board proclaimed the status of all the surrounding roads. It was then we realised that we would not be driving to Bourke. We had known that the road was unsealed, but the notice flatly informed us that the road between Wanaaring and Bourke was 'never maintained'. Perhaps I would have to forego my Bourke's Parrot.

Small groups of White-breasted Woodswallow huddled together on the overhead wires. It was disappointing to see that House Sparrows had made it to Tibooburra, and were apparently thriving without any discouragement.

Early the next morning we visited a waterhole on the Tibooburra Common. Although it was early September, it was clear, even at this early hour, that Tibooburra was going to live up to its reputation as New South Wales' hottest town. A White-faced Heron was unconcerned by our presence; a Black-fronted Dotterel was more wary. Little Corella and Willie Wagtails were busy nesting and Australian Ravens were feeding fully fledged chicks that looked large enough to leave the nest.

All this pre-breakfast activity augured well for our day's sightings. I was optimistic as we entered the National Parks office the moment it opened its doors. The ranger soon changed that. Without a hint of remorse, he told us that it was impossible to drive to Pyampa Station in a 2WD. Goodbye grasswrens.

Was this to be the story of my life — missing out on grasswrens?

We'd spent a week at Hattah in Victoria looking unsuccessfully for Striated Grasswren and a day at Port Augusta looking unsuccessfully for Thick-billed Grasswren. We'd missed out on seeing Black Grasswren at the Kimberley and could not access the escarpment at Kakadu to see White-throated Grasswren.

Our one and only grasswren success was the Dusky Grasswren that we'd happened upon by accident at King's Canyon. We did not see them as stipulated at Simpson's Gap or Ormiston Gorge, but found ourselves almost tripping over them in the early morning in the base of King's Canyon. So we'd tried hard to see four species of Grasswren and happened across a fifth. Now I was being told that I couldn't even look for a sixth species, the Grey Grasswren.

The ranger restored his humanity a little — in our eyes at least — by telling us that a Grey Falcon had been sighted yesterday at Fort Grey. What's more we could get there easily in our car. Fort Grey was where Sturt had built a stockade to protect his sheep and supplies. It is located in the western section of Sturt National Park, where I wanted to look for Banded Whiteface. Not a bad consolation prize for missing out on Grey Grasswren: Grey Falcon and Banded Whiteface. I smiled sweetly at the ranger as we left his office. After all, I told myself, he's only doing his job.

Much to my surprise, one of the first birds we saw that morning was Bourke's

Parrot. My pre-holiday reading had led me to believe that we were more likely to see them to the east of Tibooburra, and this was the main reason I had wanted to visit Bourke. But here they were at Tibooburra, very common and cooperative. These unusual small parrots have beautiful subtle warm grey and pink colours, and just a touch of blue under the tail. No illustration I've ever seen has done them justice. Even photographs don't seem to capture their true beauty. I had imagined them to be nondescript — dull even. Nothing could be further from the truth. They are delightful little birds, with their delicate hues and parrot personalities.

While we stumbled accidentally onto Bourke's Parrot, we were constantly on the lookout for Crimson Chat. These gorgeous little birds should be highly visible, I thought. We looked for them everywhere, but could see only Orange Chat. I consoled myself with the thought that Orange Chat are far more beautiful — which is undoubtedly correct. Orange Chat are a deep intense golden orange colour with a dramatic black bib: very colourful birds. From my inspection of the illustrations, I thought that the male Crimson Chat was not so brilliant. His chest and cap are more of a pink than a crimson, he has a brown back, a black mark through his eye and a white bib. And the pink (or so-called crimson) is not so intense as the vibrant golden-orange of the Orange Chat.

I told myself that I could survive without Grey Grasswren. Not gleefully, but I could survive. Grey Grasswren had, after all, been described only in 1968. However, I simply could not return home without ticking a Crimson Chat.

It is 110 hot kilometres from Tibooburra to Fort Grey and it took us nearly three hours. It's fair to point out that it would be quicker in a 4WD. The brochures advise that it takes two hours to drive from Tibooburra to Cameron Corner, a further 30 kilometres. Of course we did have to stop every time I thought I saw a whiteface, but nevertheless that time gives a fair indication of the state of the road. In fact we saw several whitefaces but they all turned out to be Southern Whiteface, not a Banded one amongst them.

I saw one LBJ with a distinct coloured chest band and urged Rog to stop the car so I could investigate it. It moved uncooperatively under a bush. I perse-

We saw few trees along the road to Fort Grey.

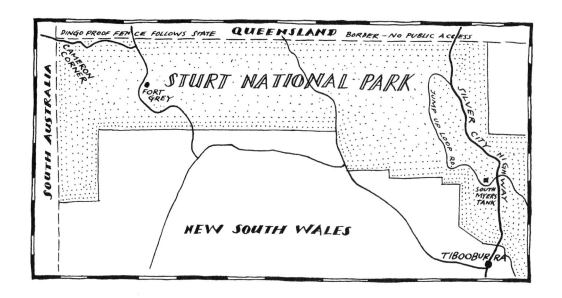

vered, looking for some sparse shade to stand in. I stood stock still. The bird
ignored me, while I tried hard to ignore the heat. Eventually it came towards me
and let me have a good look at it. It was not a Banded Whiteface: it was a female
Crimson Chat! From my point of view, at that moment, almost as good. At last,
that embarrassing omission from my lifelist was corrected.

From then on, it seemed almost every small bird we saw was a Crimson Chat.
We had stumbled upon a local irruption of Crimson Chats, with an occasional
Orange Chat for variety. The gorgeous male Crimson Chats are very pretty, but I
decided that I had been right: the Orange Chat is by far the more spectacular bird
with much more brilliant plumage.

We had wonderful views of Brown Songlarks, singing loudly while flying with
their distinctive dangling legs. And Richard's Pipits! I have never seen no many
Pipits. Of course each one was closely examined in the hope that it might prove
to be a Gibberbird. Unhelpfully, they wagged their tails up and down — a characteristic of both Gibberbirds and Pipits. But no, they were all streaked and had
pink legs. I couldn't turn them into Gibberbirds no matter how hard I tried.

At Fort Grey we had a cup of tea in the shade of a beefwood. It was the
middle of the day and there were very few birds around. The inevitable Yellow-
throated Miner came to investigate our menu. A male Mistletoebird drew
attention to himself by his song. But there was no hint of any falcons, grey or
otherwise. The wildflowers were prolific: white and pale blue and bright
sunshine yellow. There were Fleshy Groundsel, white paper daisies and exotic,
but nevertheless colourful, hops. There were hakea and acacia and lots of
beefwood. We'd seen few trees along the road.

If we were going to see Red-browed Pardalotes, this seemed the most likely
spot. I always associate pardalotes with eucalypts, but Red-browed are often seen
in mulga. These birds were proving to be untickable, no matter how hard I tried.
I'd hoped to see them in the Kimberley but had no luck there. When we were in

Alice Springs, I looked for them every morning and evening for a week in the tall gumtrees at the Telegraph Station, because some guide book had advised it. What a waste of time. There were no pardalotes there. Who knows when they'd last visited? Local knowledge is essential. Local, current knowledge. No one had told me there were Red-browed Pardalotes at Fort Grey. Sure enough, there weren't.

Being only 30 kilometres from Cameron Corner, we felt that we had to do the touristy thing and sight the spot where three states meet, I'm not sure why. Why does everyone feel compelled to visit this location? There is a plaque in place of the original hand-hewn wooden post placed by John Cameron, surveyor of New South Wales in 1880. There is a corner store or, more correctly, a pub that sells a few general items. And there is a large carpark to accommodate the constant flow of 4WDs that speed along the road from Tibooburra, stop long enough to take a photograph of themselves at Cameron Corner and then drive back to Tibooburra, so fast

At Fort Grey, a Yellow-throated Miner inspected our menu.

they can't appreciate anything along the way. Some had come down the Strzelecki Track from Innamincka and some, like us, took time for a cold beer and (as far as is possible amidst a 4WD convention) to drink in the atmosphere of the outback, and to inspect the dog fence — the longest fence in the world, going all the way from the Gulf of Carpentaria to the Indian Ocean. Built originally by the Queensland Government to keep rabbits out, it is now maintained to ensure dingoes don't get in.

It's impossible to visit these places without considering what manner of man was Charles Sturt, or James Poole, what deprivations were suffered by Burke and Wills or even John Cameron in 1880. They couldn't pause for a cold beer or jump back into their air conditioned vehicle when the heat became too oppressive.

On the return journey to Tibooburra, about 50 kilometres before the town, we noticed flocks of Budgerygahs and Cockatiels flying in to a waterhole for their afternoon drink and decided to stop and sit in the car for a while and see who else came in for a drink. There was one lone Hoary-headed Grebe on the water and one Hardhead without a white eye, making it either a female or an immature male. A pair of Crested Pigeons walked timidly down to the edge of the water. The air was full of Fairy Martins gathering red mud in their beaks and flying to a large drain under the road a few metres away. I was busy watching the Fairy Martins and didn't see the grebe get out of the water. But there it was, walking most awkwardly along the bank. The Hardhead was shadowing it from the water.

The grebe appeared to be trying to escape from the duck, which was undoubtedly pursuing it. We watched fascinated for over an hour. Sometimes the grebe dived under the water, apparently to escape from the duck, and sometimes it seemed to invite the Hardhead's attention. Both birds did a good deal of head bobbing at each other. We had no idea what was going on. We could not

I didn't like the idea of Jump Ups until I learnt they were simply Mesas by another name.

determine the sex of either bird, but we suspected we were watching a very confused couple.

We were not significantly restricted driving around Tibooburra without a 4WD. We had chosen not to drive to Bourke (who cares — we got the parrots anyway) and could not get to Pyampa Station. Other than that, we could travel most tracks: it simply took longer. The ranger (who probably wouldn't know a Grey Falcon from a Grey Grasswren) showed us two circular drives we could do in our 2WD. The Gorge Loop Road (100 kilometres, two hours) to the east through Mitchell grass or gibber plains depending on the season; and Jump Up Loop Road (110 kilometres, three hours) through the catchment area of Twelve Mile Creek. On both roads the maps showed lookouts and camping areas.

I was alarmed by the term 'jump up'. It was suggestive of the stump jump plough we'd been taught about in primary school. I'd heard of huge holes in outback roads full of bulldust and invisible to the innocent driver. Were these holes going to jump up at me? Roger scoffed at my concern, but the ranger didn't laugh. He probably didn't have a sense of humour. He told me that 'jump up' is the local name for mesas. They are flat-topped hills that have harder rock on top and erode from the sides.

Thus reassured, we set out first on the Jump Up Loop Road. First stop: South Myers Tank. There was a bird hide at one end — not where I would have positioned it, but no doubt there for a reason. The 'tank' was in fact two dams, divided by the road. A very sleek black feral cat was sunning itself on the bank. We could hear both Little Grassbirds and Clamorous Reed Warblers in the cumbungi and I feared that the abundance of little birds explained the cat's well-nourished appearance. We set up the scope and had a good look at the water. Every decent dam in this part of the world seems to be home to both Hardhead and Darter. We saw Black-tailed Native-Hen (always a favourite of mine), Grey Teal, Australasian Shoveler and Pink-eared Duck, Black-fronted Dotterel, Cockatiels and Singing Honeyeaters. Some Galahs landed on the far bank and

Both Hardhead (left) and Darter (right) were on every significant waterhole.

waddled down for a drink. Best of all, we had a brief but unmistakable glimpse of a pair of Flock Bronzewing. Tick number three. Although the identification was without doubt, the sighting had been too quick to allow the proper unrestrained twitching deserved by such a bird.

We finished the drive, along the way seeing several Emu, Crested Pigeon, Little Crow, Red-capped Robin, Zebra Finch, Inland Thornbill and more Bourke's Parrot. We reported the cat to the humourless ranger, then considered the best way to spend our remaining few hours in Sturt National Park. Should we explore new territory and hope for new birds? Gibber plains did suggest Gibberbirds, maybe even Cinnamon Quail-thrush, but, in this season, Mitchell grass seemed far more likely than gibber plains, which would make it difficult to see anything. Or should we return to where we'd already seen Flock Bronzewing and try for a better look?

Cockatiel were common in Sturt National Park.

We both agreed we wanted to get a better look at Flock Bronzewings. They are unusual looking birds, the male in particular with his bold black and white facial markings. Last century there were huge flocks of them — tens of thousands — hence the name. Today the numbers are declining — we had seen a pair, not a flock, and they are classified as near threatened. The explorers reported they were good eating, although the introduction of cattle has doubtless had more to do with their declining populations. Foxes, too, have taken their toll.

It was still hot at a quarter past four when we arrived at South Myers Tank to position ourselves in the bird hide and wait for Flock Bronzewing to come in to drink. My earlier suspicion that the hide was badly built was confirmed. It was impossible to position the scope anywhere. The viewing slots were at the wrong height. There was very poor vision of the water surface and virtually no views of the water's edge where birds were likely to come in to drink.

It was hot outside and hotter within. It was also very windy. We watched several Emu come in to drink at the far side of the dam, next to the road which divided this dam from the next. An Australasian Grebe kept us amused swimming past the hide, then allowing the wind to blow him back. Again and again he swam past our window. A Darter flew in and landed on our left, out of sight. One Little Pied Cormorant joined him. Two hot hours passed and nothing else happened. Hot and bored I ventured outside and watched a mob of Emu in the shimmering distance making its way slowly over the plains towards the dam. The heat was making me irritable. Why hadn't we tried our luck with the Gibberbird? Who had selected this stupid spot for a bird hide? Probably the ranger. If I were a Flock Bronzewing, I'd drink at the far side of the other dam where we'd watched Galahs drinking earlier in the day. I told Rog I was going to find a spot on the other dam and set off imagining all the Gibberbirds and Quail-thrushes we were missing out on in order to watch an Australasian Grebe and a few Emu. My camera always weighs more in the heat. A Variegated Fairy-wren trilled at me from a low saltbush and instinctively I stopped to focus on it. At that moment Rog emerged quietly from the back of the hide and gestured frantically for me to return. Fairy-wren quite forgotten, I returned immediately, travelling up the hot hill much faster than I had travelled down.

Rog was sitting in the hide, binoculars glued to a pair of Flock Bronzewing on the bank nearest to the hide. There was a small bush between me and the birds. Deservedly, Roger had much better views. Still, I saw the male with his unusual face. The backs of the birds were the same reddish brown as the colour of the soil. The birds were skittish, as if they were aware of our presence. I don't think they had a drink at all. If they did, it was a mere sip, not enough to sustain them for 24 hours.

We returned to Tibooburra vindicated. We'd made the right decision not to do the Gorge Loop Road. We'd had good sightings of Flock Bronzewing. And good twitching too.

Apart from Flock Bronzewing, there are other pigeons in the dry country. There are Diamond Doves and Crested Pigeons and, one of my favourites, Spinifex Pigeon. Spinifex Pigeon always make me laugh. All crested birds seem like clowns to me. We'd first seen Spinifex Pigeons in 1982 when we drove from Perth to Darwin. I remember them cheekily walking across the road in front of the car. When we visited the Centre in 1996, I decided that I'd try to photograph them. The guide books informed me that if I took some rice to the carpark at Ormiston Gorge, I could attract them to my desired spot long enough to admire them properly and presumably to photograph them. Ideally they are seen in the early morning. We were staying in Alice Springs. Ormiston Gorge is the furthest of the gorges in the West MacDonnell ranges — 135 kilometres from the Alice, so it was an early start that morning. We had breakfast at six, left at six-thirty and arrived at the Gorge carpark at eight. Immediately we enjoyed lovely views of Western Bowerbird.

I clutched my well-travelled container of rice and wandered hopefully around the carpark. No pigeons of any sort. When I ventured into the camping area I saw why. Some German tourists were feeding Spinifex Pigeons with left-over break-fast. My uncooked rice could not compete. Of course the Germans fed the birds where it suited them, in the shade. I had intended trying to lure them into the sun for a photograph. Suffice it to say that I did not succeed.

The amusing codicil to this story is that my mother saw Spinifex Pigeons in the Alice Springs Telegraph Station, right where I had been daily searching so unsuc-cessfully for Red-browed Pardalotes.

The day that I did not photograph Spinifex Pigeon, I had a minor triumph that I did not fully appreciate at the time. I saw a Grey Honeyeater. This nondescript little bird is most unobtrusive. Any new tick is cause for excitement, and I twitched a bit, but I would have been more excited if I had known then how lucky I was to see it. It is very rarely recorded, although this is because it is so unob-trusive rather than rare. And because it chooses to live in the arid outback. I have since learnt of two well-known members of The 600 Club who have never seen this bird. In both cases, it is the only honeyeater they have not seen. If I'd known that then, I would not have been lamenting my failure to photograph the Spinifex Pigeon. I would have been celebrating my exceptional sighting of the Grey Honeyeater.

But back to Tibooburra. We left the morning after we'd seen the Flock Bronzewings and felt more pleased with ourselves than a 30 per cent success rate probably justified. We'd spent two full days at Tibooburra, and made three new ticks out of our wishlist of 10 species.

Instead of going east to Bourke, we were travelling north to Noccundra along the Silver City Highway. It was undoubtedly the worst road we've ever driven on. It was dirt, and can't have been graded for years. If the road to Bourke was 'never maintained', this road must surely classify as 'hardly ever maintained'.

After we crossed the Queensland border (a rickety gate) the road deteriorated further. At least the Queensland authorities did not pretend it was a highway. Cattle roamed freely, but we saw many more kangaroos. It took us six hours to cover the 240 corrugated kilometres to Noccundra. In that time we saw one other car. I couldn't help wondering how long we'd be stranded if we broke down. But I suppressed the thought. We were on holiday.

The sight of a magnificent Black Falcon sitting still beside the road helped to buoy our spirits. He was as shiny black as yesterday's feral cat. There were only three colours visible. Against the red soil, his pale blue beak contrasted artisti-cally with his glistening black feathers. We'd never seen a Black Falcon at such close range before. Rog was driving slowly and didn't decelerate and the bird didn't flush. It sat proudly tolerating our presence, giving us a very good look. Previously, we'd only ever seen Black Falcons in flight — streaking across the sky as fast as Peregrines. It was very special to see one eye to eye.

Once in Alice Springs (at the sewage farm actually) we met a German tourist who was in Australia attempting to see every species of Falcon. He worked at Hoescht and Peregrines had nested on a high chimney stack. This had developed his interest in Falcons and he spent his annual holidays travelling the world try-ing to see every species. There are 61 falcons in the world, six in Australia, of which two are endemic. These two are the only rare ones: the Black and the Grey. He told us he'd seen Grey Falcons nesting beside the road between Darwin and Alice Springs, and asked us where he could see a Black Falcon. Alas, we could not help him. At that time, as we'd only ever seen Black Falcon on three occasions and then always in flight, we were not in a position to offer any advice. I gave him a couple of phone numbers of experts who might be able to point him in the right direction. I hope he achieved his goal.

Another raptor we've only ever seen in flight is the Black-breasted Buzzard. Obedient fellow, he'd read the guide books and turned up on cue at King's Canyon. Identification was easy when we saw two large white bull's eyes on the underwings. Although the buzzard soared high, the bull's eyes were unmistakable through our binoculars.

But back to Noccundra (population four). The road improved and we drove on to Thargomindah, looking in the acacia scrub for any sign of babblers. We were searching for Hall's Babblers.

There are only four species of Babbler in Australia, so you'd think it would be an easy family to tick off. In Victoria we are most familiar with the White-browed Babbler. These friendly birds live in family groups and bounce along the ground constantly chattering to each other. They have a range of calls from whistles to squeaks and chatter to clucks and are full of character. They build huge bulky nests in wattle trees conveniently at eye level or not much higher.

Identification of Babblers is easy north of the Tropic of Capricorn, as only the Grey-crowned Babbler is seen there. We'd seen the western race in Broome and the eastern race in places as far apart as the Barmah Forest on the New South Wales-Victorian border and Georgetown in Queensland.

We'd seen Chestnut-crowned the first time at a spot near Robinvale thanks to Barry McLean. As often happens, we worked hard to get a good look at the rich chestnut crown of these cheeky mobile birds, then the next day they were playing under our feet, distracting us as we were sitting waiting for a Spotted Bowerbird to return to its bower.

Hall's Babbler has a small range in south-western Queensland. I'd read that our best chance was east of Eulo. Just to make life interesting, both Grey-crowned and Chestnut-crowned can also occur in the same area.

From my inspection of the illustrations in the field guides, it seemed to me that Hall's Babbler was very like a White-browed. Perhaps a tiny bit larger, maybe a little darker. Its eyebrow was thicker, but who could observe that on a bouncing babbler in the bush? The one identification mark I had to see was the clean cut-off between its white throat and its dark breast below. I needed good light, cooperative birds and a fair portion of good luck.

On the road between Thargomindah and Cunnumulla, there were a few red termite mounds to match the red soil, lots of gidgee, an occasional gum tree with smooth orange limbs (Yapunyah, *Eucalyptus ochraphloia*) and one or two wild pigs. At five to three we saw our second car for the day. It was 30 degrees when we stopped for lunch and the only bird present was a very vocal male Crested Bellbird sitting high on a dead wattle and drawing attention to himself. He'd learnt his words right and expressed a satanic opinion of Dick.

It was after five by the time we reached Lake Bindegolly — reputedly a reliable spot for Freckled Duck — but we didn't have time for a proper look around. Vehicles are not permitted in the national park and it was a 4.5 kilometre walk to the bird hide. The lake was very full, leading me to believe that we'd be lucky to see anything special. According to the brochure it is empty one year in 10. I'd like to visit some time just before it empties.

We saw many suicidal Bearded Dragons on the road and almost as many Frill-necked Lizards sunning themselves in the straggly trees. I was admiring a pretty purple eremophila flower when a small flock of babblers flew across the road in front of the car. We stopped and looked and stood and listened and waited. We walked a little in each direction but there was no joy. Those babblers had simply disappeared off the face of the earth. Birds do that.

It was getting late, so we drove on to Cunnamulla for the night. Early the next morning we returned to the same spot, driving slowly with the windows down, concentrating hard, listening for babbler calls. There was 8/8 cloud cover, intermittent rain and some lightning. Hardly ideal bird watching conditions. Yesterday I'd noticed purple eremophila; this morning I saw an orange-pink variety. Suddenly we heard babblers!

We saw a small group, five I think, travelling fast away from us. Quickly and quietly we followed on foot. Babblers often chatter as they travel, giving the observer an even chance. These babblers covered a lot of ground between calls. They were dark brown babblers bouncing away from me, how could I inspect their throats?

I couldn't get a good look at their crowns either, or their eyebrows for that matter. The acacia scrub which seemed so open when we weren't following birds now seemed chock full of ground cover. They hid under twigs, took cover under dead branches, scurried under fallen limbs. A male Variegated Fairy-wren sat beside me and sang beautifully, trying hard to distract me from my mission.

I was aware that we had many kilometres to travel that day, that we couldn't sit and wait for the babblers to return. There was an urgency to this quest: it was now or never.

The babblers bounced through a barbed wire fence — we hadn't seen a fence for a long time. Stock all roam free in the outback — and that seemed appropriate to me. The first fence since the Queensland border and the babblers were on the wrong side of it. But then they turned! Three babblers bounced my way. For only a minute I had an excellent view of the clear demarcation between their white throats and dark breasts. These were Hall's Babblers indeed. An extremely elusive bird, and a well-earned tick. I had all four babblers at last. It's always very satisfying to tick off a whole family.

Now if I could just get a Gibberbird, and a Yellow Chat . . .

11

Beautiful one day…

BIRDS OF QUEENSLAND

On our most recent trip to far north Queensland we had limited time — as always — and I was determined not to waste a minute of it. It was September, a good time to travel to north Australia — not too hot, and not too wet — and a good time to see many species of birds. Sadly we would miss out on Buff-breasted Paradise-Kingfishers and (most likely) on Blue-faced Parrot-Finches. Paradise-Kingfishers migrate from New Guinea during the wet season and don't arrive in Queensland until October-November according to my guide books. Blue-faced Parrot-Finches are uncommon birds, rarely seen and their movements are

Great Bowerbird's Bower.

unknown. However, they are more often seen from January-April.

We had four weeks away. The last two were school holidays in all the eastern States, but the Olympics were on in Sydney and we hoped that the crowds would all congregate there. We planned to give Sydney a wide berth.

We'd been to Queensland on four previous trips, so we'd ticked many species already. We'd been to Lamington National Park twice (once to O'Reilly's and

The termite mounds change colour according to soil colour. This is just outside Georgetown where Australian Bustards were common, but Gouldian Finches were not.

once to Binna Burra), we'd been to Pajinka at the tippy-top of Cape York, we'd been to Bedarra twice and we'd driven up the coast as far as Cooktown.

So, in planning this trip, I knew that we had to visit central Queensland where we'd never been, but I wanted to spend most time in the wet tropics where the birds are concentrated. I wanted to see every available bird. A friend had told me that I must visit the Undara lava tubes. It is, he said, a fascinating geological formation not to be missed. I'd seen it on TV. Yes, it was interesting, but I didn't have time for the merely interesting. I was on a quest. There was but one purpose in my visit to far north Queensland: to get as many ticks as possible.

There are more species of birds in Queensland than in any other state and there are more guide books purporting to explain where each one can be seen. I reckon I'd read them all, and planned the trip accordingly. We were going to Winton for Rufous-crowned Emu-wren and (my old favourite) Striated Grasswren, and Cloncurry for Slaty-backed Thornbill and Normanton for Sarus Crane. But most of our time would be spent on the Atherton Tablelands where I hoped to do lots of ticking.

We were reasonably flexible in our arrangements. We extended our stay in Georgetown in order to search Cumberland Dam thoroughly for Gouldian Finches because the guide book said they were there. Imagine my annoyance when I was later told that Gouldian Finches had not been seen at Cumberland Dam for four years. We did see Red-tailed Black Cockatoos and I had a lovely look at a Banded Honeyeater. And, best of all, I did find a Great Bowerbird's bower — it's always so much better when you discover them yourself unexpect-edly. But for all this, I didn't like Cumberland Dam. It is signposted as a picnic spot, but cattle have the run of the place, accompanied by their inevitable foul smells, filth and flies. Naturally, had we seen Gouldian Finches, these minor inconveniences would have been quite purged from our memories, but as we did not, it's the cattle that come to mind when Cumberland Dam is mentioned, rather than the cockatoos.

Of course we did not see Striated Grasswren. Nor did we see Rufous-crowned Emu-wren or Slaty-backed Thornbill. And we had to drive a lot further than Normanton to see Sarus Crane. We saw Squatter Pigeon in Georgetown, a welcome tick, and some consolation for missing out on Gouldian Finches.

I am pleased to report that on several occasions birds did perform on cue, according to my copious pre-holiday notes. The Red-necked Crake and the Lesser Sooty Owl were both in attendance at Kingfisher Park Birdwatchers Lodge in Julatten, the Bridled Honeyeater did eat from the hand in the carpark at The Crater, the Channel-billed Cuckoo was seen on the Daintree River, Cotton Pygmy-Geese were swimming amongst the lily-pads in the quiet inlets of Lake Tinaroo and the White-browed Crake presented himself most cooperatively at the Cairns crocodile park.

Sadly, I have a list of another 63 species that I had hoped to see but didn't. The three most frustrating were the Chestnut-breasted Cuckoo, the Barred Cuckoo-shrike and the Bush-hen. If there were any justice in the world (which there clearly isn't) all three would be proudly ticked on my lifelist. The birds had other ideas.

In my more philosophical moments I reflect that birdwatching would not be so exciting if every species always turned up on request. If all you had to do was to put in your order for, say, a Night Parrot, then go to the right place (supposedly Cloncurry) at the right time of day (presumably night) in the right season (spring?) and there, presto! was your Night Parrot — it would all be too easy, wouldn't it? Where's the challenge in that? Why do fishermen get so much pleasure relating the tale about the one that got away? Because it makes what they do catch seem so much more significant. Seeing birds is so much more rewarding because you know that they do not always cooperate, they like to surprise us and obstinately refuse to read the field guides. But that's only in my more philosophical moments. Most of the time, I curse the little beggars for not cooperating.

From its description in the field guides, I deduce that the Chestnut-breasted Cuckoo must be a beautiful bird. It's small — about the size of a blackbird, but slimmer — with rich chestnut underparts, blue-grey above, yellow eye-ring and a longish, barred tail. It is not common, but can be seen on Mt Lewis, not far from Kingfisher Park Birdwatchers Lodge at Julatten where we were staying. We visited Mt Lewis on five occasions looking for this bird.

On the morning we were due to leave, before breakfast we made our ritual pilgrimage up the mountain. We parked just over the Bushey Creek bridge, checked the creek quickly for platypus and set off in search of Chestnut-breasted Cuckoos. We saw Grey-headed Robin, Grey Fantail (the darker, northern race), Eastern Spinebill, Red-backed Fairy-wren, Yellow-throated and Atherton Scrubwren, and had excellent views of a Little Bronze-Cuckoo and the northern race of the White-throated Treecreeper (which the experts tell me is smaller and darker than its southern relative, but which, to me, appeared to be more heavily streaked). With such beautiful birds, how dare I complain at the dearth of Chestnut-breasted Cuckoos?

We bumped into some American birdos on the mountain that morning, eager to see Lovely Fairy-wrens. These are unusual wrens in that (in my opinion) the female is the more spectacular bird. The male resembles a male Variegated Fairy-wren: light blue cap, shiny black throat, blue and russet back, brown wings and the distinctive, perky, cocked dark blue tail. But the female is something else. All the other female Fairy-wrens are brown. They might have a blue tail. They could wear a little eye make-up. But they are basically little brown birds. Not so the female Lovely Fairy-wren. She is indeed lovely. She is bright blue above and clean white below. She has white around her eyes and a deep blue tail. It is quite understandable that people would travel from California to far north Queensland to see her.

Unfortunately we were unable to help our American visitors and we returned to the lodge to pack, disappointed yet again that Mt Lewis was so bereft of Chestnut-breasted Cuckoos.

It didn't take long to breakfast, pack, pay the bill and say farewell to the Orange-footed Scrubfowl and Emerald Dove in the garden. The Red-necked

Crake was so upset at our departure that he could not bring himself to say goodbye.

As we were driving off, turning our minds to our next challenge (the Eungella (pronounced Young Galah) Honeyeater), our American friends ran out in front of our car, waving frantically. They had just returned from Mt Lewis. Yes, they had seen Lovely Fairy-wrens, but, more important, they'd seen a Chestnut-breasted Cuckoo. They'd rushed back to tell us. It was 800 metres beyond Bushey Creek and was calling in response to their tape recording.

The Eungella Honeyeater had waited 17 years for my attendance — it was first described in 1983. I figured it could wait another couple of hours.

And so we made our fifth visit to Mt Lewis in quest of the Chestnut-breasted Cuckoo, this time knowing that it had been seen not half an hour before. While Rog drove, I cued the tape. This time, this time surely we'd be lucky.

Alas, it was not to be. We found the spot, played the tape, scanned the rainforest. If wishing could produce a bird, we would have been smothered in Chestnut-breasted Cuckoos. As it was we saw no more Chestnut-breasted Cuckoos on Mt Lewis that morning than we had on every previous trip. Zilch. But no one can say we didn't try.

The Barred Cuckoo-Shrike was perhaps even more frustrating than the Chestnut-breasted Cuckoo, because we knew it was there. We could hear it calling. Carol, the resident guide at Kingfisher Park Birdwatchers Lodge, described the call as the start of the Laurel and Hardy theme tune. I thought it sounded like the tune kids play with their knuckles on the black notes of the piano:

Anyway, we'd been hearing the calls for days, before we found out what it was. We were never able to see the birds. It is not a common species, but it is very irritating to know it is present and not be able to tick it.

This bird used to be called the Yellow-eyed Cuckoo-Shrike. The new name is better because the bird is clearly barred and if seeing the bird is so difficult in the canopy of the rainforest, consider how likely you are to get a good look at the colour of its eye.

Perhaps the most frustrating of all my unticked birds was the Bush-hen, because I really believe I did catch a glimpse of it. It's a member of the rail family, smaller than a coot, and pretty nondescript according to all the photos I've seen.

Apparently it's very vocal and very obvious during the wet season when it's breeding. At other times it is difficult to see. We were advised that, if we were to see it, it would be by accident, along the grassy verges beside the road. Where, throughout the Atherton Tableland, we'd been seeing Buff-banded Rail. These gorgeous birds were remarkably common — I'd have gladly traded a few for one Bush-hen.

One evening at Kingfisher Park, we strolled to the river at platypus time (six-thirty). Chuck, another friendly Yank, was sitting quietly, watching the water through his scope, hoping to see a platypus. We conversed in whispers so as not to frighten any shy ornithorhynchus which might be lurking nearby, and admired the birds coming in for their evening sip and splash. Like all other American birdos we have met on our travels, he identified every species without hesitation. By contrast, when I was in America, I had difficulty distinguishing between the local Blackbirds and Cowbirds.

While Roger and Chuck concentrated on the platypus pool, I searched the grassy verge downstream. Although it was early evening, the light was still quite good — out of the rainforest anyway. Some sort of black bird emerged from the grass on the left bank and flew across the river. Neither Rog nor Chuck saw it: I couldn't yell out. In any case the bird disappeared so quickly there would not have been time. I reckon it was a Bush-hen. What else could it have been? A Scrubfowl would have trailed orange legs and this dark bird had no identifying features at all. If Chuck had seen it he would have identified it confidently, unerringly. But he only had eyes for his platypus. We left him to it and were almost as pleased as he was when he later reported his success.

Those birds (the Chestnut-breasted Cuckoo, the Barred Cuckoo-shrike and the Bush-hen) were frustrating because we ALMOST saw them — it was our fault we didn't. Many other species didn't even give us half a chance. We did our part all right. We deprived ourselves of sleep, tolerated March flies and heat and explored likely haunts rather than lounge by the pool with a beer. Did the birds respond to this attention? Did they appreciate our sacrifices? They did not.

Perhaps I expect too much. Am I the only person ever to visit Lacey Creek State Forest Park and be confronted by a male Southern Cassowary with three darling striped chicks, and have the gall to complain that I didn't see a White-eared Monarch? Am I alone in visiting the Mossman Golf Club in search of Double-eyed Fig Parrots and retire lamenting their absence, instead of admiring the Osprey on its nest on the nearby communications tower? Would other people resent the hours spent searching for Black-throated Finches (either black rumped or white rumped form) when they had seen instead Red-backed Button-quail?

On one of our many expeditions targeting Black-throated Finches, we discovered (quite by accident) the Mareeba Wetlands. My notes told me to look for drinking pools along Pickford Road at Biboohra, seven kilometres north of Mareeba. We found Pickford Road and followed it to the wetlands, which had been opened very recently, and was mentioned in only one of my guide books. Interestingly, we had seen a brochure advertising the place, featuring David Bellamy, and on the basis of the brochure we had decided not to visit. It seemed to us to be a pleasant spot for a family outing — somewhere to go canoeing rather than birdwatching. How wrong we were. The volunteer guide was extremely helpful. He chatted about concerns that Sarus Cranes now outnumber Brolgas. Apparently Brolga numbers are stable, but Sarus Cranes are increasing rapidly. Sarus Cranes were first identified in Queensland in 1967. Like Cattle

We saw lots of Brolga in north Queensland, and few Sarus Cranes, notwithstanding concerns that Sarus Crane numbers are increasing rapidly.

Egret, these birds arrived in Australia after humans had replaced the natural environment with farms. He told us that there are populations of both forms of Black-throated Finches on the reserve. We admired the caged Gouldian Finches being bred to re-populate the reserve. These gorgeous little birds really are as spectacular as they appear on film. We watched a Black Kite catch a fish — something we didn't know they did. We knew they'd eat just about anything, alive or dead, so it shouldn't have taken us by surprise.

The Mareeba Wetlands is a spot that I'd recommend to any birdo — despite the fact that we left without seeing any Black-throated Finches, either black rumped or white rumped. I did flush a Red-backed Button-quail, we had lovely views of Comb-crested Jacana and romantic sightings of Brolgas coming in to roost at sunset. We arrived too late to join the guided tour. If the knowledge of the volunteer we spoke to is any indication, the tour would be well worthwhile. When we were there the entry fee was $7.70 per person and worth every cent, with or without the Black-throated Finch.

12

...Perfect the next

MORE BIRDS OF QUEENSLAND

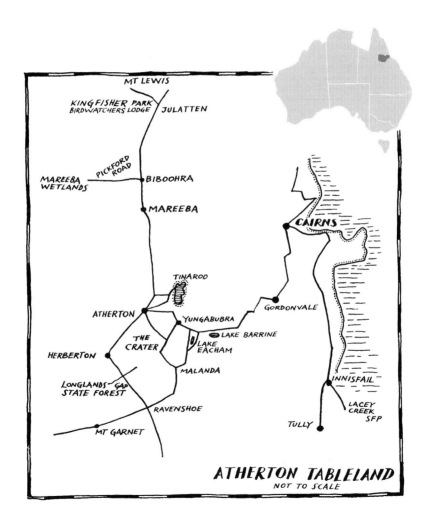

ATHERTON TABLELAND
NOT TO SCALE

Having failed to see Gouldian and Black-throated Finches, having missed out on Red-browed Pardalotes, Slaty-backed Thornbills and Rufous-crowned Emu-wren, with no sign of Letter-winged Kites or Grey Falcon, instead of wallowing in self-pity, I set myself what I thought would be a manageable target of seeing all 13 of the species endemic to Queensland's wet tropics. I'd seen some before, but I decided I'd try to tick all 13 on this trip. They are:

Lesser Sooty Owl
Fernwren
Atherton Scrubwren
Mountain Thornbill
Macleay's Honeyeater
Bridled Honeyeater
Grey-headed Robin
Chowchilla
Bower's Shrike-thrush
Pied Monarch
Victoria's Riflebird
Tooth-billed Bowerbird
Golden Bowerbird.

When I saw seven of them on the first day, I thought maybe I had set my sights too low. Wisely, before I revised my target, I decided to tick all 13 species and it's just as well I did, because some of those birds were extremely elusive.

Australian Brush-Turkeys were common and friendly throughout the Tableland.

Quite fittingly, the first of my target species we saw was the most common. The Grey-headed Robin is aptly named. It is confiding, like most robins. These dear little birds seemed to be everywhere in the rainforest. There should be a word to describe the way robins sit sideways on the trunk of a tree. Instead of having their feet parallel horizontally on the ground, they are parallel vertically on the trunk. How about 'vertisit'? It's a habit that seems peculiar to robins. Often we'd go for a walk, especially in the middle of the day, and return having seen nothing other than Grey-headed Robins. We saw them every day we spent on the Atherton Tablelands — along with Australian Brush-turkey, Spotted Catbird, Black Kite and Cattle Egret. And, unfortunately, Indian Mynah, which were far more common this time than on our previous trips to far north Queensland.

The second bird that I saw on the list was Bower's Shrike-thrush. He drew attention to himself by his musical thrush-like call. He was most uncooperatively sitting high up in the canopy, and I strained my neck trying to get a good look. I could see his streaked, cinnamon breast and grey back and head. The field guides mention that he has a short tail, but anyone who is able to judge the length of a bird's tail when it's in the top of the rainforest canopy and the birdo is 50 feet below, either has phenomenally good eyesight, or the imagination of an author of a guide-book.

I lowered my gaze to give my neck muscles a rest and almost immediately saw both the Atherton Scrubwren and the Mountain Thornbill. This was too good to be true!

I was familiar with the Large-billed Scrubwren. I'd had excellent sightings at Tarra Bulga National Park in Victoria when I was searching for Pilotbirds. The Atherton Scrubwren reminded me very much of its large-billed cousin. We saw them many times over the next few days and judged them to be very common.

I wasn't quite so confident of my identification of the Mountain Thornbill. I was happy it was a thornbill, but precisely which thornbill it was I couldn't say for certain. I was reassured when I checked the bird books to find that there is only one thornbill in this part of the world. The next day at Longlands Gap I had better views and could even see its white iris. I did not see any green or yellow on its plumage, but apparently its colouration varies greatly. To me it looked grey above and buff below. There again, perhaps it's my ageing eyesight.

Spectacled Monarchs were common throughout the Tableland, but I wanted to see Pied (and, if I am honest, White-eared as well). The Pied was on my list of endemic species, so it was a must.

The rainforest walk where I saw the first five of the birds on my Atherton Tableland wishlist.

The White-eared was supposed to be easily seen at Lacey Creek State Forest Park, where most people go to see the Southern Cassowary. I told Rog that we were looking for Macleay's Honeyeater, but I doubt he was fooled. We had, after all, seen Macleay's Honeyeater on previous trips, and I was unlikely to take us out of our way to see a bird we'd seen before, notwithstanding my self-imposed game of ticking all the endemic species. I'd been told that Pied Monarchs like to hide within the canopy of a tree, while the White-eared flit around above the tree-tops. On this basis, I figured that White-eared would be easier to see.

My neck still sore from craning to see Bower's Shrike-thrush, I climbed a hill to a vantage point where I could look straight across at the canopy. There was a black and white monarch in the tree. I couldn't believe my luck. I had a good look. His large white collar unmistakably went all around his neck. It was undoubtedly a Pied Monarch. I wondered if they were more common than I'd thought. As it turned out, that was the only Pied Monarch I saw on the trip.

The Bridled Honeyeater performed on cue in the carpark at The Crater.

Lewin's Honeyeater, too, frequented the carpark at The Crater.

Indeed, it is the only Pied Monarch I have ever seen. I have not yet seen a White-eared, despite visiting all its publicised haunts.

It was when I saw that Pied Monarch, the fifth tick on my list of 13, that I thought I'd set myself too easy a task.

I turned to suggest to Rog that we might cut our stay short and spend some more time on the Cairns Esplanade (renowned for excellent sightings of waders), when I noticed some Wompoo Fruit-Doves feeding in a fruiting tree. They really are gorgeous birds, quite incongruous, as if a child were colouring in a pigeon in a colouring book as imaginatively as possible. What fashion designer would think to coordinate purple and yellow with bright green? And as for their ridiculous call, it's a joke on all bird watchers. No bird could be taken seriously making a noise like that. Except perhaps a Trumpet Manucode. It sounds more like a frog than a bird. The person who named them 'Wompoo', thinking that was the sound they make, had hearing as deficient as my eyesight.

In the tree with the Wompoo Fruit-Doves that had caught my eye was a female Victoria's Riflebird. Tick number six. This really was going to be too easy.

There was one (only one) bird I was sure that we'd tick easily. My notes assured me that the Bridled Honeyeater feeds from the hand at the carpark at The Crater. Indeed I can confirm that it does. Or, it did in September 2000. Right on cue, this obedient little bird did exactly what the guide books claimed it did. Having admired (and photographed) the honeyeater, we dutifully did the walk to The Crater. Along the way, there are several information signs about the geology of the area, if that is of interest. It being school holidays, the walk was very popular. The scenery was pretty but there were too many happy, noisy people for good birding. As far as I could tell, no one was pausing to read the signs. I wished I'd stayed in the carpark with the friendly honeyeaters.

I now had seven birds on my first day and was brimming with confidence, a very dangerous attribute for a bird-watcher. I had not allowed for the elusive Fernwren in my assessment. This is an extremely difficult bird to see. We spent six days looking for it before we resorted to the tape recorder and found it immediately.

On one Fernwren hunt, I saw a small black tyre someone had nailed on a post about 30 feet up in the air. Now why would anyone do that? I asked myself. I looked again and it moved. It was not a tyre at all. It was a male Victoria's Riflebird displaying. Rog was a hundred yards away. What should I do? Watch the bird or go and get Roger? I compromised. I had a good look and then hurried off to tell my husband what I had found. We returned together and the bird was still there, sitting on his perch, but he seemed to have lost interest in imitating a tyre and moved his wings only half-heartedly.

I've seen film of riflebirds displaying but nothing could have prepared me for the magnificent spectacle I saw that day. It was literally breathtaking. We returned to the same spot several times (it was here we eventually saw the Fernwren) hoping that the post was a favourite perch for the riflebird. However, we did not see it again.

Am I the only person ever to visit Lacey Creek State Forest Park and lament the lack of White-eared Monarchs, instead of celebrating sightings of Cassowarys?

I saw the Tooth-billed Bowerbird at the same place, high up in the canopy. I was attracted by the call, which was rich and unusual. The bird was extremely difficult to see, very high in the tree, hidden by leaves and branches and constantly hopping around. I also thought its call was ventriloquial, although this is not reported in the field guides. Eventually my patience paid off and I got good enough sightings for an unequivocal identification. It was an unremarkable looking bird, with a striated front and a thick stubby bill. Later I saw them again, at more sensible heights, but I didn't ever hear such a vocal repertoire again.

The Chowchilla was more difficult to see than I'd expected. We looked mornings and evenings in high rainforest, but saw few ground-dwelling birds anywhere. Despite being assured that Chowchillas are easily seen at The Crater and Mt Lewis, this was not our experience. My notes also said that

This beautiful Black Butcherbird liked having his photo taken.

Chowchilla were usually seen in small groups, but we (eventually) saw just one pair. It was at Wabunga Wayemba Rainforest Walkabout (otherwise known as Charmillon Creek Rainforest Walk) in Ravenshoe State Forest. We went back to this spot again and again and, while the carpark at The Crater overflowed with tourists, we never encountered one other person at Ravenshoe State Forest.

The Chowchilla were not very cooperative, walking slowly away from us into the dark rainforest. However, I was able to see their pale eye rings and the female's orange throat.

I had now seen nine of the 13 endemic species, and I knew that Macleay's Honeyeater would not be too difficult. We'd seen it before. I told Rog that was our reason for visiting Lacey Creek State Forest Park (where I was really looking for White-eared Monarchs and instead encountered an endless stream of vicious march flies and three darling striped Cassowary chicks). I ticked Macleay's Honeyeater at the picnic grounds at Henrietta Creek, in between photographing a Black Butcherbird. We'd gone to Henrietta Creek looking for Double-eyed Fig-Parrots. Later, at Kingfisher Park Birdwatchers Lodge, Macleay's was the most common of the eight species of honeyeater we saw at the several birdfeeders in the garden.

Only three species to go and time was running out. I knew that I would never see a Lesser Sooty Owl without assistance and I needed advice about where to look for Golden Bowerbird — most of the guide books were remarkably coy about this, and I'd by now lost faith in the one that gave directions. As for the elusive Fernwren, we decided to resort to the tape recorder and, as mentioned above, achieved immediate success.

We thought the rainforest at Ravenshoe State Forest was a likely spot for Fernwren. This location also had the added attraction of no people. So we cued the tape and toddled off, not really expecting success. Everyone seemed to agree that this was a very difficult bird to see. We chose the edge of a patch of dense rainforest where we'd seen and heard absolutely nothing. Rog held the tape recorder and I held my breath. After about one minute, there was a response to the tape. We couldn't believe our ears. Some people describe the call as morse code. What we heard was a pretty whistle. The bird came closer and closer to investigate the intruder on its territory. Although the undergrowth was dense, it came within a couple of metres and we both had excellent views. He sat under twigs and branches and put his head back and sang his little heart out, pro-claiming this territory as his. It was a tiny little olive-brown bird with an obvious white eyebrow and white throat with a black band across his chest. We turned off the tape and looked our fill, then tiptoed away. The brave little bird had defended his territory very courageously.

Eleven down, two to go. As advised by the guide-books, we 'sought local knowledge' as to the whereabouts of the Golden Bowerbird. We were directed to Longlands Gap — to a spot we'd visited previously and had such lovely views of the Mountain Thornbill.

My camera with its 300 mm zoom lens is very heavy and I don't like using a flash. That's my story anyway. Foolishly, I didn't take my camera when we went looking for the Golden Bowerbird. I didn't know how far we'd have to walk. In truth, these are mere excuses. I did not expect to see the bird at all. It was September — a little early for the bird to be seen reliably at its bower. This is done from October to January. I thought I'd have to be happy with 11 out of 13 — not bad really. As good as 85 per cent. Clearly honours material.

We walked along the well-worn track that many birdos had trod before. We saw Yellow-throated Scrubwren — their beauty can never be spoiled by their prevalence — and Sulphur-crested Cockatoos cried harshly at us as they flew overhead. We walked quietly and slowly, listening for any songs or movements. We explored a few side tracks (of which there were several) until they disappeared into the rainforest. We walked until the track itself petered out, overgrown with lantana. We were forced to turn back, on this occasion not really disappointed, because our expectations had not been high. I decided to explore one more sidetrack and crept soundlessly into the rainforest. It was quite quiet and very beautiful in the dappled sunlight and I stood still to enjoy it. Suddenly a large golden bird landed on a branch beside me. Instinctively my hand went to my mouth to stifle my cries of joy. The bird looked at me and I looked at him. I turned and beckoned Roger urgently.

We saw Grey-headed Robins every time we went into the rainforest.

Together we stood enthralled by this gorgeous creature. He seemed to be just as interested in us as we were in him. Then he serenaded us. For about five minutes he demonstrated his repertoire. Right beside us it was very loud and most distinctive: a mixture of full rich notes and strange whirring rattles. No one has ever had better sightings of a Golden Bowerbird. The bird got bored long before we did and flew away, immediately invisible in the rainforest. I had now seen all 10 Australian bowerbirds.

Elated, we returned to the car, my joy only slightly diminished by the fact that I hadn't had my camera with me. We returned to the spot on two other occasions with the camera, and discovered that we had been very close to a bower. The bower of the Golden Bowerbird is different from the avenue construction of other bowerbirds. It is called a maypole, but when complete over many years is in fact two piles of twigs with a horizontal perch between them. This bower was well on the way. On one visit, we stood quietly, patiently waiting for 40 minutes expecting the bird to arrive to check on his bower. All I saw for my trouble was a Grey-headed Robin. Rog did better — he saw a tree kangaroo. Once years before, at Lamington National Park, I sat by a Satin Bowerbird's bower waiting to photograph the bird. It returned regularly about every 20 minutes. I thought there was no good reason for the Golden Bowerbird to be less diligent. Except that it was only September, and he was supposed to tend his bower from October to January.

Only after these two later fruitless trips did we truly appreciate how special our sighting had been. It is a rare bird, difficult to see and one of Australia's most beautiful.

Twelve out of 13.

The only way to see a Lesser Sooty Owl is to be shown by an expert. Carol, the resident guide at Kingfisher Park Birdwatchers Lodge, is an expert.

We called in at the lodge on our way to Daintree in the hope of seeing a Red-necked Crake. It was the middle of the day, not the best time for birding. We saw a Noisy Pitta, a Russet-tailed Thrush and several Emerald Doves and we heard,

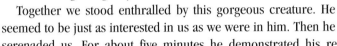

but did not see, Barred Cuckoo-Shrikes. We were about to leave when the Macleay's Honeyeaters at the birdfeeders attracted my attention and I walked into the garden shelter. I stood for a few minutes admiring the honeyeaters. Another feeder was overflowing with Red-browed Finches. Then a Red-necked Crake walked right in front of me! Rog and I both admired him appreciatively before he returned to the undergrowth.

We had to go to Daintree. We had booked (months before because it was school holidays) to do a river cruise with Chris Dahlberg. This is essential for any birdo in the area.

As we drove to Daintree, I lamented the fact that we hadn't stayed at Julatten. I couldn't help feeling we'd have seen more birds if we had. We'd made our choice of accommodation while in Melbourne, based mainly on information on the internet, thinking, mistakenly as it turned out, that we should book in advance because of the school holidays. Everywhere we went there were vacancy signs displayed.

We did our Chris Dahlberg tour in the pouring rain. Once again, I hadn't packed raincoats. I'd put in an umbrella just in case. It was brand new, and when we reached for it, it wouldn't open. We were soaked to the skin, sitting on wet towels in his open boat, but I would not have missed that trip for anything. Notwithstanding the weather, we saw 35 species of birds (including two new lifers for me — Channel-billed Cuckoo and Gould's Bronze-Cuckoo). Most frustratingly, we did not see the Double-eyed Fig-Parrot that flitted overhead at about the speed of sound. We did see Spectacled Flyingfox and a very beautiful green tree snake — just the second snake we had seen on the trip. The first one was an Amethyst Python in the ceiling of the women's toilets at Lake Tinaroo. I found it quite distracting.

Chris has an encylopaedic knowledge of the wildlife of the area and it was fascinating to listen to him. He told me that I sat in the very seat that Nicholas Day had sat on, and I wondered what I was supposed to say to this apparent honour. It didn't stop the rain being wet.

After the tour I handed Chris my wishlist and sought his advice. He shook his head discouragingly, said I had some rare birds on my list and suggested the only way to see the Lesser Sooty Owl was to go to Kingfisher Park Birdwatchers Lodge.

We were disappointed in our accommodation at Daintree. It now seems churlish to find fault with it. Apart from the exorbitant prices and the plastic smiles and forced niceness of all the staff, it really was very good. The food was excellent, the service was prompt and the setting was perfect. The truth was there were no new birds for me at Daintree.

So we cut our stay short and returned to Kingfisher Park Birdwatchers Lodge, which we had visited very briefly on our way north. With her partner Andrew, Carol was minding the lodge while the owner was on holiday. Like so many Americans, this young English couple put us to shame with their prodigious knowledge of Australian wildlife. Yes, they went spotlighting every night and usually saw the Lesser Sooty Owl. Except they weren't going tonight.

We looked at our maps and calculated distances and decided that we could stay at Julatten two nights. That gave the Lesser Sooty Owl just one chance to perform.

We spent that day and the next looking unsuccessfully for Bush-hen, Superb Fruit-Dove, Chestnut-breasted Cuckoo, Barred Cuckoo-Shrike and White-eared Monarch. Instead we saw Yellow-breasted Boatbill, Fairy Gerygone, Red-backed Fairy-wren, Noisy Pitta and oodles of Forest Kingfishers, Metallic Starlings and White-rumped Swiftlets. All lovely birds but not new ticks.

The pressure was on for the Lesser Sooty Owl. I felt (rather peevishly) that I'd missed out on seeing so much that I was entitled to see the owl.

That evening, a group of us gathered at twenty-five past six precisely, several of us with torches, all of us eager to see just one bird. Carol and Andrew, led us to the tree where the owls had nested and told us that the male had been killed on the road. There were two young, still being fed by their mother. We all stood anxiously waiting for them to appear. Carol heard the call of a Barn Owl ('kshsh') at the far side of the clearing and we all unhappily trudged after her. I overheard one man with an English accent say to his wife: 'Bloody long way to come to see a Barn Owl.' My sentiments exactly. All any of us wanted to see was a Lesser Sooty Owl.

Like me with my tape recordings, Carol was reluctant to call the owls and confuse the youngsters. At six-thirty I admired her attitude; at seven-thirty I was not so sure.

Carol and Andrew shone torches into well-known crooks and crannies to show us various frogs, spiders, possums and a platypus. I felt sorry for the little creatures for whom this was a nightly ritual. The group of us looked politely at everything we were shown and listened attentively to Carol's words of wisdom.

Then Andrew caught a cane toad and I assumed we were in for a lecture on the foolish introduction of these exotic amphibians from Hawaii in 1935 to control cane beetles in the interest of the sugarcane industry. I thought Carol would tell us that the toads did not eat cane beetles, bred rapidly and their toxic glands killed many native animals that preyed on them. But Carol did not deliver the expected address. What she said shocked and dismayed me. She said that cane toads were now part of the Australian environment and pointed out that Macleay's Water Snake ate them with impunity. Furthermore, she said, many native birds, such as White Ibis, have now learnt to eat cane toads, turning them on their backs and avoiding the poisonous glands. There is no point in trying to eradicate cane toads now, said Carol, and with that, Andrew let the animal go. I was horrified. Cane toads do not belong in Australia, I wanted to scream at these two poms. Was it politeness that stopped me from debating the issue with her, or was I simply avoiding an argument until I'd seen my Lesser Sooty Owl?

I don't know whether Carol felt vibes of mutiny but very soon after the release of the cane toad she relented and uttered a perfect imitation of a falling bomb — the call of the Lesser Sooty Owl. To my ear it is identical to the call of the Sooty Owl. Little wonder the two were thought to be conspecific until very recently.

The reaction was immediate. Two young owls called in response and were captured in the spotlight. They were just as beautiful as the photos I'd seen.

Everyone was delighted. Carol was a hero and the young owls were confused.

The call of a young Lesser Sooty Owl resembles the call of a Barn Owl but it is more drawn out ('kshshshshsh'). When the young owls heard the falling bomb they believed their mother had arrived with food.

So on the last night of our stay in Queensland's wet tropics we HAD achieved our 13 endemic species. I felt absurdly pleased with myself. After all, it was Carol who had made it possible. I almost forgave her misguided attitude to cane toads. Almost.

And so on to the next challenge: the Eungella Honeyeater (pronounced Young Galah).

There are 67 species of honeyeater in Australia. Having seen the Bridled Honeyeater at The Crater, we'd now seen all of them except three: the Green-backed Honeyeater, which is found in a tiny area on the east coast of Cape York; the Black-eared Miner, which we'd spent one whole hot day pursuing in South Australia; and the Eungella Honeyeater, which also has a ridiculously small range in the Eungella rainforests near Mackay.

This honeyeater was discovered in 1961 and not described until 1983. Until then it was thought to be a Bridled Honeyeater, and a quick look at the illustrations in any field guide will explain why. They are both small olive-brown honeyeaters with a pale mark along the gape and under the eye and a white mark above the eye. The differences are: the Eungella has a streaked breast; the mark under the Bridled's beak is yellow, while the Eungella's is cream and the Eungella has a white cheek patch, lacking in the Bridled. Now if a Eungella Honeyeater would like to eat from my hand as the Bridled did at The Crater, I might be able to observe all these points. However, if it flits about from flower to flower high up in the rainforest, it could well be another story.

Our chances of seeing a Eungella Honeyeater seemed to be diminishing the closer we got to its range. In Melbourne I'd been very hopeful. Surely, to see the Eungella Honeyeater, you go to Eungella. But we'd spoken to many birdos on our travels and no one we'd spoken to had seen it. Several people (including the clever Chris Dahlberg) had been to Eungella on more than one occasion looking for the bird and still been unsuccessful. What hope did we have with our track record? If we couldn't see Chestnut-breasted Cuckoos or Barred Cuckoo-shrikes, why should we be any more successful with a Eungella Honeyeater?

Andrew and Carol at Julatten told us that they had seen Eungella Honeyeaters at Mackay. Andrew said that the bird is so difficult to see because it moves around according to what is flowering. It may not be at Eungella at all! We'd need local knowledge.

We'd booked to stay at Broken River Resort, which is located in the Eungella National Park. I decided to chat to the park ranger and, if that didn't work, contact someone in Mackay.

It's 900 kilometres from Julatten to Eungella and we set off with our confidence ebbing. If all these experienced birdos (people who HAD seen Barred Cuckoo-shrikes and Chestnut-breasted Cuckoos) couldn't see Eungella Honeyeaters were we wasting our time? It was a long drive back to Melbourne.

Should we cut our losses, forget about Broken River and set out for home now?

We spent the night in Townsville and the next morning I was far more optimistic. We had the advantage over those who hadn't seen the honeyeaters, because we knew it moved around. We'd just have to find someone to ask.

We had morning coffee at Muller's Lagoon at Bowen where the birdlife was prolific. We sipped our coffee watching a Black Swan with four fluffy cygnets. As well as a large number of waterbirds, there were some well-named Noisy Friarbirds and some equally loud Rainbow Lorikeets, Figbirds and Blue-faced Honeyeaters. Much more sedate were the Crested Pigeons, which are one of my favourite birds. Could anyone stay in a bad mood watching these comical creatures?

Then Rog and I saw a Crested Pigeon splashing about in the water. It was not having a bath. It was trying to escape from a large black corvid — most likely an Australian Raven, I think. The corvid was persistent, pecking at the pigeon, and soon had its prey in its claws. Rog said he'd seen the corvid chasing the pigeon earlier. It seemed an extraordinarily large bird for the corvid to attack: the pigeon was more than half the size of the corvid. I rushed to get my camera which I'd left in the car but by the time I returned, all that was left at the scene of the crime were a few pathetic feathers.

I didn't think much of the road to Broken River. It was narrow and windy and declared unfit for caravans. However, it was deemed fit for milk tankers (much larger than many caravans), as the surrounding countryside was predominantly dairy farms.

As soon as we arrived at the resort I told the receptionist that we'd come to see the local honeyeater and asked where to go for advice.

'And what honeyeater would that be?' she asked and my hopes fell.

'The Eungella Honeyeater,' I replied and she corrected my pronunciation. Then she said that they were only present when the pandanus vine flowered and even then they were very rare. I think she used the term 'hens' teeth'. She'd seen one once four years ago at her sister's place and that was a long way away. Then she prattled on about canoeing and platypus and various walks, but I wasn't listening.

'I'll ask the ranger,' I said, rudely interrupting her explanation of breakfast arrangements.

'Simon won't know anything,' she said very cheerfully. 'He's only just arrived. Anyway there won't be anyone at the office until half past three.'

The National Parks Information Office was a short walk across the river from the resort. On the dot of three-thirty I was there, only to be greeted by a large hand-written sign: 'OFFICE NOT IN ATTENDANCE TODAY'. I looked at it in disbelief. For 17 years I'd wanted to come to Eungella to see the honeyeater. I'd booked this accommodation seven months ago and planned the holiday around it. Now we'd negotiated that dreadful entrance road and come all this way to be greeted by a cheerful receptionist who told us that we had no hope of seeing our bird, and an unmanned national parks office. As I stood there, I heard a child speaking to its father and being instructed in a hushed voice to talk softly.

Nothing ventured, nothing gained. In a loud voice, I addressed the hand-written sign.

'I know that the office is unattended today, but could I just ask one simple question? I've come a long way to see a Eungella Honeyeater.'

A young man with a pleasant smile and wearing a National Parks uniform emerged, followed by a small boy.

'Well, you couldn't have come at a better time,' he told me. 'They're all over the place right now. They're here in the carpark in the callistemons. They're in the camping ground. They're in Schumann Road off Dalrymple Road in the Eungella township.'

I could have hugged him.

'You'll hear their call,' the wonderful man from National Parks told me.

'I've seen them,' volunteered his son.

'We've got them in our front yard at home,' said this exemplary father. 'We've had the experts up doing a survey.'

Funny how your mood can change so quickly. I rushed back to get Rog, barely noticing the squillion Scarlet Honeyeaters or the kangaroo on the lawn. We played the tape to familiarise ourselves with the call, then systematically examined the flocks of honeyeaters in the callistemons. Most of them were Scarlet, but there were also Lewin's and Dusky and others I didn't identify. We could definitely hear the Eungella's call. The birds were moving fast from flower to flower with no consideration for how difficult they made identification. But, yes! That one there was definitely a Eungella! Look at his facial markings. See the white mark on its cheek? We both got good if fleeting views of Eungella Honeyeaters. It had taken less than half an hour!

The next morning was overcast and there were very few birds around. We rose early and again examined the callistemons in the carpark. Nothing. Not even Scarlets, which had been so numerous the day before. We walked through the camping area, then drove to Schumann's Road. No luck anywhere. It occurred to me that if we'd arrived one day later we wouldn't have seen the bird. As it was, it was a most satisfying tick, knowing that so many others had failed.

When we booked out, Rog told the receptionist of our success. Rather than share our joy, she simply said we were mistaken.

'They only come when the pandanus vines are flowering,' she said with finality.

Fleetingly, I considered inviting her opinion of the differences between the Eungella and Bridled Honeyeater (or, even Lewin's and the Yellow-spotted, or, for that matter, a Eungella Honeyeater and a Sarus Crane), but with the superiority of a birdo who's just ticked a difficult bird, wisely I kept my counsel.

13

Palm cockatoos at Pajinka

BIRDS OF CAPE YORK

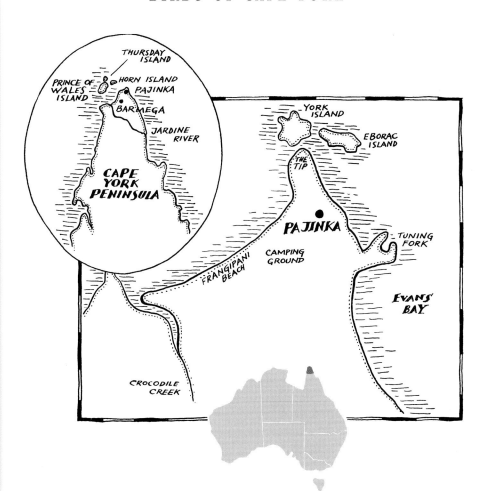

Pajinka Wilderness Lodge is 400 metres from the tippy-top of Cape York. Although there is no air conditioning, the accommodation is comfortable, the food is very good, the hospitality is unsurpassed and the weather is hot. Very hot. At least it is if you're foolish enough to visit in November as we did. Of course the best time to visit is January, when the weather is worse, but the New Guinea migrants are present — migrants like the spectacular Red-bellied Pitta and the gorgeous Buff-breasted Paradise-Kingfisher.

These migrants seem to be a bit of a movable target. When we on the Atherton Tablelands in September, we were told that Paradise-Kingfishers would arrive in November. When we were on Cape York in November, we were told they would arrive in January. Chestnut-breasted Cuckoos that were seen in September on Mt Lewis (but not by us!) were not present on Cape York until January. I can only assume that the birds arrive in different places at different times, even though logic would suggest that they'd arrive in Cape York first, not last. Reading the various texts in an attempt to make head and tail of all this, the thing that has struck me the most is how little is known about some of these species, for example, the Chestnut-breasted Cuckoo. Its eggs and nestlings have not been described and its hosts are not known for sure, although there is evidence that the Tropical Scrubwren may be host at least some of the time.

The only solution to this problem that I can come up with is that Rog and I should do another trip to Cape York, in January. We can put up with the weather. We managed last time.

We visited Pajinka in 1994, years before we saw the Red-necked Crake at Julatten, the Lemon-bellied Flycatcher on her nest at Darwin, and Beach Stone-curlews in the Kimberleys.

We flew from Cairns in a Dash 8 which had a particularly relaxed atmosphere. The plane was full of barefooted islanders. Without apology or explanation, a huge parcel occupied our allocated seats, so we sat at the back. The schedule showed us stopping at Horn Island on the way to Jacky Jacky airport at Barmega. But the tarmac at Horn Island was being resurfaced and the pilot was concerned about the weight of the plane, so he decided to drop off the Barmega passengers first. Consequently we missed out on a glimpse of Horn Island and arrived an hour early. As we disembarked, we were greeted by a blast of hot air. Not surprisingly there was no one there to meet us. There was no air conditioned Golden Wing lounge to wait in. In fact there were no airport staff or facilities at all. One very basic building provided a little shade but nothing else. A group of happy black children with wide infectious smiles had come to watch us arrive. When the plane took off again, their day's entertainment was over and they had nothing to do. We had a long, hot wait for our transport to arrive.

Eventually Chris, the resident naturalist at Pajinka, came to pick us up, bringing his delightful daughter, Christobel, with him for the ride. Chris had just returned from paternity leave and Greg, a young student from Rockhampton, had been filling in for him in his absence. Greg was nominally a botanist, but in fact was an all-round naturalist. He was about to commence his PhD studying Amethyst Python on Millman Island. These snakes fast for nine months of the year then gorge themselves on Pied Imperial Pigeons that come across from New Guinea to nest. Now Chris was back and Greg was staying on for a few days so we had two guides all to ourselves, for it turned out that, initially at least, we were the only guests at the lodge.

I gave Chris my wishlist — 26 species. He immediately crossed off five: you must visit Adolphus Island for the Pale White-eye he said, and then he crossed off the migrants: Chestnut-breasted Cuckoo, Buff-breasted Paradise Kingfisher, Red-bellied Pitta and Black-winged Monarch.

I wish I had quizzed Chris about this at the time, but I was concentrating on the remaining 21 species. Three he classified as rare: the Red-necked Crake, the White-faced Robin and the Northern Scrub-robin. Two others he told me were present but were difficult to see: the Yellow-billed Kingfisher and the Yellow-legged Flycatcher. Another four could be seen at Jardine: Yellow, Brown-backed and White-streaked Honeyeaters and the Black-backed Butcherbird. He estimated that we had an 80 per cent chance of seeing the remaining 12. Twelve is good, I thought, but 16 is better. Could we fit in a trip to Jardine?

That evening we went spotlighting. We saw Papuan Frogmouths and a Barking Owl. We heard blossom bats chattering in the flowering eucalypts and Marbled Frogmouths calling and bill clacking but we did not see them. Chris picked up a huge Children's Python — at least a metre long: the average length is supposed to be 75 centimetres according to the textbooks.

The next morning we were up at five-thirty for a six o'clock start to enjoy the dawn chorus with Chris. We saw four new species before breakfast! Lemon-bellied Flycatcher, Tawny-breasted and Yellow-spotted Honeyeaters and Magnificent Riflebirds. We watched a Cuscous eating the poisonous fruit of the *Antiarus toxicaria*. Chris was fascinated that it could digest the toxic fruit.

We saw a colony of Metallic Starlings' nests in Morton Bay Ash (*Eucalyptus tessellaris*). Chris explained that the birds select this tree because snakes can't navigate the smooth trunk.

*Metalic Starling nest in Morton Bay Ash (*Eucalyptus tessellaris*) because snakes cannot navigate the smooth bark.*

At Pajinka, the middle of the day is spent waiting for the heat to dissipate, occupying yourself with whatever distraction you can find to take your mind momentarily off the temperature. I don't know how anyone can choose to live in these conditions.

The buffet lunch was served from twelve-thirty till two. We knew we were the only guests and arrived at one-fifteen. Most of the food had gone! People appeared from everywhere as soon as the food was put out. The 'diningroom' was an awning between two buildings. I suppose some of the multitude were staff. The identity of the remainder is an abiding mystery. One friend we learnt to look out for at mealtimes was Precious, a Northern Bandicoot that called in occasionally, quite unperturbed by people.

Chris took us out again that afternoon. A tree hide had been constructed so that birds in the rainforest canopy could be viewed on their own level. Chris suggested we climb this daunting structure. Foolishly believing that people wouldn't go to the trouble of building such a hide, unless it provided good views of something, I climbed the 12-metre vertical ladder. Wisely, Roger did not. Later we learned that the ladder had fallen down the year before! It was a steep and sweaty climb. Chris kindly carried my camera for me. When we reached the canopy the only visible life was Roger standing below looking very smug.

When I climbed down from that great height and got my land legs back, we started to see birds. We were frilled to see a Frilled Monarch, a funny looking black and white flycatcher with a blue bill and eye-ring. The Yellow-breasted Boatbill is just as extraordinary as it seems in the birdbooks. Its bill looks as if some amateur busybody interfered with its creation. This is one bird that is appropriately named: its breast is sunshine yellow and its bill is definitely boat-shaped.

We had good sightings of the Palm Cockatoo.

That afternoon we had Palm Cockatoos in our sights. Chris knew all the likely spots. He could do a fair imitation of most of the local bird calls and had the Palm Cockatoo's call perfected.

Looking back now it seems all too easy. Go to Cape York, get yourself a knowledgeable guide and see the Palm Cockatoo. For see it we did. We had excellent views. But it took hours of hot searching. There were no Palm Cockatoos sitting obediently in the first clearing we visited and they did not respond to Chris' first calls.

There is something very special about black cockatoos. They are stunning birds. And Palm Cockatoos are the biggest and the best. They have as much character as any bird. The Latin name *Probosciger aterrimus*, very black nose, tells only half the story. The first thing you notice is the spiky hairdo, then perhaps the red facial skin, then the unnaturally large bill. It is called a Palm Cockatoo because it eats the young tender shoots and fruit of palm trees. It uses its strong bill to crack nuts, including the hard nuts of the nonda plum.

That evening we were joined at dinner by an Irish couple, escapees from a very cramped and bumpy two-week 4WD tour of Cape York. They decided to treat themselves to a night of luxury at Pajinka, and the next morning they joined us on our early walk with Chris and Greg. We were rewarded with Tropical

Scrubwren and Trumpet Manucode. Manucodes make the most extraordinary noise; it doesn't sound anything like a trumpet to me. It's more like a cross between the mating call of a bullfrog and someone vigorously vomiting .

When we returned to the lodge, Rog made himself comfortable on our balcony with a cold beer. The Irish couple were going to look at the bower of a Fawn-breasted Bowerbird, and invited me to tag along. There was no respite from the heat so I figured I might as well be out in it. Greg had provided directions of how to find the bower and the nearby hide, and strict instructions not to go any closer to the bower than the hide. It was far too hot for lugging a camera around, so I left it in our cabin. The three of us walked along Frangipani Beach, the heat reflecting off the sand, while we searched desperately for anything to take our minds off the temperature. A pair of Lesser Frigatebirds entertained us for a while. It took us exactly 60 hot minutes to reach the hide. My first thought was that it had been built in the wrong spot. It was very difficult to view the bower from the hide. Now I understood the instruction to go no closer. It was very tempting to sneak just a little nearer. Out there in the wilderness, who would know? We kept each other honest and were rewarded for our hot walk and integrity by the bird arriving almost immediately and giving us a good look. Why didn't I take my camera? It looked very similar to a Great Bowerbird, perhaps a little smaller, and its breast was buff not grey. The bower was similar in construction to others of the avenue variety, green was his choice of colour for his carefully selected treasures.

On the hot walk back, I concentrated on congratulating myself for having seen 11 new species in 48 hours, and repressing thoughts of the photos I didn't have. I knew I would not be doing that hellish walk again.

After lunch we set off again with Chris, to show our Irish visitors Palm Cockatoos. We repeated yesterday's steps, following Chris through the scrub, while he imitated cockatoo calls. Eventually three Palm Cockatoos flew overhead, giving just a fleeting glimpse. That was the best our Irish friends were to have. Rog and I appreciated then how lucky we'd been to get such good views the day before.

A White-lipped Tree Frog sat on our bathroom window that evening and watched me count my sandfly bites. I had at least 50 on each hand. Rog had about 200 on each leg, but he's used to bites. I'd never had sandfly bites before and I was not reacting well. I'd worn repellant but the insects found crannies between my rings and under my watchstrap. I figured it was a small price to pay for 11 new species. Little did I know that those bites were to remain with me for six weeks, reminding me of Cape York every time I put my hands into hot water.

The next morning I walked to Evans Bay before breakfast and had one of the most exciting and unexpected sightings of my life. In fact it was so unexpected that no one would believe me when I reported it at breakfast. High on the cliff, a White-tailed Tropicbird took off not far from me. It was the last thing I anticipated seeing, but quite unmistakable with its long trailing streamers. This occurred two years before we visited Lord Howe Island and watched Red-tailed

Tropicbirds on the cliffs. At that time I had no reason to associate cliffs with tropicbirds.

That morning we went looking for Beach Stone-curlews — another hot walk. We saw Little Curlew, Whimbrel, Marsh Sandpiper, Red-capped Plover, Yellow-spotted Honeyeater and Shining Flycatcher, but no Beach Stone-curlew. I was so buoyed by my Tropicbird that I didn't mind.

The next day Chris scheduled a boat trip and advised us to wear long sleeves and long pants, shoes and socks and hats. All good advice in the mangroves. We motored slowly along the coast, past the Fawn-breasted Bowerbird's bower, admiring some beautiful coral on the way. As soon as we entered Crocodile Creek we saw Collared Kingfisher, Large-billed Gerygone, Red-headed Honeyeater and Rose-crowned Fruit-Dove. We saw several nests of these Fruit-Doves — skimpy, like all pigeon nests, and each containing just one egg. We saw several Large-billed Gerygone's nests, too — untidy structures with a side entrance, hanging precariously by a thread.

The next day we did a trip to Jardine. There were three honeyeaters I hoped to see: the White-streaked, Yellow and Brown-backed. We saw all three plus four other ticks: Fairy Gerygone and Lovely Fairy-wren at Cypress Pine, and Cicadabird and Graceful Honeyeaters at the Jardine River. At one stage Greg, who was walking a little ahead of us, hurried back to ask if we'd seen the Black-backed Butcherbird that had flown in our direction. Of course we hadn't. Human nature being what it is, I cursed missing out on that butcherbird, instead of rejoicing in my seven new species. Sounds like the parable of the lost sheep. I always thought that shepherd had his priorities wrong.

The botany in this part of the world is just as fascinating as the avifauna. There were eight known eucalypts. We found a ninth. There were pitcher plants, wattles, *Morindareticulata* with large white bracts, Orange grevillea (*Grevillea pteridifolia*), peanut trees and nom de plum, a favourite with the birds. We saw one dingo, one huge Golden Orb Spider, several black baby piglets and a few Ulysses butterflies.

The Jardine trip was on Thursday. We were leaving on Saturday morning. We'd already seen 19 new species but I was greedy. I wanted more.

So on Friday morning, our last full day at Pajinka we got up at four-fifteen to have another attempt at spotlighting the Marbled Frogmouth. We heard a Large-tailed Nightjar — we were familiar with this bird from our trips to Bedarra. It is sometimes called the Axebird because of its monotonous 'chop chop chop chop' call. It was no substitute for a Marbled Frogmouth.

Later that morning we heard Yellow-billed Kingfisher (or more accurately, Chris did) and most frustratingly, Chris, who was standing right beside me, saw it. I looked where he was pointing but I couldn't see a thing. It flew and I saw movement, but I couldn't possibly call it a tick. That was two birds I'd missed out on that I felt I really should have seen.

Chris did show me a Brush Cuckoo and a Grey Whistler. This is when you really appreciate having an expert along. I wouldn't have been able to tick the Grey

Whistler without Chris' expertise. It could easily have been a Yellow-legged Flycatcher.

Rog found a Noisy Pitta — the only pitta we'd seen all week. Oh, how I wished it could have been a Red-bellied one.

Every time Chris had taken us into rainforest, we'd looked for Northern Scrub-robin. Whenever Chris heard the call, he'd respond and we'd all have a thorough search. On my original list, Chris had classed this bird as 'rare' and I didn't really expect to see it, but that didn't stop me looking. It was so frustrating being able to hear the bird so close — both calling and hopping about in the dense under-growth— and yet not be able to see it. On that last morning I was rewarded for my effort. Chris and I both saw the beautiful cinnamon bird while Rog, standing with us, did not.

At dinner on our last evening, Greg came over to say goodbye and we told him that we had a White-lipped Tree Frog on our bathroom window and had had a Common Tree Snake on our balcony that afternoon. Unimpressed, he countered by saying that he had a Marbled Frogmouth outside his window earlier that evening. Now, where's the justice in that?

14

If only…

There's no doubt Rog and I are enjoying our travels and my attempts to join The 600 Club. Of course I'd be there already if those pesky grasswrens and emuwrens were a little more cooperative. Not to mention the Red-browed Pardalote.

If only we'd seen the Hudsonian Godwit at Werribee, and the Fluttering Shearwater on our pelagic trip off Portland. If only we'd accurately identified those Kermadec Petrels at Ball's Pyramid. If only we hadn't been such wimps in the heat and had stopped at the Leanyer Sewerage Ponds to erect our scope, we might well have seen the Garganey hiding amongst the Plumed Whistling Ducks. If only we'd looked up in time to see the Double-eyed Fig-Parrots whizzing past at the speed of sound at the Daintree. If only we'd seen the Chestnut-breasted Cuckoo on Mt Lewis and the Barred Cuckoo-shrike at Julatten. If only I'd been quick enough to see the Yellow-billed Kingfisher at Cape York and the Marbled Frogmouth we heard calling and bill clacking so frustratingly close. If only we'd seen the Black-backed Butcherbird at Jardine. . .

If everything had always gone perfectly, if we found every bird we looked for, then, of course, I'd be in The 600 Club already. Some people would have counted Kermadec Petrels and the Yellow-billed Kingfisher. That's fine. Some people count heards and would have added Barred Cuckoo-shrike and Marbled Frogmouth. That's entirely up to them. I know for a fact that some people count subspecies, and why not?

Twitching is one of those wonderful hobbies where you set your own goals and apply your own standards. If I say I saw a White-tailed Tropicbird at Evans Bay, then I did. If I don't believe you saw a Night Parrot, so what? As long as I don't waste a lot of time and money trying to emulate your sighting just on your say so, then it's neither here nor there.

One day soon I'll achieve my goal. It's inching slowly within reach. I know that six hundredth bird will get one hell of a twitch. And then, of course, there's The 700 Club. But don't tell Roger.

1 Birding Organisations

BIRD OBSERVERS CLUB OF AUSTRALIA
183-185 Springvale Road (PO Box 185)
Nunawading, Victoria 3131
Phone: (03) 9877 5342
Or toll free: 1300 305 342
Fax: (03) 9894 4048
Email: boca@ozemail.com.au
Website: www.birdobservers.org.au

BIRDS AUSTRALIA
415 Riversdale Road
Hawthorn East, Victoria 3123
Phone: (03) 9882 2622
Fax: (03) 9882 2677
Email: raou@raou.com.au
Website: www.birdsaustralia.com.au

2 People

Mike Carter — Mike coordinates pelagic trips out of Portland in Victoria For up to date information, see the pelagic website mentioned below under Tony Palliser's name.

Chris Dahlberg — Chris runs excellent cruises on the Daintree River, not to be missed. His phone and fax number is (07) 4098 7997, or email him on chrisd@internetnorth.com.au

Peter Langdon — Peter runs birdwatching tours out of Pandurra Station, near Port Augusta, where they have recorded over 140 species of birds, including (so they tell me) the Thick-billed Grasswren. He will pick you up at your motel, or you can stay at Nuttbush Retreat Tourist Park at Pandurra Station (see below for details).

Phillip Maher	Recognised as THE expert on the Plains-wanderer, Phillip conducts tours to the Riverina between November and January each year. Contact:

Phillip Maher,
PO Box 38,5South Yarra, Victoria 3141
Phone: (03) 9820 4223
Email: mahert@patash.com.au

Niven McCrie	For information about birds of Darwin, visit Niven McCrie's web site. His address is PO Box 41382, Casuarina, Northern Territory 0811. Or email him: niven@taunet.net.au

Barry McLean	Barry runs 4WD camping tours throughout the Victorian Mallee. If you want to see a Malleefowl, or a Red-lored Whistler, he's your man. His email address is bmclean@vic.ozland.net.au

Clive Minton	Clive runs the Victorian Wader Study Group and is always keen to hear from volunteers to help with his banding projects. His phone number is (03) 9589 4901.

Tony Palliser	For information about all pelagic trips around Australia, see Tony's web site: http://users.bigpond.net.au/palliser Pelagic trips depart from Wollongong, Sydney, Eden, Portland, Robe, Perth and Eaglehawk Neck.

George Swann	George Swann conducts bird tours around Broome. He will most likely show you a Black Grasswren and a Gouldian Finch. I have not been out with him (yet) but my parents recommend him highly. Contact:

George Swann
PO Box 220, Broome, Western Australia 6725
Phone/fax: (08) 9192 1246
Email: kimbird@tpg.com.au

3 Places to stay

BIRD OBSERVATORIES

BIRDS AUSTRALIA runs four bird observatories at Rotamah Island in Gippsland, Victoria, Broome, Eyre on the Great Australian Bite and Barren Grounds in New South Wales. They all run courses of various kinds.

Rotamah Island Bird Observatory
PO Box 75
Paynesville, Victoria 3880

Phone/fax: (03) 5156 6398
Email: rotamah@i-o.net.au

Broome Bird Observatory
Crab Creek Road (PO Box 1313)
Broome
Western Australia 6725

Phone: (08) 9193 5600
Fax: (08) 9192 3364
Email: bbo@tpgi.com.au

Eyre Bird Observatory
Cocklebiddy
via Norseman
Western Australia 6443

Tel: (08) 9039 3450
Fax: (08) 9039 3440

Barren Grounds Bird Observatory
PO Box 3
Jamberoo
New South Wales 2533
Website: www.users.bigpond.com/barren.grounds

Phone: (02) 4236 0195
Fax: (02) 4236 0537
Email: barren.grounds@bigpond.com

BIRDS AUSTRALIA also owns Gluepot Reserve, where you can camp and look for the Black-eared Miner.

Birds Australia Gluepot Reserve
PO Box 345
Waikerie
South Australia 5330

Phone: 08 8892 9600 (6-8 p.m.)
Email: gluepot@riverland.net.au

GIPSY POINT LODGE

Richard Jordan of Emu Tours runs bird weeks at Gipsy Point Lodge from time to time. For details contact:

Libby & Ian Mitchell
Gipsy Point Lodge
Gipsy Point
Victoria 3891
Phone: (03) 5158 8205
Fax: (03) 5158 8225
Freecall: 1800 063 556
Email: thelodge@bigpond.com

KINGFISHER PARK BIRDWATCHERS LODGE has self-contained units, a bunk-house and camping sites. Write to:

> Ron Stannard
> Lot 1
> Mt Kooyong Road
> Julatten
> Queensland 4871
> Phone: ((07) 4094 1263
> Fax: 07) 4094 1466
> Email: stannard@tpgi.com.au
> Website: www.birdwatchers.com.au

PAJINKA WILDERNESS LODGE

> c/- Post Office   Phone: (07) 4069 2100
> Bamega   Fax: (07) 4069 2110
> Queensland 4876

PANDURRA STATION

> Stay at:
>
> Nuttbush Retreat Tourist Park
> Pandurra Station
> PMB 15
> Port Augusta
> South Australia 5710
> Phone: (08) 8643 8941
> Fax: (08) 8643 8906

BIBLIOGRAPHY

Blakers, M., Davies, S.J.J.F. & Reilly, P.N., 1984. *The Atlas of Australian Birds*, Royal Australian Ornithologists Union and Melbourne University Press, Melbourne.

Boles, W.E., 1988. *The Robins & Flycatchers of Australia*, The National Photographic Index of Australian Wildlife, Angus & Robertson.

Cayley, N.W., 1978. *What Bird is That?* Angus & Robertson.

Christidis, L. & W.E. Boles, *The Taxonomy and Species of Birds of Australia and its Territories*, Royal Australasian Ornithologists Union Monograph 2 RAOU, Melbourne.

Collins, P., 1995. *The Birds of Broome, An Annotated List*, Broome Bird Observatory, Broome, W.A.

Crome, F. & J. Shields, 1992. *Parrots & Pigeons of Australia, The National Photographic Index of Australian Wildlife*, Angus & Robertson.

Cupper, J. & L. Cupper, 1981. *Hawks in Focus,* Jaclin Enterprises, Mildura.

Donato, D., Wilkins, P., Smith, G., & Alford, L., 1997. *Finding Birds in Australia's Northern Territory*, CSIRO Publishing, Collingwood, Victoria.

Emison, W.B., Bearsell, C.M., Norman, F.I., & Loyn, R.H., 1987. *Atlas of Victorian Birds*, Department of Conservation, Forests and Lands, Royal Australian Ornithologists Union, Melbourne

Enticott, J. & , D. Tipling, 1997. *Photographic Handbook of the Seabirds of the World*, New Holland.

Flegg, J. & , S. Madge, 1995. *Reader's Digest Photographic Field Guide to the Birds of Australia*, Reader's Digest.

Garnett, S. (ed.), 1992. *Threatened and Extinct Birds of Australia*, Royal Australian Ornithologists Union, Australian National Parks and Wildlife Service.

Garnett, S.T. & , G.M. Crowley, 2000. *The Action Plan for Australian Birds 2000*, Environment Australia.

Higgins, P.J. (ed.), 1999. *Handbook of Australian, New Zealand and Antarctic Birds. Volume 4: Parrots to Dollarbird,* Oxford University Press, Melbourne.

Higgins, P.J., and S.J.J.F.Davies, (eds), 1996. *Handbook of Australian, New Zealand and Antarctic Birds. Volume 3: Snipe to Pigeons*, Oxford University Press, Melbourne.

Hutton, I., 1991. *Birds of Lord Howe Island Past and Present*, Ian Hutton.

Lindsay, T.R., 1986. *The Seabirds of Australia, The National Photographic Index of Australian Wildlife*, Angus & Robertson.

Longmore, W., 1991. *Honeyeaters & their Allies of Australia, The National Photographic Index of Australian Wildlife,* Angus & Robertson.

Macdonald, J.D., 1973. *Birds of Australia*, AH & AW Reed

Marchant, S. & P.J. Higgins (co-ordinators), 1990. *Handbook of Australian, New Zealand and Antarctic Birds. Volume 1: Ratites to Ducks,* Oxford University Press, Melbourne.

Marchant, S., & P.J. Higgins (eds), 1993. *Handbook of Australian, New Zealand and Antarctic Birds. Volume 2: Raptors to Lapwings*, Oxford University Press, Melbourne.

Morcombe, M., 2000. *Field Guide to Australian Birds*, Steve Parish Publishing.

Nielsen, Lloyd, 1996. *Birds of Queensland's Wet Tropics and Great Barrier Reef,* Gerard Industries Proprietary Limited.

Olsen, P., F. Crome & J. Olsen, 1993. *Birds of Prey & Ground Birds of Australia, The National Photographic Index of Australian Wildlife*, Angus & Robertson.

Pizzey, G., 1997. *The Graham Pizzey and Frank Knight Field Guide to the Birds of Australia*, Angus & Robertson.

Pringle, J.D., 1987. *The Shorebirds of Australia, The National Photographic Index of Australian Wildlife*, Angus & Robertson.

Reader's Digest, 1976. *Complete Book of Australian Birds*, Readers Digest Services Pty Ltd: Sydney

Serventy, V.N. (editor-in-chief), 1982. *The Wrens & Warblers of Australia, The National Photographic Index of Australian Wildlife*, Angus & Robertson.

Serventy, V.N. (editor-in-chief), 1985. *The Waterbirds of Australia, The National Photographic Index of Australian Wildlife*, Angus & Robertson.

Simpson and Day, 1999 (sixth edition). *Field Guide to the Birds of Australia*, Viking O'Neil.

Slater P., P. Slater & R. Slater, 1986. *The Slater Field Guide to Australian Birds*, Rigby.

Strahan, R. (ed.), 1994. *Cuckoos, Nightbirds & Kingfishers of Australia, The National Photographic Index of Australian Wildlife*, Angus & Robertson.

Strahan, R. (ed.), 1996. *Finches, Bowerbirds & Other Passerines of Australia, The National Photographic Index of Australian Wildlife*, Angus & Robertson.

Wieneke, Jo, 2000. *Where to find Birds in North-East Queensland*, Jo Wieneke.

Index